D1484052

Live to Look Again

Flying Officer (Retd.) D.A. Fraser, qualified as a Lieutenant (Machine Gun) during his 1937-40 service with the University of Toronto COTC. After service with the RCAF as a pilot attached to RAF Bomber and Coastal Commands, he returned to the University of Toronto COTC. After service with the RCAF as a pilot attached to RAF Bomber and Coastal Commands, he returned to the University of Toronto for his Ph.D. in Ecology and Geography. He headed Land Use Surveys in Northern Ontario with the Research Division of the Ontario Dept. of Lands and Forests, then lectured at the University of Alberta and was Head of the Tree Physiology Section Petawawa Forest Expt Station, Chalk River, Ont. 1949-70. In 1970 he was appointed as Chairman of the Dept. of Geography, Sir George Williams University. He retired as Professor of Geography, Concordia University, Montreal, in 1983.

His United Nations (IAEA) appointments included service as Vice-Director, Radioisotope Training Courses in Germany and Finland. He was a National Research Council Canada — USSR Academy of Sciences exchange scientist in 1969.

Live to Look Again

Memoirs of a Canadian Pilot with the
RAF during WW II

by
Donald A. Fraser

Mika Publishing Company
Belleville, Ontario
1984

LIVE TO LOOK AGAIN

ISBN 0-919303-80-3
Printed and bound in Canada

This book is dedicated to the memory of Warrant Officer James Patrick McGrath, RCAF, Rear Gunner, and Sgt. John Smith, RAF, Wireless Operator, and all those who did not return.

A McGrath — Smith Memorial Prize was established in 1981 at Concordia University, Montreal, PQ, Canada.

The author in 1941 when he was a Pilot with 150 *Wellington* Bomber Squadron at Snaith, Yorkshire, England.

Contents

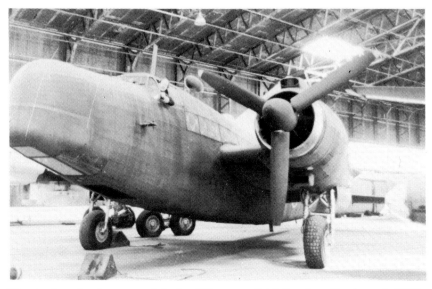

The Author "at the controls" of a *Wimpy* at RAF Station, Henlow, in 1971. Since then this machine has been moved to the RAF Museum at Hendon.

VICKERS WELLINGTON

Famed for its geodetic construction, the *Wellington* was designed by Barnes Wallis, who was also responsible for weapons which broke the Ruhr Dams, and who designed the R-100 Airship. The aircraft was known affectionately as "Wimpy" after the cartoon character J. Wellington Wimpy.

Wellingtons were in action from the outbreak of hostilities until V-J Day, flying as bombers, minesweepers, patrol bombers, anti-shipping aircraft, air-sea rescue, transport and glider tugs. Eleven RCAF bomber squadrons flew *Wellingtons* from 1941 until 1944. Two other RCAF squadrons, Nos. 407 and 415, flew *Wellingtons* in Coastal Command. No. 407 sank four U-boats with *Wellingtons* fitted with Leigh Lights. No. 415 attacked German shipping with *Wellingtons* until the summer of 1944, when the squadron converted to *Halifaxes* and was transferred to Bomber Command.

Of the two RAF Leigh Light *Wellington* Squadrons the author flew with, 172 sank nine U-boats and shared in the sinking of one other, whereas 179 carried out 64 attacks which resulted in seven U-boats sunk by squadron aircraft, and sinking of a further two was shared with other forces.

From first flight in June 1936, there were 11,461 *Wellingtons* produced in Marks I to XIX. Versions had Bristol Pegasus, Bristol Hercules, Pratt and Whitney twin Wasp or Rolls-Royce Merlin engines. *Wellingtons* remained in RAF service as transports and trainers until 1953.

Acknowledgements

The day-to-day records of my five-year tour of RCAF duty as a pilot would not have been kept had my high school classmate, the late Douglas Horniblow, not presented me with a five-year diary on the day of my departure overseas.

I wish to express my appreciation to my wife, Dr. Erika E. Gaertner, who helped with archival research in London, Germany, and Rome and with the interviews of Grand Admiral Karl Doenitz, Captain Klaus Scholtz of the *U-108*, Sir Barnes Wallis, Marshal of the Royal Air Force Sir Arthur Harris, Air Vice Marshal John Russell, Air Commodore Geoffrey Greswell, Captain (USN) Wiley Howell, and Captain (Italian Navy) Migliorini. Thanks also for her patience and careful scrutiny of the many drafts of my manuscript. My son Steven and daughter Spruce located on their own initiative the Turbinlite of Group Captain Helmore in the Science Museum in London and assisted in the early search for documentation of my wartime activities. Wing Commander Humphrey de Verde "Sammy" Leigh encouraged my endeavours and supplied me with original records pertaining to the development of the Leigh Light. Col. C.P. Stacey's valuable suggestions for the first draft of the manuscript are gratefully acknowledged.

Dr. Alex Douglas, Director of the National Defence Directorate of History, Ottawa, made pertinent information available and facilitated examination of Squadron records in London. The Canadian Armed Forces contributed to my efforts by permitting me to join their flights to and from London during my 1980 sabbatic leave.

Members of the Royal Air Force, the Royal Navy, the *Luftwaffe*, the Italian Navy, the Public Records Office at Kew, and the Imperial War Museum were all of inestimable assistance. The editorial work of Heather Ebbs and Carl Vincent of Canada's Wing is acknowledged with thanks.

The initial phase of this study was facilitated by a Canada Council grant in 1971.

Sanders Associates, Inc., Nashua, N.H., U.S.A. was the donor, and Mr. Alfred "Chief" Johnson the artist of the picture on the dust jacket.

Introduction

Aviation in itself is not inherently dangerous;
even more than the sea, it is unforgiving of any
carelessness, neglect, or incompetence.
Lt. Gen. Elwood R. Quesada, United States Air Force

IT IS JULY 1971, and I am in a little churchyard on a peaceful North Devon hillside overlooking Royal Air Force Station Chivenor. I am standing beside the last resting place of Pilot Officer H.W. Russ, RCAF. Near his grave and the graves of his crew are the mortal remains of many airmen from the Commonwealth, the United Kingdom, and from the Czech and Polish squadrons which had been trained and based at Chivenor during the Second World War. Hawker *Hunter* jet fighters flash overhead, but I see the station as it was when I first arrived here in early February of 1942.

It was not my first operational posting. I came here from RAF Bomber Command to join an exciting detachment of the RAF's Coastal Command Development Unit, the nucleus of 1417 Flight. This team refined Squadron Leader Humphrey de Verde Leigh's idea to mount a moveable searchlight mid-position on the underside of a twin-engine Vickers *Wellington* bomber. The *Wellingtons* of Coastal Command were already equipped with the brand new radar installation known as ASV (Air to Surface Vessel) radar, and the devastatingly explosive, shallow-fused Torpex depth charges. This combination constituted the new concept of a correlated weapons system and was designed to challenge the supremacy of the German Navy's U-boat arm. On this lovely summer day I look at the rows of graves and see again those days of early 1942 when, as the pilot of one of the first four "Leigh Light" *Wellington* bombers, I took off to search out and destroy German and Italian U-boats in the Bay of Biscay.

Chapter One
Early Days

MY MILITARY EXPERIENCE DATES back to my early days at Eglinton Avenue Public School in Toronto in the late 1920s and early 1930s when cadets in high-collared red uniforms were an integral part of school life. The cadets' most important function in those days was to take part in their school's activities and to participate in the Armistice Day parade on November 11. We were still parading in fours at that time, and I well remember the orders "Form Fours" and "Form Two Deep". When columns of three were introduced to the drills we felt that we had taken a great step forward in efficiency simply through the elimination of these commands.

I had always wanted to fly. I made model aircraft, read such biographies of First World War pilots as Floyd Gibbons' *The Red Knight of Germany*, and felt tremendous pride when I learned that it was a Canadian, Captain Roy Brown, who shot Von Richthofen down. Other Canadian pilots, such as Billy Bishop and William Barker, were heroes to my young mind.

My boyhood neighbour, Tom Kerr, three years older than myself, was always making model aircraft which, with the aid of rubber bands, could actually fly. Together we made many visits to the Leaside aircraft dump, where remnants and wrecks of aircraft from a huge First World War training school were piled one on top of another on the steep slopes of the Don Valley ravine behind the hangars. There I appropriated a number of treasures, such as an old aircraft ski which, with infinite labour, I pushed home to use in the construction of home-made skis. One day in 1927, when I was nine years old, Tom and I were walking home from school when a neighbour shouted to us, "Lindbergh has just flown the Atlantic!" This was incredibly exciting news even in those days of repeated aviation spectaculars, but the excitement was just beginning. Three years later the *R-100* dirigible crossed the Atlantic and moored to a newly-constructed mast at St. Hubert airport in Montreal. I saw its silver-coloured cigar shape floating up toward Bloor Street in Toronto from the hill on Manor Road; it was an unforgettable thrill.

Then in 1934 General Balbo of the Italian Air Force led a group of multi-engined flying boats from Italy to the Chicago World's Fair. They passed over our heads while my family was vacationing at Sparrow Lake, Ontario. Balbo's name was to become a wartime synonym for large formations of aircraft.

In 1936 I was awarded a provincial Edward Blake Scholarship in Botany and Zoology at the University of Toronto, and began an academic career in Honour Science. Physical Education was compulsory, and I opted to obtain the credit as a member of the machine-gun company of the Canadian Officers' Training Corps (COTC). Money was scarce in those days, and the small payment I received for each drill period was a welcome boost to my finances.

Pilot Officer H.W. Russ, age 21, RCAF, killed in *Wellington* crash, April 13, 1942. Braunton Cemetery, North Devon, England.

Cadet Don Fraser at Eglinton Ave. Public School,
North Toronto, 1930.

Summer jobs in the thirties, even for university students, were few and far between. One afternoon I spent hours cycling to the de Havilland airport and factory, north of Toronto, only to be told there were no jobs available. The lean years passed slowly. My answer to a Royal Canadian Air Force advertisement for pilots brought the reply: "Finish your degree; we consider only university graduates for training." This attitude was to induce many young Canadians interested in flying to make their way to England to join the RAF.

Hitler's assumption of control in Germany in 1933 and the 1934 assassination of Chancellor Dollfuss in Austria were early indicators of the impending war. During my university years I often went to the home of Professor McBroom, who taught German at Victoria College, to listen to Hitler's speeches over the radio. Our ensuing political discussions did nothing to relieve my apprehension.

Then, in 1938, Hitler marched his forces into the Sudeten area of Czechoslovakia. The uneasy peace there was followed by a final takeover in the spring of 1939. Where would Hitler's demands end? One could feel only a deep skepticism when Chamberlain, announcing "I bring you peace in our time", brought back Hitler's promise that the takeover of the Sudeten was to be his last territorial demand in Europe.

September 1, 1939—I was cycling up Yonge Street hill below St. Clair Avenue with some plants I had identified at the Botany Department of the U of T when I saw Constable Bob Garioch walking his beat. We paused to talk, and he told me of Hitler's invasion of Poland. This development had almost been expected, for only two weeks earlier Hitler had signed a non-aggression pact with Stalin. In his book *Mein Kampf* written over fifteen years earlier, he had outlined his determination not to fight a war on two fronts, and now his hands were free. I cycled on wondering what was to happen next. Two days later Britain declared war on Germany, and France followed suit.

Canada followed Britain's declaration of war with a formal parliamentary approval on September 9, 1939. My older brother George's regiment of the Non-Permanent Active Militia, the 48th Highlanders of Canada, had already been warned during the night parade on Friday, August 31, to expect active service. George, who at 24 had risen from the rank of private to sergeant in just seven years, was to go overseas with his regiment as part of the 1st Canadian Division, with the strange rank of Warrant Officer Class III. This was a new and short-lived British army rank for platoon commanders with the duties of a commissioned 2nd Lieutenant. George had been working in Eaton's of Toronto, a company that gave its employees leave without pay for the duration of hostilities and assured them their jobs upon return. They retained employees' benefits and were even allowed purchase discounts for their next of kin, a welcome relief for our widowed mother.

One Saturday afternoon that September I drove with my mother and younger brothers out to Barker's Air Field near Toronto to spend a hard-earned dollar on my first aeroplane flight. If I was to become an Air Force pilot, as I had resolved, then I had to at least find out what it was like up in the air. The little single-engine biplane took off into the warm, blue skies, circled the neighbourhood for about five minutes, and returned for a smooth landing. As I looked down from my perch in the sky, exulting in the sensations of flight, I grew more determined than ever to become a pilot. Besides, having lugged a heavy Vickers water-cooled machine-gun while with the COTC, I saw distinct advantages in having an aeroplane do such work for me.

After the Polish campaign Europe settled down to a *"Sitzkrieg"*. There were, of course, some flashes of activity. On 3 September, the same day war was declared, *Oberleutnant* Lemp, commander of the

U.30, torpedoed and sank the British passenger ship *Athenia.* One hundred twenty-eight lives were lost, including some personal friends of mine from Toronto. This was the beginning of the longest battle in the Second World War, the Battle of the Atlantic. I was to take an active part in that battle.

In our COTC military studies class we followed closely reports of the war in Europe, reports that were primarily concerned with the Navy, but also, to a lesser extent, with the Air Force. At the beginning of the war the Royal Navy had commandeered a number of large merchant ships, armed them with a variety of guns, reinforced their structure under the gun mountings, and sent them to sea. These armed merchant cruisers were sometimes used to act as convoy escorts, for there were not enough naval ships for the job. At other times they patrolled areas through which German merchant ships might seek passage or where German sea raiders could break out into the Atlantic Ocean. In late November 1939 two German battle-cruisers, the *Scharnhorst* and the *Gneisenau,* intercepted the armed merchant cruiser *Rawalpindi* and sank her south of Iceland. This sinking was followed by the much publicized Battle of the River Plate in mid-December, in which the German pocket battleship *Admiral Graf Spee* was cornered off Montevideo in the South Atlantic. Her fight against three British cruisers, *Exeter, Ajax,* and *Achilles,* resulted in severe damage to both herself and her adversaries. Captain Langsdorf of the *Graf Spee* sought refuge in the neutral waters of the River Plate off Montevideo to unload his wounded, bury his dead, and make temporary repairs. With a depleted crew, he then steamed out of the harbour in his damaged ship, not to fight to the death with the waiting British cruisers, but to scuttle his ship and save what was left of his crew. The popular view in my military studies class was that this act of self-destruction was not what a ship of the Royal Navy would have done under similar circumstances.

Our attention also focussed for a time on the RAF *Wellington* bombers. The type's much-vaunted bottom turret, housing a machine-gun and operator, and its front and rear powered turrets were of no avail when some twenty-two of them attacked the German Navy off Wilhelmshaven in December 1939. Half of the twenty-two were shot down by *Messerschmitt 109* and *110* fighters, which had quickly discovered that a beam attack on the *Wellingtons* not only eluded the latter's full defensive fire, but also brought the fighters into position to shoot up the wing petrol tanks. As a result, the *Wellington* attacked would lose a substantial amount of fuel and was easily set on fire. After this tragic incident a formerly undisputed tactical belief, that daylight bombers in numbers could protect one another from enemy fighters, had to be swept under the carpet, and RAF heavy bombers were relegated to night-time sorties. It was not until about four years later that Allied heavy bombers, this time American, ventured over Germany in daylight, only to once again learn the hard way that to do so without fighter escort was to risk appalling losses. Little did I realize in those college days how intimate I would become with the *Wellington.*

In December 1939 the 48th Highlanders of Toronto began their move overseas, entraining at Toronto one dark, stormy night. I was unable to see George off, as my COTC mid-term examinations took place that night. I was busy until almost midnight, while my brother's train steamed eastward out of Union Station, the beginning of his voyage to Europe.

COTC parades and lectures continued several times a week throughout that dark winter, and I was becoming increasingly disenchanted with the prospect of fighting my war as an infantryman. Several Reserve Officers from the faculty joined our machine-gun company as "seniors" when war was declared to drill us in our parades. Their lack of familiarity with the drill exercises became apparent one night when they marched us over an embankment and sent us tumbling into a small valley near the main library of the University. Another time they marched us into a wall before they could think of an appropriate command to turn us. These incidents made me realize how little personal control one would have over one's fate as an infantryman. I had submitted my application for pilot training at the outbreak of the conflict in September, and as the COTC drills stumbled on, I became increasingly convinced that my choice had been the right one.

At long last there was some indication that my wish might come true. I was directed to report for my medical to the RCAF's Toronto Manning Depot at the Canadian National Exhibition grounds during the 1939 Christmas holidays. I took the streetcar down one cold Saturday morning and had a thorough examination. The medical officer seemed satisfied and I passed the medical first class, although I had to squint, not too obviously I hoped, when identifying letters for the eye test. I knew that I had slight astigmatism in my right eye, but I could usually get 20/20 vision if I peered through the corner of my eye so that the crystalline lens gave an unaltered line of sight. This problem passed unnoticed until I was an operational pilot and one of my crew observed that I automatically tilted my head each time we flew over the control tower prior to landing. Only that tilt enabled me to see the wind sock and any special landing instructions that might be marked on the ground near the flying control office.

Studies and parades continued as the winter of 1940 changed into Spring, and the *Sitzkrieg* in Europe ended. The German invasion of Denmark and Norway came first, followed in May by Hitler's sweep through Holland and Belgium and into France—the miracle of Dunkirk, then French capitulation, and the rallying of the Free French under

De Gaulle. My brother nearly saw action at this time. Few people know that three Canadian battalions, including the 48th Highlanders, were landed in France south of the Seine as part of the Second British Expeditionary Force after the Dunkirk evacuation. They were moving up to reinforce the disintegrating French forces when, on 14 June, it became obvious that the situation was hopeless, and the Expeditionary Force was ordered to retreat. "Better to fight and run away and live to fight another day," as the old saying goes. The train carrying my brother's battalion was delayed when the French engineer absconded. The Commanding Officer eventually found a Canadian soldier who could drive a locomotive, and they reverse-steamed back to the port near Brest, where a cross-Channel steamer waited patiently. Lack of space meant that the Canadians had to push their brand-new vehicles off the dock into the water to deny them, at least temporarily, to the pursuing Germans. The Canadian artillery regiment refused to give up its guns, and they were packed onto an already overloaded boat. Somehow the Canadian units returned safely to the United Kingdom, where they were to form the backbone of a force to repel the expected German invasion.

In early June 1940, after my graduation, I moved with my COTC machine-gun company to summer camp at Niagara-on-the-Lake for field examinations and exercises. Webbing and accoutrements were issued from the COTC armouries before we boarded the Lake Ontario passenger ship *Dalhousie City*. Four hours later we landed at Niagara-on-the-Lake and moved by bus to our canvas encampments. A real *esprit-de-corps* existed during our stay at the camp. The officers were of our own company and were well trained. The Sergeants and Corporals were from all walks of life—professionals, businessmen, even Members of Parliament who had been active in the militia.

Every morning at 0530 our kilted piper would march up and down the rows of tents playing "Hey, Johnnie Cope, Are You Waking Yet?". This was the signal to turn out, clean up, head off to breakfast, and prepare for practical training: map reading, marching, and firing machine-guns. One officer, Jeff Dale, had been a teacher at Trinity College in Port Hope. Midway through camp his younger brother, Bob Dale, turned up in his blue RCAF uniform, with a white flash on his cap denoting that he was "aircrew in training". To my envious eyes he was far ahead of me, and I little realized that I was to follow him through aircrew training by only a month, I as a pilot, he as a navigator. We were both to end up in 150 Squadron of RAF Bomber Command, and later, much later, we would serve together on the staff of 180 (*Mosquito*) Squadron of the Royal Canadian Air Cadets in 1947 and 1948.

I successfully passed my Lieutenant examinations at camp and in late June returned to Toronto for my appointment as supervisor at the

Bessborough playgrounds, North Toronto. I was scheduled to enter the Ontario College of Education that September to begin studies for my secondary school teacher's certificate. But my planned life of peaceful study was not yet to begin.

Author's older brother, George, of the 48th High-landers.

Chapter Two
Trials and Tribulations of a Pilot-in-Training

ON THE LAST FRIDAY in June 1940 a telegram from the RCAF arrived: "Report Monday Toronto General Hospital for medical pending aircrew enlistment." I hesitated over the telegram for some hours, for I was not particularly eager to interrupt my carefully planned career. But the walls of Europe were crumbling: had I any real option? A telephone call to my supervisor, Mr. Bartlett of the Toronto Board of Education, produced a sensible alternative. Bartlett suggested that I remain on as swimming instructor for the summer, finish my academic training that Fall, and join the service after accepting a teaching position. By that time not only would I be older, and more prepared for my part in the war, but my formal education would be completed, to say nothing of the fact that seniority and pension benefits would accrue during my service career. It was tempting advice, especially since I had borrowed more than $150 to help me through my final year at University, a grand sum in those days. But allegiance to my country finally triumphed, and I decided to report for the examination. Mr. Bartlett kindly held my position at the playgrounds open for a few days pending the results of my medical.

Monday morning I was at the hospital bright and early for my medical. It turned out well, and I was requested to report to the RCAF recruiting office on Bay Street the next day. At the appointed time and place I stood at attention as the officer in charge perused my qualifications: "Hmm, degree in Science, qualified as a Lieutenant in the COTC, machine-gunner . . . what's this? 'Well known to the Toronto Chief of Police, General D.C. Draper!'" I had to admit that it sounded rather as if I were a criminal with a long record, but the truth of the matter was that my father, until his death in 1937, had been General Draper's personal assistant at Police Headquarters. The recruiting officer's face relaxed as he read the letter of recommendation from Chief Draper: "Donald Fraser is the son of the late George Fraser, a much respected member of the Toronto Police Force." At last the officer extended a Bible, upon which I placed my right hand and solemnly swore allegiance to His Majesty the King. "You're in the Royal Canadian Air Force now, for the duration. Report directly to RCAF Manning Depot at the Toronto Exhibition Grounds." My adventure had begun.

It had always been a joke in the COTC that should a war emergency occur, at least we would not be conscripted into the Army at less than our rank of Lieutenant, with a reasonable rate of pay. Now, in December 1939, with the British Commonwealth Air Training Scheme coming into effect, all prospective aircrew, including D.A. Fraser, started out as Aircraftmen Second Class (AC2), equivalent to privates in the Army, at $1.30 per day. What a let-down. My application to the RCAF in 1939 had asked for acceptance as a pilot in training with the rank of provisional Pilot Officer, the Air Force commissioned rank equivalent to Lieutenant in the Army, at which I would have been earning $4.25 per day. Most of the money I had borrowed to pay my university fees during my graduation year had started to accrue interest at 6% as soon as I graduated on June 7, 1940, and now this unexpectedly low income would delay my payments even more. Nonetheless, my determination to fly was not weakened. Mother was worried, but, I suspect, also proud. Her uneasiness was natural, for I was a university graduate in Honour Science as well as a qualified Lieutenant and machine-gunner in the Army, and might have been able to find a less dangerous position, yet I was becoming a flyer, a reputedly short-lived profession.

Before any training began I was directed to fill out more forms and make a will, leaving my earthly goods to my mother in the event of my demise. Then it was straight down to Manning Depot, where I grabbed a lower bunk in a room for 500 recruits. My civilian days were suddenly over. Uniforms were issued the next day. "Sorry," said the Corporal in charge. "No hats over size 7." What a penalty to be born with a large head! Many of us didn't get hats and, lacking that essential item of uniform, were confined to barracks. The ludicrous situation quickly gave rise to a small business—renting hats for 25 cents per night from those with smaller heads. It was no easy trick to balance a small hat on your head while running for a street car, as many of us discovered.

Inoculations and drills followed the uniform issue. The experience gained in the COTC stood me in good stead, but some of my fellow recruits were definitely of the awkward squad. One of our drill Sergeants had been with an International Brigade in Spain, fighting against General Franco. We all respected him, but could hardly help wondering why on earth a man of his experience had been relegated to drilling our rather motley crew.

In a week we made a very smart squad, even if I do say so myself. Almost a month passed before the great day finally arrived and a list of the 600 names of those designated for pre-flight training was tacked up on the notice board. Bright and early the next morning we lined up, about fifty of us still without hats. I can still hear that awful command: "Fall out, those without hats!" We sheepishly moved to one side and were dismissed while the others boarded buses for the move to Eglinton Hunt Club for initial ground training. We large-headed recruits were given no word on our fate for the rest of the day. Would we be issued hats? Were any available? I had scoured the Toronto stores earlier and had even checked the factory which had the contract for making the hats, but all to no avail.

The next day we lined up and, to our great disappointment, were issued, not service hats, but pith helmets. Groaning under this further blow to our dignity, we were loaded into the train and were off—not to Eglinton Hunt Club, but to RCAF Station Camp Borden, sixty miles north of Toronto, to relieve the army on guard duty. Although it was a relief to get out of Toronto, our flying training seemed to recede into the distance. But at least there were planes at Camp Borden. Having had the advantage of COTC drill instruction, three of us were promoted "acting Corporals, temporary, unpaid" on our first day at camp. We were in charge of eight men; my group was detailed to No. 3 guard post at the south end of the tarmac, up a small hill. The first day on guard duty, when finally given time for a break, several of us rushed down to the tarmac and approached someone we assumed to be an instructor.

"How about a flip?" I asked. Somehow over the roar of the engine of a *Harvard* training aircraft being tested, I heard his affirmative reply. "Seat-type parachute?" I queried, for I knew there were also chest types.

Looking at me as if I were kidding, he replied, "Of course."

I strapped it on with the help of a mechanic and climbed into the front seat of the aircraft. The instructor followed in a few minutes, waved away the chocks, taxied out, and we were off into the bright blue sky. He spoke as we climbed, but I couldn't hear him through my helmet, and replied with non-committal grunts. The instructor did a loop, some steep turns, and a few incipient stalls, continuing his commentary all the while. Finally, after about forty minutes, we circled the aerodrome and lined the *Harvard* up with the runway. Suddenly the instructor's voice came in quite clearly: "Okay, you land it."

With definite overtones of panic I replied, "I've never landed a plane before!"

An angry shout burst through the ear phones as the wheels began to lower for the landing. After bumping our way down the runway the instructor literally chased me away. I had been mistaken for another instructor coming to check him out that day on *Harvards*—apparently I was not the only one who had never been in one before!

We witnessed another shaky do from our guard post when one of the aircraft dropped a smoke bomb by mistake as it taxied past. The white clouds drifted toward us and we began to cough, sputter, and grow teary-eyed. Demonstrating my powers of leadership, I called for an emergency upwind evacuation of the post. We later learned that the white smoke was trichlor acetic acid—tear gas—used to mark dropped bombs.

At the end of August, after a month of guard duty, we were posted to Regina, Saskatchewan for ground instruction. We boarded our train and set off, travelling first class—comfortable sleepers, clean white sheets, and excellent meals. Our initial exploration of the train turned up a company of khaki-uniformed infantry in a rear car. They looked a tired and scruffy lot, and their sleepless journey on hard, third-class seats would not improve their appearance to any extent. I came to the conclusion that the Air Force did have its advantages, even for the lowly Aircraftman Second Class.

Tiger Moth on the tarmack at No. 5 Elementary Flying Training School, Prince Albert, Sask.

Our barracks in Regina were in the Teachers' College, with about thirty recruits in double bunks per classroom. We did some drill, but concentrated mainly on classroom studies: Morse code, math, navigation, airmanship, and meteorology. I whizzed through most of it, having just finished my degree at university, but I had to work hard to master the Morse code. There was a rumour circulating that the trainees with the highest marks in mathematics were to be chosen for observation work—but rumours be damned! I was determined to do my best in everything and still continued to hope for pilot training.

The Regina folk were untiringly friendly. On one occasion, following a church service, I had two families pulling my arms from opposite sides to invite me home for a Sunday dinner. The one that pulled hardest had a daughter, with whom I was asked to take a walk while the roast finished cooking. On another occasion a group of us were marched to the nearest dance hall and dismissed for dancing, to find our entrance fees paid for and the dance hostesses waiting inside. What a life! There were even times when we would find children lining up in front of our barracks asking for autographs. On the other side of the Atlantic the Battle of Britain was raging, and future pilots everywhere were showered with public admiration. Later, after I arrived in England, George once remarked, "Here comes the glamour boy!" a phrase often used in reference to aircrew.

Accidents will happen... *Tiger Moth* at Prince Albert, Sask.

At last, after a month of intensive ground training, all recruits were marched out on to the parade square. Our hearts were beating rapidly, for the moment of aircrew selection had come. Which of us would be pilots and which navigators, wireless operators, or gunners? My name was called in the first batch of twenty-five. What was to be my future? As we were marched away we learned that we were the lucky ones selected for pilot training. Yet, even for us future knights of the air, there was the inevitable delay. The training station was not quite ready for us, so we boarded a train for RCAF Station Brandon, Manitoba, purportedly to cool our heels for a week. Cool our heels indeed! We roasted them on parade grounds every day.

One afternoon in late September we potential pilots, along with several hundred other Air Force recruits, were marched about for several miles before finally halting on a street near the barracks. Forty minutes later we were still standing there when one of our own number (was it Gordie Gosman, an ex-bush pilot?) decided that as future pilots we should show initiative: rather than continue to wait, we ought to march into the barracks, dismiss ourselves, and be off to supper. Accordingly, one of our members called the group together—"right turn, quick march, left wheel"—and we marched smartly past the other masses of recruits down the street and into the barracks gates. Our arrival caused a tremendous commotion amongst the Sergeants and Warrant Officers inside. They quickly ordered us to about turn and march back to our original positions. The remaining airmen were eventually marched into the barracks, but it was much later when the Sergeant Major dismissed us for supper, with a curt, "Be on the barrack square at 1930 tonight in gym clothes." We had committed what appeared to him as tantamount to mutiny. The physical education NCO was waiting for us when we reported that evening to the bullpen. He lined us up on the square and started us jumping up and down and doing push-ups (it seemed like hundreds, although it probably wasn't more than fifty). Though we grew exhausted, none of us faltered, even when ordered "around the bullpen on the double" until we were practically numb. We were finally dismissed, but only after being ordered to report the next night for the same treatment. By the third evening of extra drill we had become a co-ordinated and probably more submissive group, and our personal *esprit de corps* increased with each additional exercise.

After a week at Brandon we were off for RCAF Station Prince Albert, the site of No. 5 Elementary Flying Training School, where we were to use single-engine biplane trainers, *Tiger Moths*, for flight training. Our new base was reminiscent of our ideas of First World War fighter aerodromes, with two rows of about twenty *Tiger Moths* lined up evenly on the tarmac beside the hangars. We were billeted in an H-type barrack. The men in the senior course had one arm of the H-hut, our newly arrived junior course the other. The cross arm held the washroom facilities. A furnace with an automatic coal stoker at each end of the cross piece provided the heat, for winter was approaching. Though my bunk was in an uncomfortably hot position near the furnace, it was distinctly superior to those in the chilly farther recesses of the room.

Early one Sunday morning at about 0300 I was awakened by screams coming from somewhere near the furnace. As I peered out at the machine from under the blankets, I saw legs waving madly about. Apparently one trainee had come in very late, and being somewhat soused, had flaked out on somebody else's bed. His neighbours decreed that he should be taught a lesson, and carefully hoisted him onto the coal hopper, which fed coal to the furnace. He didn't waken until the thermostat called for more heat and the worm screw at the base of the hopper started to feed coal into the furnace. Jolted awake by the sound of the roaring furnace, the poor sod momentarily believed himself in Hell. We extracted him from his predicament and dumped him into a cold shower before he collapsed again, this time into his own bed.

For two weeks, until the temperature fell below 0°F, we had outdoor phys-ed every morning at 0700. Lectures took place later in the morning, and flying training was in the afternoon. This order was reversed about a month later when we became the senior course. After seven hours of dual flying instruction one was expected to go solo. If you didn't make it, or didn't get the nod after eleven or twelve hours of dual instruction, you could consider yourself washed out, and prepare for a posting to some other flying category. My instructor, Joe Coombes, was an ex-bush pilot, as indeed were many other instructors. He used to fly out of Northern Saskatchewan with fish in the summer and furs in the winter. While we were waiting for our plane we would often chat about the philosophy of flying. If it was a warm day we would sit on the ground behind the time-keeper's shack, and Joe would draw various aircraft movements in the dust with a stick. His most well-worn phrase was: "Don't try to be the best pilot, try to be the oldest. After all, whenever an aircraft fatality is reported in the newspapers, they always say 'he was one of the best'."

On October 18, 1940, after seven hours and twenty minutes of dual flying, including a number of take-offs and landings, Joe told me to taxi downwind and turn the plane around prior to take-off. He signalled for me to brake, then, climbing out of the rear cockpit, said, "Take her around once, and don't break her. You're ready to go solo." I had no time to worry as I watched him turn away and walk toward the flights room carrying his parachute. Turning the plane at right angles to the line of take-off, I carefully, and no doubt very slowly, did the final cockpit check. I searched sky and ground for other aircraft which might have been in the way, checked the wind sock for direction, then turned the *Tiger Moth* into the wind, slowly opened up the engine, and steadied the plane as it gathered speed. At 55 miles per hour the *Tiger Moth* bounced into the air. I held it at about twenty feet above the ground to allow the speed to build to 65 miles per hour, and then climbed, reducing power somewhat by throttling back at the same time. At five hundred feet I eased into a gradual left turn, and again searched the sky for other aircraft. At one thousand feet I brought the plane around to the left again for the downwind leg, levelling off as I throttled back to maintain a cruising speed of 85 miles per hour. The hangars slid under my port wing and, when well downwind of the field, I turned once more to the left and let down toward the field and my original take-off point. Throttling back again to keep the nose up, I neared the ground, and the wheels touched with hardly a bounce. I cut the engine. Safe. Carefully taxiing in a zig-zag, for there was a blind spot dead ahead, I headed back to the tarmac to park in line with the other planes. Joe was waiting for me in the flight room. "Nice landing," he said. "That'll be enough for today. You can go celebrate your first solo; we'll start instrument flying tomorrow." The solo flight left me with a tremendous sense of relief. Never again would I have to experience that frightening initial moment of realization that I taken my fate into my own hands.

A few days later, when most of the class had soloed and only the odd one still had to try it, we stepped out of the lunch hall at about 1240 to the sound of an engine in the air. Usually all planes were on the ground during the lunch period, being gassed up and serviced in preparation for their 1330 flights. We all raced to the tarmac and watched as a lone *Tiger Moth* came in low over the field. It dropped lower and lower, until at ten feet above the ground it levelled off and seemed to stagger. Then the engine roared back to life and the plane rose into the air again. While the plane circled we learned the rest of the story. One Groves was on his first solo and had managed to get into the air with little difficulty, but was more faint-hearted in his attempts to land. The sequence repeated itself three times. The fourth time the *Tiger Moth* came in low over the field as usual. Fire crew and ambulance were standing by expectantly, and a crowd of trainees and instructors had gathered near the tarmac. A few feet above the ground the engine of the plane started to roar as if Groves was going to repeat the performance, when the engine suddenly sputtered and died. The aircraft hit the ground with only a slight bounce and rolled to a halt with the engine stopped and the propeller still. Groves was down in one piece, thanks to running out of gas at a fortuitous moment. Next day the class was one member short.

Our flying hours started to build up, but there were still two hurdles to surmount before passing out of EFTS: the twenty-hour test and the final fifty-hour test. Joe was getting me ready for the former, and together we polished up my landings, steep turns, and instrument flying; I wasn't doing aerobatics yet—at least, not officially. The moment eventually arrived when my test was only one hour away. Joe advised me to take up *Tiger Moth* 414 for a few circuits to get the feel of the wind and the field, as well as the plane. It was a brisk, sunny day in late October as I taxied out. There was one plane in front of me, zig-zagging across the field, and one far behind me. The plane in front turned across wind preparatory to its cockpit check, final turn into the wind, and take-off. I zagged to the right to be well out of his way, stopped my aircraft, and looked over my shoulder to see where the other *Tiger Moth* was, for until then I had been concentrating on the one in front. Horrified, I saw it, engine roaring, just starting to chew its way up my tail. I immediately jammed the throttle wide open to escape this reckless onslaught, but the other aircraft also lurched forward and my tail disappeared into the maw of its propeller. As I continued my efforts to pull ahead, a final leap of the plane behind me brought it down on my fuselage. Its wooden propeller snapped off at the hub and the machine settled just six inches behind my head. I cut my engine and slowly got out of the cockpit. Furious, and still shaking, I looked at the mess that had once been the tail of my plane. The pilot of the other, Alcazar from Trinidad, came very close to being dragged out of his cockpit and having some free dental work done. I'm not quite sure how, but I managed to restrain myself, and Alcazar climbed from his aircraft without my assistance. In several succinctly chosen phrases, perhaps best left to the imagination of the reader, I expressed my feelings on the incident, and suggested that he quickly report his incredible blunder. He said nothing, and meekly walked the three-quarters of a mile back across the field to the tarmac.

After what seemed to be an eternity he finally disappeared into the flight hut. Almost immediately, the sound of sirens exploded in the distance as a fire truck and a station car with the Chief Flying Instructor and Joe Coombes tore across the field to where I was waiting beside the remains of the two *Tiger Moths.* As I rode back with Joe in the back of the car, he asked me how I felt. Aside from a severe mental shaking up, I felt fine, and was ready for my test. It was just as well, for another *Tiger Moth* was being warmed up at the flight hut. Flying Officer Gardiner, the testing pilot, motioned to me, and a few minutes later our *Moth* was climbing into the sky.

The routine exercises of the test were anticlimactic after the earlier crisis, and we landed safely forty minutes later. Gardiner gave me the OK, and I was relieved to have yet another hurdle behind me.

That evening the Chief Flying Instructor, Andy Madore, called an emergency meeting of all pilots in training and their instructors. Madore went over the afternoon's incident and discussed how easily it might have been fatal—one more bounce of Alcazar's aircraft and I would have been done for. As it happened, thirty years later I was to meet another, unrelated Fraser on the staff of Sir George Williams University who had been in a similar accident—except that it was in *Spitfires* and the metal propeller had not broken off. As a result, he had lost an arm to the whirling propeller, simply because the second pilot had been careless. In my case, Alcazar said that he had seen one plane ahead of him as he zigged, then when he saw another plane as he zagged he assumed it was the same one. When the plane in front of me turned into the wind to take off, Alcazar revved up his engine to get out of the way and consequently crashed into my plane. He got off with a reprimand, but this was not to be the last of his escapades. A few days later he was practising what may have been an unauthorized forced landing when he turned across wind into a practice field. The Flight Commander and a student had also turned into the wind from the other side, and had it not been for the alertness of the Flight Commander there would have been a head-on collision. Needless to say, another trainee was washed out, and our number was down to twenty-three. Andy Madore mentioned that another accident, involving two *Ansons,* had occurred on a Calgary training station at about the same time as mine. They also hadn't seen each other and were both approaching for a landing. The one on top settled onto the one below, but fortunately—very fortunately —the pilot in the lower plane kept his head and landed both planes straight ahead, piggyback fashion.

The weather grew colder, and snow built up on the surface of the aerodrome. Only a narrow path was cleared for take-off and taxiing. Pilots flying over the Saskatchewan River just after take-off often found their cockpit hoods coated with ice and had to fly blind until it melted a few minutes later. The ice would form when the cold aircraft entered the humid atmosphere over the river.

One morning my name was called out at the flight room to report to the Chief Instructor. I marched in somewhat apprehensively, but soon found that all was well. "Get ready for a cross-country flight," said Madore. "Your instructor tells me you're a good pilot. I have some business in Saskatoon so you can fly me down and get some experience on the way." Feeling honoured, I rushed off to check the assigned plane: fully gassed up and oiled, mechanic check sheet signed, wings and tail OK, no locking devices on the elevators or ailerons, pitot tube (air speed indicator tube) uncovered, air in the tires. I obtained a map, checked the weather, plotted the track to Saskatoon, and calculated the course, taking the wind into consideration as I worked out the probable ground speed. I had my parachute ready and was standing near the plane by the time Madore walked out.

The flight to Saskatoon was uneventful save for a few moments above Gull Lake, when my thoughts drifted to history lessons and discussions of the 1885 Riel Rebellion there. The plane slipped a few degrees off course while I was poring over the scenery and dreaming of its history, but I snapped out of my reverie when the CFI gently brought the error to my attention.

The Saskatoon airfield appeared to be much larger than that at Prince Albert. There were a great many civilian aircraft as well as the twin-engine *Ansons* of an RCAF Service Flying Training School. The runways were a new experience for me, as at Prince Albert we landed and took off from a large grass field. Once on the ground the CFI took over the aircraft and parked it near the flight office. As we climbed out of the cockpits Madore told me that he would be busy for a few hours;

in the meantime I was to get the plane gassed up and checked over.

The CFI re-appeared in mid-afternoon, waving his little attache case to indicate that business was over. It was growing dark by the time we approached the town of Prince Albert, and the street lights indicated that we were on the right course. The runway landing lights were also on, and the aerodrome lights blinked above the hangar. I approached carefully, noting the direction of the wind sock that was scarcely visible in the twilight of the late afternoon. I brought the plane in cautiously over the edge of the aerodrome and touched down safely, then taxied over to the hangar where two mechanics were waiting to guide the plane into position near the open door of the hangar. As I shut off the engine, I was exultant in the knowledge that I had made what was almost a night landing, and had completed my first long-distance flight in a *Tiger Moth* under the eyes of none other than the Chief Flying Instructor. Another stepping stone in my flying career had been reached. My confidence increased, but always in the back of my mind I could hear Joe Coombes' admonition, "Don't try to be the best pilot, try to be the oldest." It reminded me of the "vaulting ambition" said to have wrought Macbeth's eventual destruction. I was determined to keep both these in mind throughout my flying career.

The days grew shorter, the weather colder, and more snow covered the ground. We now generally broke through the stratus formations into sunshine at 4000 feet, to chase up and down through the valleys of clouds with the white cumulus billowing up ahead. We would steer around some of them and through others to experience the bumpy air, ending with a slow northward descent to bring us northwest of the aerodrome. When we broke cloud, often at about seven hundred feet, we would turn on a reciprocal course, head south until we hit the North Saskatchewan River, and then turn east to follow the river back to the aerodrome. Often we were the last plane to land.

Soon I was doing aerobatics regularly. Joe liked to try out new manoeuvres, and during one flight he asked if I would like to try an inverted spin. I had full confidence in him so eagerly replied, "OK". He turned the plane upside down, throttled back, pushed the joystick slightly forward to raise the nose, and kicked the rudder to one side. We fell upside-down toward the ground in great, swooshing, flat circles. I suddenly became aware of something dripping from my nose. Was it blood, I wondered? Lifting my hand to my nose and drawing it away again I saw nothing red. The drip had stopped, but it started again as soon as I took my hand away. I broke into a cold sweat. What was it? With relief I finally realized that what was dripping down my face was not blood, but water that had condensed in the speaking tube which was now upside down.

After a few long minutes, I finally heard Joe say, "Now we'll recover from this spin: apply opposite rudder, stick back." The nose of the plane pitched toward the earth, and although we were still upside down, the spinning stopped as we gathered speed. Joe then pulled the plane right side up and opened up the engine. We returned to the aerodrome feeling jubilant at having done an aerobatic manoeuvre that was not really in the books.

The food at our EFTS was excellent: good steaks every day, lots of milk and cereal, bacon and eggs for breakfast, and tea or coffee, but it was the milk that we really poured down our throats. My weight went up from 148 pounds at recruitment to about 160-165, and stayed there, although it dropped back to about 155 before I returned from overseas several years later.

A classmate was taken to the hospital when tests showed something wrong with his heart. He had had rheumatic fever as a child, and his heart proved to have been permanently weakened. He was washed out of flying, and our number dropped again.

The people of Prince Albert were magnificent. At one time a request came in for volunteers to sing with a girl's choir, the Dolphinettes. They wanted to put on a programme in the local theatre to raise money for some worthy cause or other and needed some male singers, preferably in uniform. I volunteered along with eleven others. It was obvious that all they really wanted were some uniforms in the background, for none of us could sing, except perhaps after a few beers. We practised and practised in our time off, and as a pleasant result got to know the girls fairly well. I remember one song went: "Up boys, up in the open sky . . ." It really stirred up the audience, as the Battle of Britain had just ended and everyone felt proud and grateful toward the Air Force.

Exams came and went. Finally it was time for the fifty-hour test that would determine whether we would go on to the Service Flying School and our wings. Everything went smoothly when Flying Officer Gardiner gave me my test. I had the flying instructor's patter down almost word for word and explained every manoeuvre over the speaking tube as I performed it. My take-off and landing were good, and my instrument flying was perfect, but my aerobatics were rather weak. The one bad moment occurred when I stalled the aircraft out of a roll off the top, but I recovered safely and tried again. Perhaps I scared the instructor just a little, but he was probably used to that. I consoled myself with Joe's assertion that instrument flying was much more important anyway, as it would keep me alive in poor weather, whereas aerobatics were of little use in modern flying.

After the test Gardiner asked if I would like to be an instructor. I considered the question carefully, thinking of my brother George in the Canadian Army in England and my conviction that the Allied failure in the Battle of France had been due to a lack of pilots and planes.

Eventually, I thanked Gardiner, but told him I would rather proceed overseas. After my contribution on operational flights, I might want to return to Canada as an instructor. By that time I would have more experience to pass on to the new recruits. Gardiner later discussed my test with Joe Coombes. He had apparently been impressed with my patter during the test and my explanations of each manoeuvre. Joe also heard about my decision to go overseas, and told me he would have taken the same step had he been in my shoes.

Gradually my remaining classmates finished their tests, and news of our next posting came in late November. We were to proceed to No. 1 Service Flying Training School with its single-engine *Harvards* and *Yales* at RCAF Station Camp Borden, Ontario, presumably to be trained as fighter pilots. A tremendous celebration followed this announcement. We were sorry to be leaving the Dolphinettes chorus and all our friends in Prince Albert, sorry to part company with the *Tiger Moths,* the good meals, the excellent and friendly instructors, and the clear, cold air, but it was nevertheless remarkably encouraging to be returning "home" to the East.

It was a cold, blowing, snowy morning when our train pulled into the little railroad station at Angus near Camp Borden. Our gear was unloaded in no time, but, naturally, the transport trucks had not yet put in their appearance. We huddled around a pot-bellied coal stove in the station until the trucks arrived, then piled in for the drive to Camp Borden. At No. 1 SFTS ground instruction was not nearly as interesting, nor as well organized, as that at Prince Albert. We did a lot of gunnery and bombing work, with emphasis on the Browning machine-gun. I had already become familiar with the Vickers machine-gun in the COTC, but it was not the type used in aircraft. Our rank was now Leading Aircraftman, indicated by a little cloth propeller on our sleeves. Our daily pay went up twenty cents to $1.50, plus $0.75 extra as flying pay; a total of $2.25 per day. A small part of this magnificent sum was deducted for messing fees.

Our first new training aircraft was the single-engine *Yale,* aluminum in colour with a fixed undercarriage and spats around the wheels. The RCAF had taken these aircraft from an uncompleted French contract, and in our first cockpit drill I noticed that all instruments were gauged in metric, a type of measurement I was accustomed to in a science classroom, but totally unprepared to fly by. Fortunately, the airspeed indicator had two danger lines in red, with a green line centred between them. The red lines denoted the stalling speed and the maximum top speed, below and above which respectively it was dangerous to fly the aeroplane, and the green line indicated the optimum cruising speed.

One day I had taken off and was high in the air before I realized there were no red or green lines on my craft's speed indicator. For several shaky minutes I envisioned the crash which would inevitably result if I stalled the plane while coming in for a landing. Attempting to ignore my fears, I made a few quick calculations. I knew the *Yale* stalled at about 65 miles per hour; what was that in kilometres per hour? About 100? I prepared myself as well as possible for a crash landing, but all went well. The *Yale* was a reasonably safe aircraft, but it rattled like an old tin can when stalled and put into a spin. It was a cold plane, too; the heaters never seemed to work very well. It was designated by the RCAF as an "intermediate trainer", a category about as useful as feet on a fish.

We soon moved onto *Harvards;* fast, single-engined, yellow aircraft with retractable undercarriages, a much hotter development of the *Yale.* Like most aircraft, this type had its quirks; tending to dip a wing near stalling speed, for one thing. It was an aircraft with lots of power for aerobatics, but it also spun very rapidly, and one could easily get killed in it. One evening we heard that one of our classmates had not returned from his flight. Late that night, as we were making our way back from the canteen to the barracks, we saw a truck pull up. In the back were aeroplane pieces, so small each of them could have been put in a matchbox. The parts were the yellow of a *Harvard,* but some carried reddish-brown splashes, the blood of our late pal.

The weather at Camp Borden was what could be expected of an Ontario mid-winter, with masses of snow. Daytime flying stopped at 1700 and night flying started shortly afterward, as soon as it was completely dark. After the episode with Alcazar at Prince Albert I kept an especially sharp lookout, both on the ground and in the air, for other aircraft. This practice might have saved my life, for late one afternoon I was on the downwind leg of a circuit, just prior to turning in for a landing, when I did my habitual thorough check of the skies around me. Immediately above my plane was another aircraft, descending with wheels down and within ten feet of me. Alarmed, I pushed the stick forward and dove steeply. I don't believe the other pilot ever did see me, but I'd had enough of a shock for both of us, and was still shaking after making a second circuit and landing safely.

I wanted to get in as much flying as possible, so would often turn up at the flight hangars on Sunday, when my usual instructor was off for the weekend. One Sunday I was sitting near the crew room when a mechanic appeared and said I was to warm up the *Harvard* being pushed out of the hangar, as my instructor would be over shortly. I was surprised, but, nevertheless, grabbed my parachute and climbed into the *Harvard.* The engine was running smoothly by the time the instructor came wobbling out through the snow drifts with his seat parachute on his back. Climbing onto the wing, he motioned for me to get into the rear cockpit, where the instructor normally sat—the pupil always flew from the front seat. Once we had both settled into the respective seats, he spoke to me over the intercom. "Pull the blind flying hood over; you are going to do some instrument flying." The hood in place, he told me to taxi out.

"But I can't see where I'm going!" I replied, with some alarm.

"Don't worry, I'll tell you where. Straight ahead—turn right—I have control—you have control—you are now lined up with the runway. Take off."

"Under the hood?" I asked, astonished.

Sounding impatient with my apparent stupidity, he answered, "Yes, under the hood."

I slowly opened up the throttle and cautiously gathered speed, keeping the plane straight with the help of the gyro compass, which I had uncaged when the instructor told me I was lined up with the runway. At 80 mph I eased back on the control column and climbed straight ahead.

His voice broke through the intercom again. "Keep straight—climb to 4500 feet—turn to the right and climb to 7500 feet. I have control." The *Harvard* went through some strange antics, though what exactly I couldn't tell, as I was still under the hood. "You have control."

I decided we were upside-down and eased back on the control stick. Our speed gathered and I righted the plane onto an even keel.

"I have control," came the instructor's voice once more. He did something else with the plane. What was it? A loop? A roll off the top? We were again in an unknown position, and, sweating heavily, I did my best to recover the plane to the straight and level. Finally, after about forty minutes of this unusual and nerve-wracking exercise, the instructor said, "Turn to the left again—slow to 120 miles per hour—let down to 1000 feet—turn 90 degrees to the left, and land straight ahead." The altimeter showed that we were approaching the ground. I eased back on the stick, the speed dropped to 80 mph, and as the wheels touched the ground I cut the throttle. We were down safely. For the last time my instructor's voice came through the intercom: "I have control."

He gunned the engine and taxied the aircraft rapidly back to the tarmac hangar through the blowing snow. With a sigh of utter relief I pulled the hood off. Near the hangar the instructor asked me to pull up to the hangar door, then jumped out onto the wing and motioned me to taxi the plane back to the flight line to park the aircraft. I stopped the engine and the mechanic put the chocks under the wheels. As I climbed shakily out onto the wing and dropped to the ground, the mechanic said, "He's pretty far gone, isn't he?"

At that belated moment I realized that the instructor must have come straight from a party, and was well-elevated even before getting into the aircraft. Suddenly breaking into a cold sweat, I shuddered violently as I thought of the incredible danger I had just escaped. Someone had once told me that a climb to 10,000 feet was a good way to clear a hangover, but from then on I held the opinion that it was only a good way to get killed.

Harvard training aircraft taken over from France in 1940.

Yale training aircraft with retractable undercarriage, 1940.

Late one afternoon I was the last to land my *Harvard* and take my parachute back to the flight room. A mechanic was waiting for me: "They want you down at the Squadron Office, right away."

I grabbed my greatcoat and rushed off through the snow to the Office, where I was ushered into a room with four officers: I snapped to attention. It took only a moment to realize that they were evaluating prospective candidates for a commission. One might become a Pilot Officer on obtaining one's wings or remain a Sergeant. I was totally unprepared for this unexpected interview, and, worse luck, I was apparently the last candidate. The others had been warned earlier while I was still flying, and had had the opportunity to return to the barracks to clean up and polish their buttons.

"Who is the leader in Romania?"

"Antonescu?"

"Who was the first officer to command the first Canadian squadron to go overseas?"

"McNab," I hesitantly answered. Thus it went, question after question. They were mostly on current affairs; nothing was asked about my COTC background, nothing of my present flying. When finally dismissed, I was given no indication of how I had been rated.

At last we were given our wings test by Flying Officer Sharp, who thirty years later was to become Chief of Staff of the Canadian Armed Forces. My navigation tests also went smoothly, and having finished early in the course I was employed as an instructor of sorts, checking out other trainees in instrument flying when they needed more experience.

On February 10, 1941, one chapter of my life was brought to a magnificent close. Relatives, reporters, and dignitaries had gathered at the drill hall inside one of the large hangars to witness that long-awaited ritual, the wings ceremony. The names were called out one by one, and it was but a brief wait until it was my turn to step smartly forward and have my wings pinned onto my proudly extended chest. It was a glorious day, despite the snowstorm raging outside. That evening my picture was in the *Toronto Star*, but to my annoyance the caption read, "AUSTRALIANS GET WINGS", followed in small print by "D.A. Fraser of Toronto being awarded his wings." My friends in Toronto were astounded by my inexplicable and unheralded change of nationality.

Following the wings parade we were all given two weeks leave, after which we were to report to RCAF Manning Depot, Toronto for overseas posting. Along with the wings came promotions to Sergeant Pilots, and we began receiving $3.70 per day. As I was packing to catch a bus to Toronto, Flying Officer Hilton took me aside. "You should have gotten a commission," he said. "I recommended you, but none of my students are getting promoted to Pilot Officer. The assessment committee doesn't like me." Oh well, could an Australian from Toronto expect any better?

I whiled away most of my leave lounging around home and visiting the University, though I did manage to make it to a dance at Simpson's Academy Court. The girl I accompanied to the dance wore a long dress with horizontal bands of red, white, and blue—very striking and attractive. When, some twenty-five years later, I reminded her of the dress, she said that she had considered it very patriotic for those wartime days and nights. I squired this same girl to various functions, and we passed many pleasant hours together, but marriage rarely, if ever, crossed my mind. One or two of the fellows I had trained with used their two-week leave for a wedding and brief honeymoon, but among other reasons, I was financially unprepared for such a venture. It would, I felt, be unfair to my bride, and in any case I was determined to help my widowed mother as much as possible. I had already assigned half my pay to be sent to her automatically. During my leave I also took out a $500 insurance policy which would cover my education debts to the University and the Masonic Lodge, should I not come back. The insurance company, naturally enough, decided that I was a bad risk, and would only issue the policy to me on the condition that I pay the premium for my age plus ten years. After the war I had a hard time getting my real age back for insurance purposes. And it was only after the war, too, that I learned of the insurance company's fine-print war clause which made the policy good only if I had been killed while on the ground.

In late February a telegram was delivered to our house. This was a rare event, and our immediate fears for George made us hesitate to open it. But it was only a telegram from the RCAF. A diptheria epidemic at the Toronto embarkation depot dictated that my leave be extended until early March, when I was to report directly to RCAF Station Debert, Nova Scotia. There I would join my company, and we would proceed to Halifax to embark for overseas.

I still remember the going-away party given for me on March 9, 1941. An old classmate from North Toronto Collegiate, Douglas Horniblow, presented me with a five-year diary, remarking, only half in jest, that he hoped the war would not last that long.

I left Toronto by train the next morning at 1015, with my mother and two younger brothers there to see me off. In the station I met some of the other members of my class; one of these was Howie Davidson from Preston, Ontario, with whom I had shared living quarters during our flying training, and who had spent many evenings extolling the virtues of the CPR, for whom he worked, compared to the CNR. We were joined by more classmates when we changed trains in Montreal: Stanislaw Kozlowski from Ottawa, Gordie Gosman from the West, and Charlie Tourville from Victoriaville, Quebec. Together we boarded the sleeper for Debert.

Chapter Three
Trans-Atlantic Voyage

OUR TRAIN ARRIVED IN Debert station the following evening, and for once the trucks were waiting to take us and our gear to the camp. It was a desolate place. At this stage the camp was a makeshift establishment with the runways still under construction, although a twin-engine *Hudson* bomber did come in to land two nights after we arrived. At first we were billeted in the hangar barracks, then moved into the Officers' Quarters, even though we were all Sergeant Pilots. It was a bit disappointing that so few of us had been awarded a promotion to Pilot Officer, at least until word came that our SFTS mate Les Broad, who had been promoted to Pilot Officer and gone to RCAF Station Trenton on an instructor's course, had been killed when the wing came off his *Harvard.* Maybe I had been wise to refuse the position of instructor with its automatic promotion to Pilot Officer after my fifty-hour test.

New drafts were announced daily and trainees began disappearing one by one. Once, while wandering around the perimeter of the aerodrome, I thought the airman on guard duty looked familiar and went to speak with him. He recognized me immediately. It was Hughie Grant from my Sunday School class at Glebe Presbyterian Church in Toronto. This was the last time I would see him, as he was killed two years later while training on *Spitfires.* Another old acquaintance I ran into at Debert was Tom Kerr, the one whose model aircraft I had always admired when I was in my early teens. To our mutual disappointment, he had not become a pilot, but was instead a clerk in the Royal Canadian Postal Corps.

By March 15 I still hadn't received my pay. I had assigned $23 a month to my mother, as we were not allowed to assign any more than that. We heard that we were to get five shillings a day, about one dollar, while serving with the RAF and that the rest would be kept in Ottawa, but it was difficult to get any definite information.

That evening Punchy Archibald, a fellow Sergeant Pilot from Oakville, Ontario took me to visit some friends of his in Truro, not far from Debert. Punchy, a friendly, popular individual, was to be one of the few to go on *Spitfires,* and was later killed in France. It was rumoured he was shot down and, after setting fire to his plane, was killed by German troops while trying to escape.

There was a continual stream of new arrivals, as Debert was a staging post for aircrew going overseas. Parades were held every day, and I would spend occasional evenings in Truro at a movie with Punchy Archibald, Howie Davidson, and Matt Dunham. All three of these friends were lost in the war—Punchy I mentioned above, and Matt and Howie went missing in the Fall of 1941 while on *Blenheims.*

Rosamond, the girl with the red, white and blue evening dress, at the author's class graduation party, February, 1941.

S.S. *Rajputana* which escorted 700 ships in convoy without loss, carried its last draft of 100 British Commonwealth pilots from Halifax to Reykjavik in late March — early April 1941, to be sunk by the U-108 on April 13, 1941, while on its lonely patrol in the Denmark Strait.

(Photo: P & O Steamship Navigation Co.)

On Wednesday, March 26, 1941, our draft was told to put all luggage in No. 1 hangar. We left Debert at 1630 and arrived in Halifax three hours later, immediately boarding HMS *Rajputana,* a 17,000-ton armed merchant cruiser with eight 6-inch guns and two 3-inch anti-aircraft guns, the ship that would take us part of the way across the Atlantic.

Rajputana was built in 1926 by Harland and Wolff at Greenock, Scotland, and was originally on the Bombay mail service, later transferring to passenger runs to Japan. At that time she carried 310 first-class and 290 second-class passengers. *Rajputana* was in Yokohama, Japan when war was declared, and was ordered to proceed immediately to Esquimalt, British Columbia, where she received her armament. By the time we boarded, she had already escorted seven hundred ships on convoy without a loss.

Rajputana had altered considerably since her civilian days. Our sleeping quarters, for instance, left a lot to be desired. We were crowded into a large space below the waterline, the dance floor of a more peaceful era. Closely-laid straw mattresses were spread across the floor as our "beds". There were only fourteen Canadians from our original group among the one hundred Commonwealth and United Kingdom pilots on board. It appeared to be the intention of the RAF to get us overseas as soon as possible, with small concentrations of aircrew distributed amongst the other forty-three ships in the convoy. This strategy would keep individual losses to a minimum in the case of a successful U-boat attack. Besides their "passengers", the other ships were loaded to the top with aircraft stowed on their decks. We Canadians on *Raj* banded together and, with a little bribery, took over a small empty cabin above the waterline. Most of the cabins on the ship had had their contents ripped out and replaced by thousands of empty forty-gallon oil drums, which might keep the ship afloat should it be hit by gunfire from the German battle cruisers presently at sea.

Sgt. Pilot Jack Hallam, RCAF, from Sarnia, Ontario, standing in front of the *Rajputana* nameplate, April, 1941. Missing on operations, July, 1941.

At last we set sail at 1530 on March 27. Our forty-four ship convoy was guarded by the British submarine *Tribune*. Because the formidable German battle cruisers *Scharnhorst* and *Gneisenau* were active in the North Atlantic at the time, it was planned that if they attempted to intercept our convoy, the *Rajputana* would engage them. This would give the *Tribune* the opportunity to submerge, creep around, and torpedo the German ships. At the same time the convoy would have the opportunity to disperse. This manoeuvre, without a submarine, had already been employed by Captain Fegen of HMS *Jervis Bay,* another armed merchant cruiser, which attacked the German pocket battleship *Admiral Scheer* to allow an Allied convoy to scatter. Captain Fegen had perished during this valiant and largely successful effort, and was awarded a posthumous Victoria Cross.

Our average speed was a crawling eight knots. Every day Action Stations were called at 0700 and 1800. On our first day at sea, the 28th, I was a slightly ill mess orderly. I wasn't really seasick, but I wouldn't have wanted to try anything too energetic. American destroyers were with us all day, as well as, I believe, two submarines. None of us knew our destination for sure, but the consensus was that we were headed for Iceland. The next day I served on watch from 2200 to 2300 during the blackout above deck. We were in the Gulf Stream by that time; it was quite mild, but there was a strong wind.

On the 30th we put the clock ahead one hour for the first time. The ship was encased in a dense fog for part of the day, but by the time I went to stand watch at 0500 the following morning the stars of the Big Dipper were quite distinct. Another armed merchant cruiser followed us for a short time that day. We heard that the *Scharnhorst* and *Gneisenau* had entered the French port of Brest—for a few days, at least, we could feel safe from them. The destroyers and one of the submarines left us to return home to Halifax. We joked, uneasily, that it was getting to dangerous for them to go any farther with us across the Atlantic.

After a routine dinner of bangers and mash on April 2, I ran into another graduate of my high school, Jack Nicholson, in our group of pilots. He had just finished his final year at the Collegiate the previous June. As far as I know, Jackie later went on light bombers, *Blenheims*, and was the man who dropped replacement wooden legs to the legless RAF fighter pilot Douglas Bader, who had been shot down over France. Jackie himself did not survive the war. He was only seventeen years old when we met on board *Rajputana;* I was one of the oldest at twenty-two.

That same day brought a bit of excitement when we chased two steamers. This really wasn't too unusual—whenever smoke appeared on the horizon, Action Stations were sounded and *Rajputana* went charging off to the attack, while *Tribune* submerged. Two of the ships chased in this manner on Thursday, April 3 were found to be British steamers with a few extra passengers—survivors from a torpedoed boat. The atmosphere grew tense as we progressed further eastward, and our watch was doubled; in the previous convoy seven ships had been torpedoed within the last forty-eight hours. We inspected the mute evidence of this tragedy as we ploughed through the flotsam and overturned lifeboats; there was no sign of life. Orders were issued to wear lifebelts at all times, even to bed.

One morning we woke to a rough sea and scattered convoy. We spent the whole day rounding up a group of forty-one ships. After twelve days at sea we expected to leave the convoy soon, to be replaced by an escort of destroyers that was supposed to be refuelling at Reykjavik. I hoped that we would go to Iceland ourselves. The next evening, at the end of a foggy and rainy day, we finally met the expected escort and were free to speed alone toward Iceland at nineteen knots—two knots faster than *Raj's* nominal maximum cruising speed. We saw one iceberg and passed the battleship *Resolution* and six destroyers before landfall at 1030 on April 10. Rain was falling as we anchored in Reykjavik harbour, and we airmen were quickly transferred by the tug *Jokul* to His Majesty's transport *Royal Ulsterman,* with Scots troops and Royal Engineers already aboard. To our pleasure, we found that although the food in *Royal Ulsterman* was rationed, with no sugar and just condensed milk, generous and surprisingly delicious meals were served. It was Good Friday when we boarded—there were one thousand troops on the ship, and most of the Sergeant Pilots were pickled. We inspected the land from the ship, but Iceland is one of the countries where I have, as yet, never set foot.

Rajputana left the harbour on another mission on April 11. Some of its crew had mentioned to me that they had not been home to the UK for two years and almost hoped to be torpedoed so that they could get survivors' leave. Their jestful wish was to be fulfilled within forty-eight hours. We watched *Raj* steam out, not realizing how thankful we should have been that we had parted company with her.

After dropping us off at Reykjavik, *Rajputana* headed out alone into the Denmark Strait between Iceland and Greenland on patrol for blockade runners, and to warn of the presence of any enemy surface ships. No one on *Rajputana* suspected that their ship was being stalked by *U.108,* a submarine that had sighted its funnel smoke at 0945 on April 11 off the northwest coast of Iceland. All day long *U.108* tried to manoeuvre into firing position, but was thwarted by *Rajputana's* continual changes in speed and direction. At 0608 *U.108* fired two torpedoes from a range of two thousand metres. Both shots missed. The following day at 2246 and 2248 two single torpedoes were again fired, from a range of one thousand metres, and again both missed. Finally, at 0715 on April 13, *U.108* sighted *Rajputana* on a reciprocal course and submerged to attack. A single torpedo fired at 0740 from a range of eight thousand metres missed the cruiser, but another, fired three minutes later with the range closing, struck the ship. *Rajputana* had been completely unaware of her pursuer until this sixth torpedo found its target between the aft mast and the funnel. The engine and boiler rooms were seriously damaged—three men were killed instantly. *Rajputana*, at last drastically aware of the presence of the U-boat, opened fire on the visible periscope, hoping to keep the enemy out of effective range. Captain Klaus Scholtz of *U-108* ordered a dive under the sinking ship, and the U-boat came up to periscope depth on her opposite side. Scholtz watched while *Sunderland* flying boats circled the sinking ship and a destroyer from Reykjavik picked up survivors. *Raj* was slow in sinking, probably because of the thousands of empty forty-gallon drums in her cabins. Assuming most men had evacuated the ship, Captain Scholtz fired a final fan of three torpedoes. Two struck *Rajputana,* and she sank to the bottom. It was a credit to *Rajputana's* Captain and the ship's company that the evacuation of the sinking cruiser resulted in the rescue of 283 men, although the Captain himself perished.

We first learned that *Rajputana* had been sunk shortly after we arrived in the United Kingdom when we saw a newspaper note: "Canadians rescue British oilers trapped in hold of *Rajputana.*" The notice had originated in Glace Bay, Nova Scotia on May 21, 1941, and described the actions of Chesley Barford of Glace Bay, L. Basset of Windsor, Ontario, and T. Shepperd from Prince Edward Island. These *Rajputana* crewmen went below the waterline into the engine room after the torpedo hit the vessel and carried the injured men on deck. One of those rescued later died of his injuries.

In March 1980 I located Frigate Captain Klaus Scholtz, commander of *U-108* when it sank *Rajputana* off Iceland. He welcomed my wife and myself when we stepped off the train at Lubeck in West Germany. After a sight-seeing trip around that old Hanseatic port he took us to his home, where his wife had tea and cakes waiting for us. We reminisced. He remembered the torpedoing of *Rajputana.* He had been on patrol in the Denmark Strait where he was to work in conjunction with *Bismarck,* the German super-battleship that would shortly be sailing through those waters. Captain Scholtz was interested in my experiences with *Rajputana,* and wanted to know if there had been a great loss of life. He seemed pleased and relieved to learn that most of the company had been saved.

To return to 1941, we stayed on *Royal Ulsterman* in the harbour at Reykjavik until Easter Sunday—April 13, the day of the sinking of *Rajputana.* Our departure on that day was cut short by a well-founded U-boat scare, and we returned to harbour. We finally got away on the following day, accompanied by our sister-ship, *Royal Scotsman* and two destroyers.

Ulsterman rolled incessantly despite the calmness of the waters, and many soldiers and airmen were seasick. As a defence measure our ship did a lot of zig-zagging, and after three weeks we were still at sea. Land, the Isle of Lewis, was finally sighted at 0930 on the morning of April 16. We hoped to be in Clyde that night, for the Hebrides were in sight all day; several wrecked steamers could be seen on the rocks. On April 17 we saw the Clyde lighthouse, and we soon found ourselves anchored in Greenock Bay, landing at Gourock the following morning. The trip from Toronto to Gourock had taken thirty-eight days, only twenty-one of them actually on board ship. Yet despite the hopes of some and the fears of others, the war was not over before we got there, after all.

Chapter Four
Introduction to the Wimpy

IN UXBRIDGE (WHERE I met my first Woman's Auxiliary Air Force [WAAF] personnel) I filled in papers for aircraft preferences. Everyone's first choice was fighters, and then, if they were not available, four-engined flying boats. That first night we visited the town and saw a show. Movies were at their peak of popularity and were the universal entertainment of the era. This evening also brought home to us a new part of our daily life—we were now in the land of the blackout. This and the all-day rain made for a gloomy welcome. The next day it was still raining, but clear skies in the afternoon and my initial pay of twelve pounds cheered me considerably. Howie Davidson and I went to town again that night to see another show. At 2140 another element of life in the UK startled us when the theatre trembled as bombs exploded nearby. The screen immediately flashed a message: "Anyone who wants to go home can leave now." Our thoughts were literally, "Let's go home to Canada," but noticing that few other patrons were moving we stayed and saw the whole show, before staggering out to the sound of still more bombing. As we made our way back to the station Howie and I wondered, with far more than a casual interest, whether it was safer to walk on the inside, next to the houses, or out on the street.

On the first Sunday at our new station there was a clothing parade, during which we were issued anti-gas equipment, respirators, and helmets. That night I went to a service at a nearby church, one that had been built in 1622. There were not many worshippers in the congregation. I had my helmet and respirator with me, and they clanked noisily whenever I knelt for prayer. Few people had brought them there, but it was compulsory for service personnel to carry them at all times when off the base. I returned to play snooker in the Sergeants' Mess before retiring to write the first of my letters from England.

Monday, April 21, dawned a lovely day. Rumour had it that we might be posted soon, and it became fact later that day. I was posted to RAF Station Benson, near Oxford; Howie Davidson was to go to Bicester to fly *Blenheims*.

The crew of aircraft J for Johnny of 114 Squadron, RAF, that went missing October 14, 1941.
Sgt.-Pilot Howie Davison, RCAF (centre) from Preston, Ontario,
Sgt.-Observer Paul, RAF (left) from Plymouth, England,
Sgt.-Air Gunner Peppler (right) from Southampton, England.

For once no time was wasted, and I arrived at Wallingford station near Benson at 1630 hours the next day. As we new airmen debarked from the train, we saw several huge (at least in our minds), black, twin-engined bombers, with a single tail fin stretching high in the air: *Wellingtons.* They reminded me of large sharks as they sailed slowly through the skies. "Slow" was the right adjective to use for these planes. I found out later that even the *Harvard* trainers I had flown in Camp Borden had a higher cruising speed than these operational aircraft.

A truck soon arrived to take us to the aerodrome three miles away, where we soon learned we were to fly these *Wellingtons,* affectionately known as *Wimpys.* This was a bit of a disappointment; they were neither the single-engine fighters nor the four-engine planes we had asked for when we filled in the papers at Uxbridge. We were assigned surprisingly clean barracks and granted leave until Saturday midnight. With only a few days leave I decided to visit George, stationed somewhere south of London. There were no buses to town, so I walked out on the road near Benson and, for the first time in my life, started to hitchhike. I hadn't long to wait before a chap in an English Ford came along and drove me right into London. My first stop was the Beaver Club, sponsored by the Canadian High Commission in London, where one was actually able to get pancakes with real maple syrup. This club was to become a regular eating place for me every time I passed through the city. By good chance I met Jim Monroe from the 48th Highlanders, who would be driving back to the Regiment a little later that same evening. Thus I managed a fast trip to Kingswood, near Sutton, to visit my brother. He was surprised when I walked in, but was quick to fix me up a bunk for the night. By the following evening George was able to get a 48-hour pass and we bused to Perley to see a show: *The Mark of Zorro.* We then became tourists, travelling the next day via Leatherhead to visit Windsor Castle. We also stopped at Eton College, where the bursar, whom we met on the grounds, took us around and showed us through a chapel that had recently had a close shave with an enemy bomb. That night we went to a dance at the Sergeants' Mess of the Grenadier Guards, before slipping into lovely, soft hotel beds. On our last day together George and I saw the Changing of the Guard at Windsor Castle and followed it with breakfast at the Royal Albert Institute. We parted at noon, returning to our separate stations.

On Sunday, April 27, a large group gathered at Station Headquarters to learn more about our posting. I was assigned to No. 3 Squadron, located a mile away on the far side of the aerodrome, right next to the fence that separated it from the village of Benson. We were to undergo training for six weeks, with lectures from 0900 to 1230 hours and flying from 1330 to 1700, except when on night flying.

It was very chilly weather that first week. We were issued flying kits with oxygen equipment and had our pictures taken, but little else took place for several days. Finally, on the 30th, I managed to get two hours as a passenger in a *Wellington,* the plane I would come to know so well. We landed at a nearby aerodrome, Harwell, where I saw Westland *Whirlwinds,* twin-engined fighter-bombers. The type looked very sleek, but was somewhat under-powered and hence did not have the performance of the twin-engine *Mosquito* that later replaced it. I was to visit Harwell again just after the first British atomic reactor had been constructed in one of its hangars. At this later date one of the hosts commented in the course of his remarks that none of the visiting scientists had been in the Harwell hangar before, and was somewhat taken aback when I casually mentioned that I had parked a *Wellington* outside its doors some thirteen years earlier.

Our training continued for days in disorganized fashion. Some of the lectures were rather inadequate, as, for many of the instructors, it was their first time in front of a class. There was much less flying than we would have liked because the *Wimpys* were in such short supply. The machines used were old ones which, as they had been shot up on squadron operations over Germany, were unserviceable much of the time. We made up for this to a degree by spending many hours on the Link trainer, a small cockpit and fuselage mounted on a system of wind-operated bellows in which we could simulate blind flying. Flight efforts were traced out on a sheet of paper by an electronically-controlled crab.

RAF force U-boat to surrender
A *Hudson* aircraft of RAF Coastal Command sighted and attacked a U-boat in the Atlantic. Close-up picture as she lay helpless in the heavy seas awaiting a boarding party from HM ships.   (Imperial War Museum)

Aircrew in the summer of 1941.
Left to right: Sgt. Jerry Burns, RAF Malaya to the Middle East; Sgt. Bennet, RAF; Sgt. Post, RAAF, missing in action; Sgt. Geard, RAF; Sgt. Twydall, RAF on 33 course; Sgt. Mackillop, RAF, killed in action, Bicester Station; Sgt. Anderson, RCAF; Sgt. Jack Hallam, RCAF, Windsor, Ontario, missing on active service, July, 1941; Sgt. Macguire, RCAF, three ops crash landings so far.

On Monday, May 5 a *Wimpy* crashed near No. 3 Squadron flight office, one of its engines having failed on takeoff, a nightmare that haunts every pilot. That night we had a lecture on Bomber Command's new "secret" Astrograph, a celluloid roll with position lines calculated for certain stars. When bearings were taken with a portable bubble sextant on two different stars and plotted on the Astrograph, the position could be rapidly and accurately determined. This worked well on clear nights, but, of course, was of little use under cloud.

The maintenance on No. 3 Squadron was simply terrible, but flying time gradually increased. After three hours in a *Wellington* I went solo on the second Saturday in May, with no real problems. After our solos we started instrument flying in earnest, in the air for three hours at a stretch. We were flying whenever there was a plane serviceable, even missing pay parade!

It was about this time that I found they were taking two shillings a day off our pay for British income tax. I objected to this deduction, because under the British Commonwealth Visiting Forces Act of 1933, military men were under their own country's laws, including income tax, even when serving abroad. Now it looked as though we were not only to fight the war, but to pay for it through the nose. Nevertheless, the RAF authorities were adamant. The final word in any argument was always: "You're in the RAF now," and some of the RAF officers began to refer to us as "you Colonials". I finally wrote to the Canadian High Commissioner in London, Vincent Massey, and to Mr. Hoblitzel, Liberal MP for my riding in Toronto, about this income tax situation.

I still had some Canadian money with me, and one day I tried to send a ten dollar bill in a letter to Mother. The letter and the bill were both returned to me by the censor, which confirmed that our letters really were read by someone other than the senders and receivers.

Two of the last heavy *Luftwaffe* bombing raids on London took place while I was at Benson. We could see the flames in London from our second floor barracks window; Benson was only forty miles west of the blitzed city. As we stood there watching in helpless sympathy and anger, one of our number tuned in the radio. A retired Army general from the First World War was comparing that war and the present one.

"You know," he said, "England had a great shortage of trouser buttons in 1914, and it was very difficult to equip all the army's trousers with a sufficient supply of them. However, in 1939, realizing that a war might be on its way, the Government stocked up a large supply of these buttons, and we need not fear a shortage."

Screaming with laughter, we all had to support ourselves against the nearest wall or chair to keep from falling over. "These bastards don't even know when they've lost the war! Here's London going up in flames, the British Army has been chased off the continent, and we're told that only the RAF Bomber Command can take the fight to the enemy—in these old *Wimpys!* The British will never lose this war because they won't even know when they're beaten!"

On May 19 I flew with Scottie, one of our instructors, on landings at satellite aerodromes, but fog came in at 600 feet and further flying was scrubbed. Later that day, important enough in wartime Britain to note, I bought two oranges and a chocolate bar in the mess. Although I don't particularly care for oranges, I was planning to save them and give them as a treat to my young cousins in Stafford, England, when I next visited them on leave.

The following day was quite cloudy again—visibility two miles with low ground haze. I did instrument flying for three hours with Kozlowski in preparation for the triangular cross-country under the hood the next day, when we had to end up where we started after two hours of flying. Accurate instrument flying could save your life in bad weather.

At about the same time we heard that the German super-battleship, *Bismarck,* had sunk His Majesty's Ship *Hood,* the world's fastest and largest battle cruiser. We also heard that parachutists were landing in Crete. Undisturbed by all this news of the war, I played a quiet game of chess that evening with Charlie Tourville from Victoriaville, Quebec. Later that month I started low-level bombing exercises.

There was still a low, 600-foot ceiling on May 29 when I flew on instruments to Swindon, a nearby satellite aerodrome. This trip was enlivened by my *Wimpy* blowing her tail wheel as I was landing, but I had no trouble bringing her to a safe stop. The next morning, with a 36-hour pass under my belt, I hitchhiked to Oxford to catch the London Midland and Southern (LMS) train to Bletchley. There I changed trains, finally arriving at Stafford early in the afternoon to visit my uncle, Dr. Horace Binks, his wife Mary, my mother's sister, and cousins John, Roy, and Heather. The highlight of my brief visit was a horseback ride in a forest known as the "Chase". But my pass was a short one, and the next day after lunch I caught the 1413 train to begin my seven-hour journey back to Benson.

That night I heard two satisfying pieces of news: the *Bismarck* had been sunk, and, on a far more personal level, I would have my own crew for my first cross-country flight on the following day. I didn't recognize any of the names of my crew, which consisted of a Pilot Officer Scott, second pilot, Sergeant Foster, navigator, Sergeant Grieve, wireless operator, and Sergeant Hart, rear gunner. I hunted them out in the crew room the next morning, and they all seemed to be pleasant chaps. We chatted for a bit before the navigator and I plotted the course to Shrewsbury near Birmingham. The meteorology office forecast rain and low clouds, but I anticipated few problems on the fairly straightforward run.

Our plane was ready at about 1430 hours, so we all climbed aboard and began the starting-up procedure. I signalled to the groundcrew to start the engines, and the starboard one roared into life, but the port just backfired and stopped. After ten minutes of futile efforts to get the port engine going, a mechanic came running up to wave us out of the machine. Apparently he still had something to repair on the port engine and had not seen fit to inform us earlier. Highly disappointed and put out, we trooped back to the flight room with our maps and parachutes to wait for a serviceable aircraft to become available. At long last, about 1600 hours, we got the engines going on another plane and were ready to taxi out, when, to our intense disgust, yet another mechanic signalled us to shut down, whereupon he ran up and pumped more oil into the engines. Praying that it would be third time lucky, we fired up again, and finally were off the ground. Clearing the fence around the aerodrome, we climbed to about 1500 feet, just under the cloud ceiling, and headed northwest. I was at last off on my first cross-country flight with a full crew, one that had even less experience than myself.

We eventually reached Shrewsbury, turned toward Manchester, and headed back. By this time it was after 1800 hours. I was flying low, keeping below the clouds at 900 feet, when I observed an aerodrome in the distance on our starboard side. Checking my map, I found that we should have been directly over Pershore aerodrome, but if it was the one away to our right then we were north of our prescribed track. I called the navigator on the intercom, pointed out our actual position, and suggested that I whip the plane over to Pershore and then turn on course again.

"No, no, that isn't the way it's done," he replied. "Wait a second and I'll give you a new course for Benson."

I waited with rapidly escalating impatience until, when ten minutes later he still hadn't given me any directions, I called him up again on the intercom: "Hurry up with that new course!"

Hustling up to the cockpit, he handed me a small piece of paper and said, "Here's the new course—ETA Benson is 1746 hours."

With what I still feel was superhuman patience, I pointed out to him that the chronometer now read 1830, so he must have made a mistake. He went glumly back to his calculations. In the meantime I asked Pilot Officer Scott, my second pilot, if he could pinpoint our current position. A drizzling rain had begun, we were down to 800 feet, and the windscreens were obscured with condensation. Things didn't look good, to say the least, and they didn't get any better when Scott slid open the window to get a better view; a blast of air whirled around the cockpit and all his maps went sailing out the window. He looked forlorn.

Despairingly I recalled my fighter training on single-engine *Harvards*. What was I doing wandering around, lost, in a lumbering old *Wimpy?* Suddenly I remembered my lectures on QDM, the magnetic direction to base. All might not yet be lost. I called up the wireless operator. "Get me a QDM to base, and fast!"

"Okay, Skipper."

He called back a minute later, and, delighted at such efficiency, I complimented him on his quickness, whereupon he said, "I can't work this wireless. It's a Marconi and I was trained on a Jeep set." I was beginning to wonder what else could possibly go wrong, but he assured me that he would get the hang of it soon, and, sure enough, he called up on the intercom ten minutes later: "Skipper, I'm through to Benson."

Relieved, I replied, "Good, get me a QDM." By now we were over unknown territory, though I believed we were still north of our track.

My thoughts were interrupted by a plaintive call from the wireless operator. "They won't answer me, Skipper. I only have the verification numbers up to 1800 hours, and it's now 1850."

What a position to be in! We would have been alright if we had gotten away on time in the afternoon, but the unserviceability and changing of kites had delayed us two hours. We were lost, our maps had gone out the window, and we couldn't get a QDM because base wouldn't answer. I called up the navigator again, and when he didn't answer I turned in my seat and peered down the fuselage. He had disconnected his intercom and was looking forlornly out the plastic transparent astrodome some twenty-five feet behind me. No help there. Angry, frustrated, and with a growing feeling of apprehension, I realized that, having exhausted the resources of my navigator, second pilot, and wireless operator, I would have to take matters into my own hands. "I'm turning to starboard and south until I pick up the Thames to follow back to base." I was sure we had overshot Benson and were flying north of it. The cloud base had lowered even more, and increasingly heavy rain was pelting the aircraft. I was down to five hundred feet trying to keep under the cloud base. We passed over a built-up area, and while I was wondering what town it might be, I saw a small aerodrome with a grass field, hangars, and a row of fighters. Anti-aircraft guns surrounded the aerodrome and seemed to be following us around. I decided to land to find out where we were.

I circled slowly—fifteen degrees of flap down—propeller pitch moved toward fine—engine petrol mixture in rich—wheels down. With the engines roaring, flaps partly lowered, and nose up, I lifted the *Wimpy* just over the surrounding buildings—full flap—and dropped it over the fence. I cut the engine and we fell out of the sky with a reasonable landing, braking quickly. Our plane rolled almost to the end of the runway, and we were down safely. I heaved a sigh of relief as I taxied over to the control tower. An erk ran over, and I throttled back the engines to ask what drome we had landed at.

"Northolt," he replied, sticking his head up through the open hatch near my feet. We were only about thirty-five miles east of Benson, a mere fifteen minutes of flying time. For a couple of minutes I debated whether to attempt the short flight, considering the diminishing ceiling. Finally I decided to try it, and I whipped the plane around on the perimeter track and taxied back to the takeoff position. The air was calm, but night, rain, and the cloud ceiling were all falling. I lined up the wings and we charged off—30 . . . 40 . . . 50 . . . 60 miles an hour. The buildings past the end of the strip loomed up like forbidding ghosts, and abruptly I realized we'd never make it. I slammed the throttles shut and jammed on the brakes, sending the protesting *Wimpy* skidding toward the end of the runway. As we slowed down I breathed my second relieved sigh of the evening.

In a very reflective frame of mind I taxied back to the control tower and told the crew to wait for me. A *Hurricane* fighter had landed just before us and its pilot followed me up the stairs to the control room. I mentioned that we were from Benson, and he remarked, "I've just come in from that area—been in fog most of the way, hedge-hopping."

A few minutes later the station duty pilot, having heard my story, asked, amazed, "How did you get through the balloons?"

"Balloons?" I repeated, "What balloons?"

"There's a red alert. A German air raid is on." I was too stunned to make a reply, and in a moment he continued, "You're damn lucky. The balloons are up to the south and east and are going up west and north of here right now."

It was obvious that we had no option, so I agreed that we would stay the night.

My crew, oddly unabashed by their parts in the day's succession of events, straightway commenced planning a trip to London. Northolt had a tube station nearby, and who were they to ignore such a golden opportunity? I managed to get special permission for them, though Lord knows they didn't particularly deserve it, to go in their flying jackets without respirators or tin helmets, and off they went, while I headed back to the plane to check that it was bedded down safely for the night. The fog had begun to swirl in over the aerodrome and my *Wimpy*, hulking through the mist, looked like a pregnant duck compared to the single *Hurricane* and the line of sleek *Spitfires* before me. Before hunting out supper and a bed, I checked in with the met office. The forecast was not encouraging.

The next morning I was ready for an early start but the fog was so thick one could almost literally cut it with the proverbial breadknife. Just as I was walking toward the control tower after breakfast, the metallic voice of the public address system squawked out, "Fraser, report to the Duty Officer."

I found him in the control tower. My Flight Commander at Benson was on the phone. "Get the hell on the next train back; the last crew that we had lob down at Northolt was there for two weeks!"

I rounded up my crew, whom I suspected would not have been averse to two weeks' access to the delights of London, and the transport truck drove us through the fog to the train station. The civilian passengers on the train looked at us with curiosity. You could almost hear their thoughts: "Wonder who these lads are? Have they just been shot down, maybe? Couldn't be fighter pilots, there are six of them." Relishing the role of operational veterans, we refrained from enlightening them. The train was slow, and we had two transfers to make before pulling into Wallingford, where I had to call for transport. We got back to the mess just before supper ended.

I was not to see Northolt again for thirty-nine years, when I visited it during my stay in London in April 1980. The Commanding Officer had to authorize my visit, for the station is now the operational headquarters of the Queen's Flight. I was met by a pleasant public relations officer and ushered into the office of a delightful, pretty, young WAAF officer. Cups of hot coffee were presented as they showed me a recent report in the local paper on the history of Northolt. The paper even included an aerial shot of the station taken by the *Luftwaffe* September 3, 1940, during the Battle of Britain. At the aerodrome control tower I watched a plane doing the circuit for landing—London's major airport, Heathrow, is only a few miles to the south, and the controller explained the difficulty of keeping the aircraft circuits in proper order to prevent accidents. Then we drove out to the runways and I was interested to see that they were much longer. Since my aborted attempt at takeoff in 1941 the runways have been extended twice for bombers and once for jets.

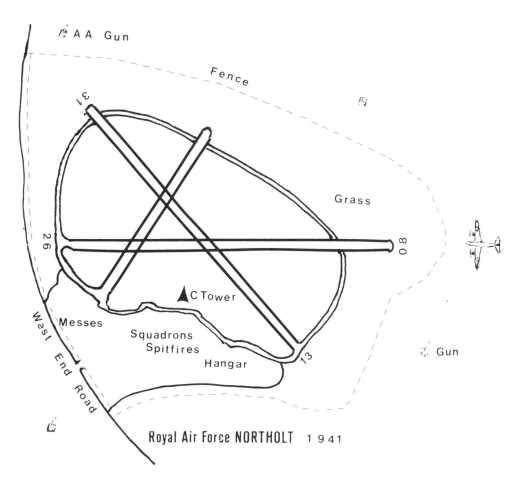

FRASER'S WELLINGTON BOMBER FORCE-LANDING

On the morning after my crew and I returned to Benson I was ordered to report to the Flight Commander's office. I marched in feeling somewhat embarrassed about what had happened—how was I to get out of this mess? The Squadron Leader looked me in the eye as I stood quaking before him: "Glad to see you back safely, but don't let it happen again. We know you Canadians, always wanting to see a bit of London."

Thanking my lucky stars, I about turned and marched out. No word of explanation had been needed—just as well!

Not many days later a group of us flew with the instructors to a satellite aerodrome for night flying practice. We arrived to find, as always, that there weren't enough aircraft for all of us. Just then a telephone call from Benson let us know they had produced another serviceable aircraft, but that there were no pilots left to fly it over to the satellite. The Squadron Commander shouted, "Fraser, get back to Benson and fly that plane back here. Take a wireless operator with you." The two of us hopped into a Humber car and the driver tore away at about eighty miles an hour. Back at Benson there was no sign of life other than the lone *Wimpy* and a mechanic with a starter battery. I climbed into the cockpit, fired up the engines, and tested the magnetos and controls—everything seemed okay.

By this time it was almost totally dark. I switched on the navigation lights and we felt our way across the darkened field to takeoff position. Runway lights were never used at Benson, as most of the crews had their living quarters there and German bombers were frequently overhead. I took off and in ten minutes was circling the satellite aerodrome.

Receiving a green light from the Aldis lamp of the duty pilot, I brought the plane in for a landing. It surprised even me how smooth it was. The agitated Flight Commander met me: "What are you doing flying at night? You haven't gone solo yet." My instructor had been looking for me to give me the first night's instruction on circuits and bumps, only to be told that I was the one coming in for a landing. After nervously watching while I landed, the instructor mustered me back into another *Wimpy* for more night flying before my official solo flight. (During that later solo I completed two circuits and then the oil temperature of the starboard engine suddenly shot way up, so the aircraft was put unserviceable. I wasn't having much luck.)

One Sunday I slept late and found the mess closed when I went for breakfast. I wandered over to the KCB—"Keep the Country Beautiful" —pub on the edge of the aerodrome to have a bite to eat. A group of RAF types were already there. One of my English mates spoke: "Say, Don, where did you learn to fly?"

"In Canada," I replied.

"You certainly picked up the Canadian brogue fast."

Thus I learned that with the British Commonwealth Air Training Plan, initiated in Canada in December 1939, the Canadians, New Zealanders, Australians, and United Kingdom types who trained under it would all be lumped together as British pilots, with little identification of their own country. The Australians were recognizable in their darker blue uniforms, and the South African pilots had their khaki uniforms, but the rest of us were all considered British. Proud of my own country, I resented such a lack of discrimination, and from then on tended to bring Canada into my conversations more frequently.

For a change of pace that evening I went to the Toc H Club to hear guest lecturer Dr. Chrystl, an entomologist from Oxford. We had a chat afterward, and I mentioned my Honour Science degree in Biology from the U of T. He subsequently extended a thoughtful invitation to me to visit the University in Oxford.

Sgt.-Pilot Donald A. Fraser. Photograph taken by the RAF on arrival at RAF Station Uxbridge. To be used by the French underground for forging an Identification Card if forced down on enemy territory.

After another flight as first pilot on a night cross-country, I had completed my course. On June 11 I did some high level bombing, which brought my flying time to a grand total of 187 hours, 45 minutes.

A five-day leave and my pay of four pounds eighteen shillings put me in an excellent position for a trip to Scotland. I sent a telegram to Aunt Jean in Aberdeen and caught the 1915 train, optimistically labelled the

Express. Naturally, it was a long, slow trip in a crowded compartment. I was seated next the aisle, while a rather less than immaculate middle-aged farmer had the window seat, and a pretty girl sat between us. The others on the train, all civilians, were an older group. The train bumped along, stopping periodically whenever a siren signalled an air raid alert.

By midnight everybody seemed to have settled down, and the compartment lights dimmed. The girl beside me looked briefly at the farmer, then cast an appraising glance at me, and, apparently satisfied, snuggled up close. I put my arm around her, her head was soon resting on my shoulder, and suddenly the train trip didn't seem so bad after all. As dawn broke my fellow travellers began to stir. The compartment emptied at Edinburgh, but I pushed on to Aberdeen, the granite city of the north.

My Aunt Jean and my old Aunt Kate both lived in Aberdeen, and I couldn't have asked for a warmer welcome. After I joined them for a delicious, hot chicken dinner a taxi rolled up and Aunt Kate took me some sixty miles up the Deeside to see Balmoral Castle, Crathie Church, and Braemar, where the Highland Games are held. I must admit I was able to do a lot of sightseeing during my service days. Next day I went to church with her, then visited old Dominie Murray, who had taught my mother. But all good things must come to an end, and that evening I caught the return train to London, arriving at Benson at 1345 the next day. I learned that we had the afternoon off, so I went on to Oxford to see a play, *The First Mrs. Fraser,* at the new theatre. While there I met other Canadian pilots from nearby RAF stations, and my leave finally ended on this congenial note.

Tuesday, June 17, 1941—I handed in my parachute harness and had my clearance certificate completed. That same day I was posted to No. 150 Squadron in RAF Bomber Command on *Wimpys,* at RAF Station Newton, near Nottingham. I was to leave Benson Thursday in the early afternoon. Charlie Tourville left for Okington, and Kozlowski was posted to 103 Squadron at Elsham near Leeds. My group from Toronto was now practically all split up.

Chapter Five
A Bomber Pilot with 150

BEFORE LEAVING RAF STATION Benson I received some welcome news. On June 18th a letter from George told me that he was on an Officer Cadet Training Course at Bordon, Hants. I was very happy for him, and the second piece of news I received that day cheered me even more. The Canadian High Commissioner in London, Vincent Massey, wrote to assure me that Canadian servicemen were indeed exempt from British income tax, as I had surmised. I took it up with the paymaster, an RAF Squadron Leader, but all I got was his obdurate reply that he did not take orders from Canadian authorities. The next day I was called into the paymaster's office; they had received a signal from the Air Ministry in London to the effect that all income tax deducted from Canadian paycheques was to be refunded as soon as possible. Somewhat smugly, I said that I would like to take mine immediately, because of my impending departure for 150 Squadron that afternoon. Checking my records, the disgruntled paymaster went to the safe and grudgingly counted out what was coming to me. I told all the other Canadians I met about the refund, and as I was leaving that afternoon I saw, with glee, a line of Canadian aircrew forming up outside the paymaster's office.

At 2100 hours that evening I arrived at RAF Station Newton, the home of 150 Squadron. I was happy to discover an old friend at the station, Bob Dale, the navigator from Toronto. The following day I was interviewed by the Commanding Officer, Wing Commander Carter. My suggestion of leave for my crew received the strange reply: "Oh, no. The stars aren't in the right position!" Rejecting the idea that astrology ruled the RAF, I was just deciding he was crackers when he went on to say that the Squadron went on bombing raids every night when the moon was up, weather permitting. As much assistance as possible was needed from the weather for bombing at that time: records would show that for the first three years of the Second World War a deplorably small percentage of RAF bombs fell within three miles of their target. The choice of bright nights for bombing operations was abandoned three years later, when blind bombing with radar assistance and target identification became the rule.

Von der Royal Air Force
abgeworfen

Nr. 23
21. Oktober 1941

**Verboten
überall, wo
die Wahrheit
verboten ist**

Russlands zweite Linie kampfbereit

L ENINS Leichnam ist aus dem Moskauer Mausoleum am Roten Platz nach einer anderen Ruhestätte im Innern Russlands überführt worden.

Schon lange vorher sind andere Transporte nach dem Osten gegangen. Denn Russland kämpft weiter, gleichviel, wie die Schlacht um Moskau enden wird.

Ein grosser Teil des Maschinenparks der bedrohten Kriegsindustrien im europäischen Russland ist schon ins Innere Asiens geschafft worden. Mit ihm sind viele Facharbeiter und ihre Familien zu den neuen Produktionsstätten gewandert, u.a. nach Sverdlovsk, Tscheljabinsk und Magnetogorsk, wo neue Flugzeuge, neue Panzer gebaut, neue Geschütze gegossen werden.

Denn Stalin hat schon vor Jahren die Gefahr eines deutschen Angriffs erkannt. Und er hat gehandelt. Östlich des Urals sind neue Kriegsindustrien entstanden. Hier werden die Erze des Urals, die Kohle des Beckens von Kusnetz und die Baumwolle von Turkestan verarbeitet.

Und hinter dem schützenden Wall des Urals, unerreichbar für die Luftwaffe, sind die neuen Armeen der Sowjetunion aufgestellt, ausgerüstet und für den Kampf geschult. Denn der Kampf geht weiter — wie oft auch Hitler ihn für entschieden erklärt.

Was nicht weggeschafft werden konnte aus dem Gebiet, das dem Feind überlassen werden musste, haben die Russen zerstört. Allein in der Ukraine waren 90 000 landwirtschaftliche Traktoren in Betrieb. Sie sind nicht mehr vorhanden. Deutschland kann sie nicht ersetzen ; denn es hat selbst nur 140 000 Traktoren. Und die Fabriken, die im Frieden Traktoren herstellten, bauen jetzt Panzer. Selbst wenn Deutschland sie ersetzen könnte : es hat nicht die Millionen von Hektolitern Benzin, die diese Maschinen jährlich verbrauchen.

Deutschland, das heute 3½ Millionen Ausländer und Gefangene beschäftigen muss, um seine Wirtschaft in Gang zu halten, hat auch nicht die Arbeitskräfte, die für die Ausbeutung des eroberten Gebietes benötigt werden. Noch weniger hat es die Rohstoffe und Menschen, um im Krieg all das wieder aufzubauen, was ein entschlossener Gegner vernichtet hat.

**DER BISCHOF
VON MÜNSTER
KLAGT AN
SEITE 3**

Ein französischer Seemann wird als Geisel in Vincennes erschossen. Nach der Ermordung des deutschen Kommandanten von Nantes, Oberst-Leutnant Holtz, wurden am 21. Oktober 50 Geiseln erschossen. Falls die wirklichen Täter nicht innerhalb von 2 Tagen verhaftet werden können, sollen weitere 50 unschuldige Geiseln erschossen werden. (Siehe „ Unsere Meinung '' S.2)

Ohne Ausbildung an den Feind

U-570, das sich am 25. August 1941 südlich von Island einem britischen Hudson-Flugzeug ergab, hatte eine Besatzung von 44 Mann.

Davon waren 42, also alle ausser dem Ingenieur-Leutnant und dem Stabssteuermann, zum ersten Male auf Feindfahrt.

Fast die gesamte Besatzung war seekrank, infolge von mangelnder Erfahrung auf hoher See.

* * *

In einem U-Boot im aktiven Dienst bildet ein einziger unerfahrener Offizier oder Unteroffizier eine dauernde Gefahr für das Schiff und die Besatzung. Durch die

DIE MORDKOMMISSION GREIFT WEITER

Deutsche Bergleute, die bisher unabkömmlich waren, müssen jetzt einrücken.

Deutschland braucht all die Kohle, die es fördern kann, für den Bedarf seiner Industrie für die Gewinnung

Leaflet dropped on enemy territory.

Le Courrier de l'Air

No. 10
6 JUIN
1941

DISTRIBUÉ PAR VOS AMIS DE LA R.A.F.

L'Amérique abandonne le pied de paix

" Plus vite nous courons, et plus loin elle est ! "

L E grand discours prononcé par le Président Roosevelt, le 27 mai, était attendu avec un très grand intérêt par le monde entier. On pensait que le Président donnerait de nouvelles indications sur la politique "d'aide illimitée" à la Grande-Bretagne et qu'il expliquerait la portée des mesures prises pour augmenter la production.

Le discours de M. Roosevelt a dépassé de beaucoup ce cadre. En effet, le Président a informé son immense audience qu'il venait de lancer une proclamation déclarant qu'il existe "un état de danger national pressant et illimité." Ceci veut dire que l'Amérique n'est plus sur le pied de paix.

Dans ce grand discours, le Président explique la technique d'agression mise au point par l'Allemagne, en montrant comment chaque conquête a servi de base pour une nouvelle agression. Il spécifie les noms de quelques unes des bases dont la possession ou le contrôle par d'autres régimes menacerait la sécurité des Etats-Unis [...]

[...] l'Afrique du Nord, les Açores, les Iles du Cap Vert et Dakar sont cités comme présentant un intérêt particulier pour la sécurité américaine.

Ensuite le Président déclare que la "résistance épique" de la Grande-Bretagne ainsi que la lutte de la Chine empêchent les dictateurs de s'emparer du contrôle des mers, contrôle qui seul pourrait leur donner la victoire. L'Amérique est décidée à aider jusqu'au bout ceux qui luttent contre cette tentative de domination mondiale.

Parlant de l'aide à la Grande-Bretagne, M. Roosevelt a dit : "j'affirme que la livraison de matériel dont la Grande-Bretagne a besoin constitue pour nous une nécessité impérieuse. J'affirme que cela est possible. J'affirme que cela doit être fait et sera fait."

M. Roosevelt dénonce alors les efforts de la propagande allemande en Amérique et dit qu'une petite minorité seule s'oppose à la politique nationale.

Plus loin le Président Roosevelt a dit : "Nous n'accepterons pas un monde dominé par Hitler, et nous n'accepterons pas un monde semblable à celui qui a suivi la dernière guerre, après l'année 1920, et dans lequel l'hitlérisme pourrait à nouveau être semé et trouver pour se développer un terrain favorable.

"Nous accepterons seulement un monde où la liberté de parole et d'expression sera garantie, où chacun aura la liberté d'adorer Dieu à sa manière, où les hommes seront libérés du besoin, libérés de la terreur."

Le discours a reçu l'approbation enthousiaste de l'opinion publique américaine. L'impression générale est que l'Amérique, ayant définitivement garanti la victoire de la Grande-Bretagne et de ses alliés, se trouve la veille de décisions historiques. Quant à l'opinion publique britannique, la déclaration présidentielle lui a apporté une nouvelle

Ce que la proclamation signifie

Voici quelques uns des vastes pouvoirs que la proclamation de l'Etat de Danger National illimité confère au Président des Etats-Unis.

Le Président peut suspendre ou contrôler les émissions radiophoniques. Il peut réquisitionner les centrales électriques, les réservoirs et usines, pour fabriquer des munitions de guerre. Il peut réquisitionner les navires ainsi que contrôler leurs mouvements. Il peut augmenter les forces armées des Etats-Unis et mobiliser les réservistes. Il peut ordonner que les chemins de fer donnent la priorité aux transports intéressant la défense nationale. Il peut suspendre les lois du travail pour les institutions qui travaillent pour le gouvernement ou sous contrat. Il peut se servir des forces armées des Etats-Unis pour défendre les communications. Il peut ordonner à toute usine de fabriquer des produits essentiels à la défense nationale et, le cas échéant, il peut faire réquisitionner les usines qui n'exécuteraient pas les instructions du gouvernement.

3 nouveaux cuirassés

On mande de New-York que le cuirassé de 35.000 tonnes *Washington* a été terminé le 15 mai, avec six mois d'avance sur les prévisions, sa construction ayant battu tous les records de vitesse. Le *North Carolina*, de la même classe, a été mis en service le 9 avril. Un troisième cuirasse, le *South Dakota*, sera lancé le 7 juin, cinq mois avant la date fixée par le programme de [...]

SYRIE

[...] situé à 200 kilomètres [...]

Le monde libre réaffirme sa foi en la France

L E gouvernement de Vichy annonça le 14 mai qu'il avait approuvé l'accord Darlan-Hitler et demanda en même temps au peuple français d'en accepter aveuglément les conséquences. Immédiatement après, on apprit que Vichy permettait aux Allemands de se servir des aérodromes de Syrie.

Cette curieuse manière de "défendre l'Empire" a valu au gouvernement de Vichy des avertissements sévères de la part du Président Roosevelt, le 16 mai, et de la part de M. Eden le 22 mai. Mais tous les deux exprimèrent nettement les sentiments des peuples américain et anglais à l'égard de la France. M. Eden a déclaré le 29 mai : "Dans nos cœurs, nous ne devons jamais manquer de faire la différence entre la France et Vichy."

Dans sa déclaration du 16 mai, M. Roosevelt, s'adressant aux Français et à leurs dirigeants, a affirmé :

"Le peuple de France chérit toujours en son cœur et en son esprit la liberté et les libres institutions, et l'on peut compter sur lui pour demeurer fidèle jusqu'à leur rétablissement.

"Il est inconcevable qu'il veuille accepter volontairement une prétendue collaboration qui impliquerait en réalité son alliance avec une puissance militaire dont la politique générale et fondamentale vise à la destruction totale de la France et des institutions démocratiques partout où elles existent."

Et voici comment M. Eden s'est exprimé, le 22 mai, à la Chambre des Communes :

"Le gouvernement de Sa Majesté est convaincu que le peuple français tiendra cette politique pour incompatible avec l'honneur de la France, et qu'il ne croira pas davantage que l'avenir de la France et de son empire puisse [...]

Leaflet dropped on enemy-occupied territory.

63

Sgt.-Pilot Don Fraser and his older brother, Lt. George Fraser of the 48th Highlanders, June 1941.

Bob Dale, who was in Al Hastie's crew, took part in a raid on Kiel that night. They returned safely, but I heard that another Canadian, McVicar, had caught a packet over Duisburg the previous Monday.

On my second day at Newton I checked in with the Medical Officer and was given a general tour of the station by one of the aircrew. I was assigned to B Flight on Sunday, June 22, as co-pilot to Sgt. Parrott, a tubby British type. It was the custom to do a half-dozen or so operational sorties as a co-pilot before taking your own crew on operations. That afternoon I did some practice bombing, and when I landed I heard that Hitler had invaded the USSR. Perhaps the war wouldn't continue for thirty years after all, as I had first considered possible, now that Hitler, in my estimation, had made the same mistake as Napoleon.

Monday, June 23, was a big day for me. I did some practice air-to-ground machine-gun firing, went on a cross-country flight to Benson via Sywell, and, that night, went on my first operational flight. It was a little bit dicy. We had old "P for Peter", an operationally-tired *Wimpy* that resolutely refused to fly higher than 11,000 feet, although we were supposed to bomb from 14,000. I still recall everything from the moment we taxied out, the third machine in a group of nineteen, to climb into the darkness with a full bomb load. I raised the undercarriage as soon as we cleared the perimeter fence, and then gradually let off flaps as we climbed above five hundred feet. We circled in the darkness and came back over the aerodrome at about 1000 feet to set course for our target. Looking down, we could see the flare path, the orange-coloured gooseneck flares, and about sixteen machines waddling like ducks as they moved toward the takeoff point. One after the other they turned into the wind, opened up their engines to full power, gained speed, and became airborne. We were the only crew on "freshers" that night, that is, the only crew on its first operational sortie. Our target was Boulogne, a channel invasion port theoretically not heavily defended by flak (*Flugzeug Aberkanone*—anti-aircraft guns) or enemy night fighters. The trip was to take four and a half hours, rather than the usual six to seven hours of longer bomber flights deep into Germany. As a consequence, our petrol tanks needed to be only partially filled, permitting us to carry a full bomb load of sixteen 250-pound bombs. In addition, we carried some "Newspapers" (or "Nickles", as they were code-named) to distribute while over the Continent as part of the British propaganda war. This particular one was *le Courrier de L'air No. 10, 6 juin, 1941,* which was *distribue par vos amis de la RAF* and headlined *"L'Amerique abandonne le pied de paix."* On the front page a cartoon portrayed Hitler, Goering, and Goebbels running toward a signpost which read *Vers la Victoire.* They were saying, *"Plus vite nous courons, et plus loin elle est"*—The faster we run, the further it is. The previous year the fresher crews had usually had just a straight "Nickle raid" as their first operational sortie. Some of the crews, especially the Canadians, would take along a few cases of empty beer bottles to drop out of the flare chute or rear gunner's turret. We did not expect to hit anybody on the head with them. The empty bottles would make a whistling sound as they descended, and it was hoped that the Germans would believe them to be bombs with a time-delayed fuse and would spend considerable time looking for them. After 1941 the war had taken a more realistic course, and there were no further raids just to drop propaganda literature.

To return to the night of June 23, 1941, the coast of the Continent appeared ahead but was lost in swirling clouds before we reached it. We circled aimlessly through the overcast looking for our target, but to no avail. I suggested that we let the bombs drop on the Estimated Time of Arrival, but no, Tiny Parrott insisted upon seeing the target before bombing. Finally we headed back to England with the full bomb load of sixteen 250-pound bombs still in our belly. I shuddered, thinking of what could happen when we landed with them. The undercarriage could collapse, and if the bombs were to explode then, there would, perhaps, be no more aerodrome, and we would have struck a blow for, rather than against, the enemy. I made a second suggestion: "Why not jettison the bombs over the Channel?" My advice was once again ignored. After all, Tiny insisted, the bombs cost so much money to make, we should bring them back. Imagine landing with two tons of high explosives! We saw the twinkling of identification lights--lights that usually spell out two letters in Morse code to identify their location —as we came over the south of England, then the beacon nearest our aerodrome. Circling, we flashed our identification light and got a green from the Aldis lamp of the aerodrome control pilot. We entered the downwind leg of that critical landing. Once again I was responsible for the flaps and undercarriage. First, undercarriage down and green lights on in the cockpit to show that the wheels were locked in place, then fifteen degrees of flap. Our plane turned left across the wind, Tiny put the propeller pitch in fine position, and the props began to whine as their rate of revolution increased. I prayed that the gasoline mixture was rich. As I lowered full flap just before the final touchdown, the *Wimpy* staggered as if we had lowered a barn door. Tiny brought the plane in over the perimeter fence. The "Chance light" at the start of the flare path suddenly blazed into life to throw a broad beam of light over the ground. The plane steadied itself and gently ran along the rough grassy ground until we gradually drew to a halt. I had already pulled up the flaps, so they would not be damaged by stones thrown up by the propellers. I was particularly careful at that moment to avoid pulling up the wheels, something that occasionally happened because the flap and undercarriage levers were side by side in the middle of the cockpit. Normally disastrous for the plane and very embarrassing for the pilot, the consequence of such a *faux pas* with our load of explosives did not bear thinking about. The Wing Commander was at the ops room to greet us. He congratulated us on our safe return, but when he learned that we had landed with a full bomb load he was furious. We could have blown up the aerodrome, or at least half of it. His advice for such an aborted mission was the same as my first suggestion. Tragically, Tiny was not to learn, and disastrous events later confirmed my apprehensions.

Following the evening's harrowing events I slept in the next morning. In the afternoon I went for a dental checkup, and had a tooth filled. It was important to keep our teeth in good shape. An abscess or local tooth infection would cause even more pain two or three miles above the earth on bombing sorties because of the lower air pressure at high altitudes. We did not enjoy the luxury of pressurized cabins.

On Wednesday, June 25, we listened to a lecture from an army anti-aircraft gunnery officer. He introduced us to the technique of locating *Luftwaffe* aircraft over England by radar, rather than by the older method of sound detectors. As he outlined new developments that would come into operational use within the following year, we all silently hoped that the enemy did not have such wizard ways of detecting us when we were over Germany. I was none too optimistic, as I had every respect for German technology. I had used much of their scientific equipment at the University prior to the outbreak of war and felt that we would indeed be lucky if we could all complete our tours of operations before the enemy brought such aircraft detection equipment into use and co-ordinated it with flak and night fighters.

The following day I slept very late, until 1000 hours, having spent my first night in my comfortable new quarters, the White House, a converted farmhouse on the edge of the aerodrome. When I reported to the hangars at 1400 hours I learned that we were on ops that night to Dusseldorf. At the briefing later that afternoon we were told that the city was more heavily defended than it had been previously. Our target was the post office, but the Operations Officer let us know that we weren't expected to hit it with pinpoint accuracy, as it was in a built-up area of the city. This was my first introduction to the concept of area bombing, a tactic with which I was never too happy. The targets were not simply selected buildings within cities, or armament factories, aerodromes, or railway stations; they included residential areas, and I was never able to completely justify this in my own mind. After the general briefing I went with the other pilots to get special information on the German defences to be expected, whether flak or night fighters, and information on what, at that time, was one of our worst enemies— the weather. A frontal condition lay between us and the Ruhr Valley where our target was located, and we could expect some severe thunderstorms. Those of us who were fortunate enough to have good *Wimpys* would be able to fly over most of the cloud and around the thunderheads. I did not look forward to the trip, for in old "P" we were unable to climb nearly as high as the other machines in the squadron.

About an hour before dusk the crews gathered in the flight room to pick up their equipment: parachutes and warm flying clothing for everybody, maps for the navigators and pilots, wireless codes for the wireless operators, and ammunition for the front and rear gunners. Trucks took the crews out to their machines. We checked our pockets before leaving, so that we would not be carrying anything that might give away any vital information, should we be shot down and killed or captured. I had already removed my Victoria College class ring some time before, after one of the aircrew jumped off a truck that was taking him to his plane and caught his ring on a nail. Part of his finger was torn off, and few of us wore rings while on duty after that.

"P", as befitted her senility, was a dribbler, and the smell of oil from the engines and hydraulic fluid from leaking pipes pervaded the aircraft. We were carrying a full petrol load as well as a 1000-pound bomb, two 500-pounders, and three small bomb containers, which were full of four-pound incendiary bombs to set fire to the houses adjacent to the Dusseldorf post office. As we climbed in I wondered briefly if the cabin heater would work—it rarely did. Then the engines were started and I concentrated my attention on the takeoff procedure. Soon we were on our way; if we were lucky we would probably not see another plane, friendly or otherwise, until we returned.

We started our climb to bombing height as soon as we crossed the English coast. Far ahead on the enemy coast a few searchlights had already begun their hunt for us, extending their icy, grasping fingers high into the sky. A few flak bursts also broke the darkness, but we continued our flight unharmed. Yet, while the enemy couldn't stop us, the weather could. We had managed to fly poor old "Peter" up to 12,000 feet when we ran into severe thunderstorms over Holland. A huge cumulo-nimbus cloud loomed up ahead, and suddenly we were pitched into it as into the darkest night—everything was black. We were buffeted by tremendous winds and turbulence, and the windscreen quickly iced over with the freezing rain. Tiny appeared to have lost control, and we began heading downward. Automatically, I checked my chest-pack chute in its storage box at my feet. It was pitch black, and my ears rang with the changing pressure. The altimeter was spinning backward; we were losing height fast. I hung onto the side of the aircraft as I stood beside Tiny, who was desperately pulling back on the control column. Our airspeed had built up to over 300 miles an hour, the pressure was terrific, and the whole kite groaned. We pulled out of the dive at about 6000 feet, travelling in a direction opposite to our target.

We had been out of control for I don't know how long, and neither of us wanted to do anything but head back toward England. We climbed to 10,000 feet and came out into open sky. When the Dutch coast appeared we identified the island of Walcheren, and made a bomb run on some enemy searchlights that were seeking us out. We weren't about to haul our bombs back to base again. It was with a great sigh of relief that we finally landed. We found that no one had gotten through to the target, except perhaps the New Zealander who had taken Hart, my rear gunner from Benson. The last signal received on the wireless was that he was ploughing through the storm. Nothing had been heard since, and they were later posted as missing in action.

The bad weather held out for some time, cancelling ops for several days. I used the time to get a haircut and see a show in Nottingham, and to visit a farmer and his family who lived across from our White House residence. After a couple of days our crew was given a 48-hour pass. I left immediately for Stafford with some chocolates and cigarettes for Aunt Mary and Uncle Horace. Once there I opened an account with Lloyds Bank and deposited twenty carefully-saved pounds. Aunt Mary and a neighbour then took me to visit a strawberry farm near Pershore, the destination of my first cross-country flight from Benson. That evening I made the rounds of the bomb shelters and air raid posts with my Uncle Horace, who was a doctor. We were welcomed everywhere. Tea and a biscuit were ready for the Doctor at each stop, and I was hosted like a long-lost friend. This continued until early morning. As we returned to the house by car, Uncle Horace said that I had really cheered him and his volunteers at the air raid posts. On this pleasant note, I tumbled into bed and was asleep before I knew it. Unfortunately, I had to catch the 0845 hours train back to the squadron. Tiny Parrot and I arrived together at Newton and found that we were warned for ops.

Our target that night was Bremen. The weather forecasters promised clear skies over Germany, although there was to be a ground mist. Our bomb load was two 500-pound bombs and ten small bomb containers, each carrying over 60 four-pound incendiary bombs. The bombing policy was changing to concentrate heavily on the use of incendiaries. We were told that it would be the fires we started that would do the greatest damage to the cities and to Germany's industrial capacity. Well, there were going to be more than a few fires in Bremen that night.

The pilots had final briefing, and we checked our planes one last time before taking off for Bremen. Tiny and I climbed as high as we could in old "P"; it wasn't as high as we would have liked to go, but we did manage to struggle up to 12,000 feet. The skies over Germany, as predicted, were clear, but there was a dense industrial haze between us and the ground, blocking out surface details. We saw searchlights ahead, and lots of flak going up. Away to the right the searchlights locked onto one of our planes. We saw a shell burst near him, then watched as a flicker of red on the aircraft intensified to a scarlet, star-like mass. The burning aircraft seemed to circle slowly, before suddenly turning toward the earth and plunging downward with ever-increasing speed. I gazed spellbound as the bright ball fell—it hit the ground with a brilliant flash. The colours of the flak bursting about us in the air reminded me of the 24th of May back in Toronto, when we used to send up sky-rockets, except that now it was a fatally serious matter. We seemed to be slipping unobserved through the searchlights when suddenly it happened. A purple master light picked us up and the other white searchlights coned in on us like the obedient slaves they were. We were blinded. Tiny went on instruments as the flak started to burst in front of us. I flicked on the IFF, "Identification Friend or Foe", radar set just behind me on the right side of the fuselage. The master beam wavered briefly, but steadied on us again. The shell bursts were getting closer—big, black mushrooms just in front of the *Wimpy's* nose. The rear gunner had never experienced heavy flak before, and shouted, "Watch out for the balloons, Skipper," under the mistaken impression that the black blobs of smoke passing his rear turret were balloons.

With far more haste than kindness, we shouted back, "You asshole; those aren't balloons; it's flak!" Our plane started weaving as Tiny swung it from side to side, alternately climbing and diving, in an attempt to evade the flak. Despite his efforts the bursts were getting closer and closer; one could smell the pungent fumes of high explosives. Suddenly a shell exploded directly beneath us. The whole plane shuddered violently, and I was lifted off my feet. I was astonished to find that we were still in the air, but the *Wimpy* had somehow recovered and we staggered on.

A mist lay over our target of Bremen. Downward visibility was nearly nil; we saw some fires burning, but they could have been dummy ones to deceive us. Nevertheless, we set course over the burning area and dropped our bombs. The searchlights were still on us, and I could scarcely see the instrument panel in front of me. The *Wimpy* continued to stagger with the explosions, which first seemed to be getting closer, then faded into the background. They persisted for almost an hour as we literally fought our way back to the North Sea coast. At last we were able to heave a sigh of relief and pass into the darkness over the water. When we landed back at the aerodrome in one piece, I jumped out of the plane and kissed the ground. Some of the other fellows followed suit. I was reluctant to look at the damage to our plane, but it had to be done. At first it didn't seem too bad—there were lots of pepper marks caused by the flak blemishing the fuselage of the *Wimpy*, but no major damage was apparent. As I walked around the tail, I discovered that large pieces of fin and tailplane were missing and a hole the size of a football had been blown through the centre of the tail. We were lucky to have made it home.

I had been having a lot of trouble with earaches at about this time, and was becoming hard of hearing, especially in my left ear. Finally I reported to the Medical Officer, who took one quick look and sent me to the hospital. That same day they operated on an abscess in my left ear. Ops were on the next night, but I was not with them. After a day or so in the hospital the Doctor put a dressing on my ear and a bandage around my head, and I was released. But the infection wasn't about to give up so easily. The ear had to be drained again later that day, but the Doctor told me I would probably be well enough to fly. I turned up at the briefing that night with my crew, but as it proceeded the Wing

Commander looked my way more and more frequently. He called me up after the general briefing. "You look terrible with that bandage, Fraser! What would the Germans say if you were shot down in a condition like that?" I replied that I felt reasonably well, and that did it. He vetoed my flying for as long as I had the bandages on.

One evening while I was still bandaged I went into Nottingham with some of my crew. The civilians on the bus stood up to give me a seat. I looked at them askance and refused, wondering at the peculiar reaction they had to a man in uniform. Then I remembered how my appearance had hit the Wing Commander. Even some groundcrew had come up to me and asked solicitously, "Was it flak?" Apparently another crew member had been shot up the previous night and the word had gotten around the station.

A little later I took a test flight to Mildenhall, another bomber station, and was pronounced fit to fly. The first ops after that were scheduled to Bielefeld in Germany, near Hanover. My navigator had gone on ops with another crew during my absence in hospital and had been shot down, so on our trip to Bielefeld we borrowed the station's navigator. The journey out was a piece of cake. There were searchlights and some flak, but none of it came dangerously close to us. We searched in vain for the viaduct near Bielefeld, and finally bombed the most probable area.

Throughout the trip I was unable to hear what the crew said over the intercom. As we were crossing the Dutch coast on the way home a black shape passed rapidly just above us on our right. It was a twin-engine plane, fairly small and fast—*Messerschmitt 110* night fighter? The rear gunner shouted something I could not make out and we dived for the clouds below, flying straight into them. Better to fight and run away and live to fight another day. We shot out of the clouds going like blazes. Something inside my ear popped, and for the rest of the trip it hurt like hell. We levelled off just above the water surface. No enemy was in sight, so we climbed up again and crossed the English coast, got a QDM on the wireless set, picked up the visual beacon, and landed back at base. My ear was throbbing with pain, and I slept little that night, what there was left of it. In the morning I reported to the Medical Officer, and was grounded pending an examination by an ear, nose, and throat specialist.

In a few days our squadron moved to a new aerodrome at Snaith in Yorkshire, and I was replaced on Tiny Parrott's crew. I was assigned, temporarily I hoped, to the position of Duty Pilot and made responsible for the co-ordination of night flying. I watched the squadron *Wimpys* take off one by one for Snaith, and I saw "P for Peter" disappear into the distance without me. I hitched a ride on the last plane to leave Newton, sharing space with mechanics and spare parts. As we landed at

Snaith sand was blowing, almost obscuring the runways. Immediately the new station was christened "Benghazi the Second", after a town in North Africa where the German *Afrika Korps* and the Italian army were fighting the British. Snaith was a new aerodrome, and for some unexplainable reason the NCOs' barracks had been built over a mile away. There were no showers at the barracks; they were back on the main drome.

Thirty years later I was to visit Snaith again to renew old memories. I stopped the car near the main gate, where a sign read *Pollington Airport,* Pollington being a pleasant little village about one mile away. The aerodrome was deserted. Signs such as *Keep Away* and *Government Property* were everywhere, but I noticed some clothing drying on the line at the old Group Captain's stucco house near the entrance. A knock at the door produced a woman with a young child. Her husband, a truck driver, wasn't home. They had lived in the Group Captain's old house for some time and hoped to buy it at some point in the future. The woman told us that the aerodrome was not used anymore except for storage and the testing of equipment for the National Fire Service. She thought there were occasional police dog patrols, but added, unconvincingly, "they won't hurt you". I turned and walked over part of the abandoned hardtop road that led to the Officers' Mess and Officers' Quarters. A row of poplar trees had been planted almost thirty years before along this short road; they now stretched over thirty feet high. The doors of the abandoned Officers' Mess were open. We entered the empty room, and found nothing but a round stone on the mantle-piece above the stove. In days long past many an aircrew member could often be seen throwing a small round stone up and catching it again, especially when he was nervous. Was this worn stone such a one? This was not the mess I had enjoyed thirty years before, for I was then only a Sergeant Pilot. My commission had come later. I looked out past the still, black hangars. Most of the runways must have been torn up and buried, for now the field was a continuous expanse of barley and oats. On the far side of the aerodrome we met a motorcyclist, who confirmed that the National Fire Service was testing new equipment and had buried most of the runways some thirty feet under the soil. We looked into the Sergeants' Mess, and I pointed out to my wife and children where I used to take a shower—all the plumbing had been ripped out. It was a very different aerodrome from the one I had known in 1941.

Shortly after the transfer to Snaith, Tiny Parrott's crew was given two weeks leave, but I was left behind as Duty Pilot. On July 16 I went to the hospital in York, where a specialist examined my ear and grounded me until further notice. An appointment was scheduled with a second specialist for a time in the distant future, and I was allowed to return to the squadron. I was made Acting Control Pilot on my return.

Even though I couldn't fly I was still near planes, so I attacked my new duties with gusto. They included laying out the flare path, which usually took from 1930 to 2100 hours. We had to be ready not only for operational sorties and night flying exercises, but also for bringing in planes that were lost or whose own aerodromes had been shut down due to ground fog or other weather conditions. One evening on duty I prepared myself for a slow night, for there were no ops or night flying scheduled. I was almost dozing at about 0100 hours when the phone rang. It was Group Headquarters, telling me to light up the flarepath and prepare to take in a number of bombers. An unexpected ground fog had developed at aerodromes to the south and their planes returning from bombing missions were unable to land. The regular Duty Officer was away on leave; I, alone, was in charge. My first move was to make several calls, first to the Orderly Officer to let him know what was up, then to the groundcrew to get the gooseneck flares lit on the runway. Finally I notified the fire truck crew and the hospital. The radio operator in the control tower with me started to receive transmissions, and I posted an Aerodrome Control Pilot out near the Chance Light at the beginning of the runway.

We started to hear the sound of aircraft engines over Snaith at about 0330 hours. We gave the planes permission to land one by one as quickly as possible. I stationed some groundcrew out near the far end of the runway with large flashlights and a tractor to guide, or tow if necessary, the planes off the runway as soon as they landed. The sky seemed to be full of milling aircraft. In some cases they had been shot up. By this time the Wing Commander had joined us in the control tower. He said nothing, but watched and listened as I gave instructions. Some of the pilots contacted us on their TR9 radio-telephone sets after landing. We told them to get their planes off the runway quickly, and to leave them there in the grass if they got stuck. I then sent the transport trucks out to pick up the aircrews and bring them back to the mess. The Orderly Officer was arranging sleeping quarters for the men while they were being debriefed. Another of my tasks was to send out signals to the various home aerodromes as the pilots arrived, so the men would not be posted as missing. At 0445 hours the fog started to build up over our aerodrome, and by 0515 I was forced to close down the drome for flying—one could hardly see a hundred yards. There were still a few stragglers up in the air. I was sympathetic toward their situation, but there was little I could do other than direct those we were able to contact north to Pocklington or some other drome that was still open. We heard some poor bloke shout on his radio telephone, "Darky, Darky." This was the signal that he was lost and badly needed help, before he had to tell his crew to bail out with parachutes and let the aircraft crash.

Sgt.-Pilot Al Hastey of Ottawa flying a *Wellington* of 150 Bomber Squadron, Snaith, Yorkshire, England, 1941.

We contacted him on the TR9: "Hello Darky, this is Snaith answering. You are now twenty miles south of York, thirty-five miles west of Hull. Do you read me?"

He answered, "Thanks", and we listened as his engines faded to the north. The fog cleared up later the next morning. The excitement of the night had kept me from my bed, and I drove around the aerodrome looking at the aircraft we had brought in. There must have been thirty or forty planes: large four-engined *Stirlings*, various twin-engine bombers —*Wellingtons, Whitleys,* even *Hampdens,* which we had thought were now relegated to Coastal Command. The night had begun quietly and then developed into a hectic, tumultuous circus as we guided the aircraft down out of the sky. I felt that I had accomplished something worthwhile that night. It was mid-afternoon before I finally got to bed.

One Saturday in July, I received a carton of 300 cigarettes from Mr. Keiling, my old high school History teacher. It is interesting to see how attitudes have changed. Cigarettes, in those days, were not regarded as one step toward the grave, but as great morale builders. They were a favourite item in Victory parcels.

Friday, July 25, I was given seven days leave, so I set out for London on the 1800 hours train. The next day, after a night spent in a room near the station, I visited George at Bordon, the highlight of my visit being a ride in a Bren gun carrier. The next evening I travelled to Edinburgh to see Dr. Marian, my old bio-chemistry Professor from the University of Toronto. He was now in Edinburgh as the head of Medical Chemistry. We had lunch together and one of the things we discussed, naturally enough, was flying. He was particularly curious about how we handled the calls of nature on a long flight. I began a description of the chemical "Elsan" toilet, but stopped short when I saw the grin on his face. Some time previously he had been brought some caustic material that had been dumped out of a German plane and which caused irritation and burns on the people who had come in contact with it. It was identified as caustic soda, or chloride of lime. They at first thought it was a somewhat inefficient form of chemical warfare, but finally realized that when a plane had been damaged the aircrew dumped everything possible overboard to lighten the plane, including the chemical toilet.

Having said my goodbyes to Dr. Marian, I just caught the train to Aberdeen and went on to Dyce, where my mother had been born in Home Cottage. I visited the Dyce aerodrome and learned that my old friend, Punchy Archibald from Oakville, was with a *Spitfire* squadron on the Shetland Islands north of Scotland. I had expected to see my Uncle Alec Fraser at Dyce, but he was away on holidays, so I went to visit the farm on the Ythan River known as *Ythanbank,* where my father had been born and raised. His older brother Tom still lived there with his wife, Annie. The farm was some ten miles up the Ythan River from the village of Ellon north of Aberdeen. There was a bus to Ellon from Dyce, but no transportation to the farm was available. I caught the bus anyway, trusting that something would turn up. Sure enough, when I reached Ellon I was able to rent a bicycle and pedal up to the farm. It was small, just a few acres altogether, with a narrow trout stream flowing along the back. After my tour in Western Canada it seemed more like a garden than a farm. The old, rambling cottage had a huge, welcoming fireplace, used for both warmth and cooking, and my relatives' hospitality was second to none. Later I meandered contentedly around the farmyard, sidestepping the many chickens running all over the place.

I had often heard of my father's fishing escapades on the Ythan

River when he was a lad. Now I just had to see if I could catch a fish there too, maybe even a salmon. I decided not to make too big an investment in equipment for this adventure, as with the life expectancy of a pilot I might never use it again. A strong ball of twine bought in the village of Ellon and some hooks and sinkers were all I needed to make a throw line. From my boyhood summers at Sparrow Lake I recalled that most fish liked worms, and figured that this preference would not be restricted to Canada. A bit of digging in Uncle Tom's garden produced a good supply of them. By this time the rumour of a Canadian pilot in the district had spread, and there were several boys of different ages standing outside the farm house. They followed as I proceeded down to the Ythan River to catch a fish. We must have been a strange-looking parade. Cutting a twig from a nearby tree, I fixed a line and sinker, with the hook wrapped over a big, fat, juicy worm, and walked alongside the quiet stream. It was disappointing in size, not even the width of the Don River near Toronto where I had swum and fished as a boy. Of course, I should have been prepared for it by then—the United Kingdom scale for land and waterways was a bit different from my expectations, after my Canadian youth and the stories I had heard from my Scottish parents and their friends. Nonetheless, there was nothing for it but to try my luck. Having selected a likely looking spot, I put a stone at the end of the line, tied a piece of wood about eighteen inches back from the stone at the end, attached a small line with hook and worm, and finally whirled this contraption around my head before letting it drop into the river like a lasso. The line dropped into a deep, quiet pool, and the wood raised the hook off the bottom. I then sat down to wait. The young farm lads were all around me. They had never seen anything like this before and they thought that I must be a true cowboy set out to lasso a fish. A little while later I felt a tug. I set the hook and pulled in. What on earth was I pulling up? A snake? No, it was a writhing four-foot-long eel. Startled, I nearly jumped back in horror. I had never seen such a creature before except in books. What was I to do with it, especially with the farm lads looking on? Courage. Grabbing the eel behind the head, I withdrew the hook and threw the eel up onto the bank. Now to try again. A little while later, there again was a pull, and the ceremony was repeated until I finally had five large eels, but no salmon. It was getting dark, and, disappointed, I decided to call it a day. It wasn't until later that I learned that salmon run up the stream in the spring, not in mid-autumn. The farm boys with me seemed to regard my catch as more than satisfactory. In the face of their admiration I hadn't the courage to admit that I had never eaten eel in my life. I gallantly offered them to the boys, who pounced on them and carried them triumphantly off to their homes. It was not until twelve years later, after I married and my wife served smoked eels as a delicacy, that I appreciated their worth.

My fishing experience on the Ythan River was repeated to some extent in 1954. My wife and I hired a Ghillie (guide) and rented a boat to fish in the mouth of the river for sea trout. For four hours we sat in a rainstorm, fishing with our legally mandatory rods and flies. It was our only chance to fish, and I refused to heed the pleas of the Ghillie or even my wife to give up. I declared that I would stay there until I caught something. All the other boats had long since departed and gone in. The Ghillie looked around: no one in sight. "Where are those worms I know you brought?" Hastily I baited the hooks with worms and almost immediately landed one small flatfish, which I carried proudly back to Aberdeen to my Great-Aunt Kate's kitchen. She was not very impressed with my expensive catch. The Ghillie alone had cost me more than a pound (five dollars). Aunt Kate said that she could get a much better fish down at the Aberdeen fish market. . . .

On July 31, 1941, I went back to Aberdeen after a good breakfast at Uncle Tom's farm. From there I went to visit another relative, a distant cousin, up the Deeside. After my first cup of tea, neighbours began walking in to have a look at and to welcome their Canadian "cousin". I knew that there were no phones in the area, and I had brought no vehicle to signal my presence to the community. I asked my hostess later how they knew I was there. "Och, aye," she said. "When we have an important visitor, I just hang out a sheet from the upstairs window and the neighbours see it and come over. We have different signals for different occasions." Just like the Indians of the old West, I thought, but rather than smoke signals, my cousins used sheet signals. Was there any way to adapt that to my *Wellington?* I thought not. And so I returned happily from my journey through that homeland of my ancestors. I arrived back at Heck, the nearest railroad station to Snaith, at 2230 hours on Friday, August 1. As I walked back to the station a flight of *Wimpys* was just taking off on ops.

Early next morning I relieved Mr. Brown, the old permanent Duty Control Pilot. Later that evening on duty I was busy laying out the flare path and regulating night flying when I heard some saddening news. Tiny Parrott and his crew had gone missing the previous Wednesday. Don Monk was gone too, with Jack Evelle. Tiny had crashed into a hill while returning to England in a mist, with a full bomb load again I believe. All were killed except the rear gunner. The rear turret broke off and rolled down a hill, and the tail gunner got out with a broken back. Such is life . . . or death.

After an unsuccessful test flight which indicated that I was still slightly deaf, I went to York hospital to see the specialist again. He ran a tube in through my Eustachian canal and did a few quick tests, only to tell me there was little change. A chronic inflammation had developed, and to relieve it he suggested an operation to remove the nasal septum. For the meantime, he gave me an oil to put in my nostrils. Upon my return to the station I went to see the Station Medical Officer about the possibility of an operation. He could not guarantee the results, and all my visit accomplished was a semi-permanent grounding. Finally I talked with Wing Commander Carter, who said that he would not have the operation if he was in my shoes. He did offer me the hope of some low-level flying. So the net result of my day's round of interviews was that I stayed on as Duty Pilot.

Ops about every third night kept the aircrew in top form, and I was glad to see Pat Geary, a rear gunner from Dublin, get the Distinguished Flying Medal (DFM) because he had shot down a few fighters. We teased him that he would soon be an ace with five enemy planes to his credit, and he wasn't even a pilot.

The days were passing. I checked astro sights, wrote letters, read, and played mah-jong to fill the hours I wasn't on duty. I also plotted out a new map for the crew room that pinpointed aerodrome locations.

In early August I went to Barnsley, near Sheffield in West Yorkshire, for a few days to handle the Air Training Corps Exhibition. I took along some parts of a *Wellington* for the Air Force display which I was to look after. One evening while walking from my hotel to the display hall I passed a photographer's shop. I decided to drop in, and an old lady cheerfully took my picture and promised me several good prints to send home. The Exhibits were a great success, and on my last evening in Barnsley I went to a dance with the Air Training Corps.

On August 29 I was transferred to the position of Watch Office Duty Pilot of Headquarters staff, under Flight Lieutenant Brown. Brown went on leave shortly afterward, and I practically lived in the Watch Office for two weeks while in charge of Flying Control.

Monday, September 8—Bob Dale heard that he was to be posted off to a Long Navigation after thirty ops, and would return to Canada for this course, which was held at Port Albert on Lake Huron, Ontario. That day also saw a courtmartial for one of the pilots for low flying. F/L Brown returned from leave for the hearing, which brought me a measure of relief as Duty Pilot.

At about this time a series of night vision tests were given. It so happened that one of the better gunners failed the tests, but the Wing Commander kept him on ops as he had already shot down several German night fighters.

I continued to be kept busy as Duty Pilot at the Watch Office because F/L Brown was often out selecting more beacon sites for Burn aerodrome, our satellite. The flights had not assigned an Aerodrome Control Pilot, so I not only had to act as Duty Pilot, supervising radio transmissions and the dispatching of planes, checking with the Met

Office for weather conditions, and assigning the correct runway, but I also had to run out to the end of the runway by the Chance Light, to give red or green light signals to permit aircraft to take off or land on the runway. To add to the confusion, ops were off and then on again with weather changes. One night Sergeant Hutchison landed in the Humber River. We thought that he might have nicked one of the balloon cables near Hull and damaged a wing, although there were explosive balloon cable cutters on the leading edges of the wings of the *Wimpy*. The idea was, that if you hit a balloon cable, it would slide along the leading edge of the wing until it caught in this device. An explosive charge would then fire and a knife edge would chop off the cable, theoretically at least. Even those who operated balloons had problems. After the war I met a friend from Montreal whose father had joined the balloon section at the beginning of the war. One day he was on a barge with a balloon to protect a convoy entering the Thames estuary. The barges were wooden to avoid detonating the magnetic mines dropped by the *Luftwaffe*. But the enemy aircraft had also dropped sonic mines. The barge passed over one and the sound of the propeller set off the mine. The resulting explosion sank the balloon barge and killed my friend's father. There really was no safe job during the war.

As autumn proceeded rain showers became frequent. On my inspection day I found a 300-foot-long wire looped and criss-crossed on one of the runways, just waiting to entangle itself in the wheels of one of the *Wimpys*. It was one of the long wire aerials which were reeled out during flight for receiving radio transmissions on medium frequencies. Someone must have landed without reeling it back in, and it had snapped off. Often the aerial looked like a snake wriggling behind the plane, especially when flying through a thunderstorm. In these cases it had picked up an electrical charge and was discharging sparks along its serpentine length.

Ops were on for Hamburg on the 29th, and one aircraft, "H for Harry", crashed on the aerodrome. I quickly dispatched the fire tender and ambulance, but the plane had only ground looped and no one was hurt. After ops the next night all planes returned except the unlucky "H", which landed elsewhere with an injured tail gunner.

On Wednesday, October 1, I was idling away my time in the Sergeants' Mess at 1830 hours when the phone rang. George had just arrived in nearby Goole. I hopped a truck from the transport section and hastened to visit him at the station hotel. He had finished his OCTU course at Bordon and had been commissioned a Lieutenant. He looked fine, and it was good to see him again. Ops were cancelled that night so I had a few hours off to chat with my brother and catch up on all the news. The next day George dropped in at the aerodrome and I took him around the Control Tower and the Met Office. He was short of cash after buying a new uniform, so with what I considered great brotherly generosity, I gave him twenty pounds. I made him work for it, though, tiring him out on practice flying in the Link trainer all afternoon. He didn't do very well, but then, I had done even worse when trying to drive an army Bren gun carrier along a narrow path through a minefield in southern England when I visited him earlier in the year. George left the next day by train for Manchester, on his way to visit Uncle Horace.

Life as Duty Pilot could be hectic with the changing weather. We had frost the night of October 11 and it was very cold in the bunks. But the frost signified clear weather, and the next morning the blue sky was cloudless, though there was some ground haze. Naturally, ops were on, and every plane got away alright. But later, as some of the planes started to land and taxi in, a German night fighter began circling our aerodrome and dropping flares. We quickly got on the radio and diverted the last three kites to the drome at Hemswell—we didn't need to have our aircraft shot down right over our own station.

The next night, with ops on again, "M for Mother" took off smoothly, but almost immediately had an intercom failure. The pilot jettisoned 400 gallons of high octane gas over Snaith village, three miles away, to lighten his plane and thereby facilitate a safe landing. If the villagers had known this would happen, those with vehicles would undoubtedly have been out with upside-down umbrellas to collect the gasoline, which was severely rationed.

I was part of a committee for the inspection of a nearby army search-light battery. The army and the air force normally had little to do with each other, but the lights could help lost planes find their way back to their base, or at least to a safe landing—part of the "Hello Darky" procedure. The searchlight could be raised vertically, with the beam shining straight up into the night sky, then quickly dropped horizontally to point toward the nearest aerodrome, which by then would be ready to lay out its flarepath and take in the lost plane.

Tuesday, October 14, another op to Dusseldorf. Blake got shot up. Two nights later there were three freshers on to Dunkirk. This and other invasion ports were usually the targets for the first ops by new Captains—often the planes were loaded with sixteen 250-pound bombs. Everybody returned that night.

I left the station on the 17th for a few days' leave to see Uncle Horace in Stafford and do the round of air raid posts with him at night. I also used the opportunity to visit the University of Birmingham, where my cousin John was a medical student. While there, I met Dr. Donald Gunn of the Zoology department, a respected scientist whose work I had studied at the University of Toronto. This visit prompted me to consider graduate work, perhaps as an external student at the University of London, to include the subjects Botany, Zoology, and Military Studies, with a thesis on distribution of airborne micro-organisms. Dr. Gunn introduced me to Dr. Chesters, a mycologist who studied fungi. During my flying from then on, I collected airborne material to study, and Dr. Chesters provided me with spore traps with agar, so that any spores caught could be germinated *in situ* and their viability directly assessed. Things were looking up. It was cheering to think that the war needn't completely interfere with my education. At the time, it looked as though the war might still go on for thirty years. It was possible that diseases caused by airborne micro-organisms could be a new weapon. Even if this proved an absurd idea, it was as well to know what was in the air, if the enemy was up to something. Years later I saw the method used by botanists studying the potential of plant dispersal when they collected pollen grains and other airborne "organisms" while flying over the North Pole.

From Stafford I headed for Rothamsted Experimental Station just north of London at Harpenden. There I met the world renowned soil scientist, Sir John Russell. He had written *Soil Conditions and Plant Growth*, another text I had used at the University. I spent two days there and was guided on some fascinating tours of the Station, by Sir John and Dr. Singh one day, and by Dr. Schofield and Dr. Parks of the Soils Bureau on the next. I looked with awe upon the historic fields where wheat had been grown for over 100 years with no fertilizer added during that entire time. Then it was back to London where I stayed at the Winston Hotel. I had my favourite lunch at the Beaver Club, pancakes with real maple syrup—it really bucked you up, and almost made you feel as though back home in Canada.

On Friday, October 24 it was back to Snaith. I was immediately notified that I was to have a medical board in London the following week. All had not gone well at Snaith while I was on leave. Two more of my friends had gone missing on ops, while a third and somehow more tragic incident had occurred right on base. Returning aircrews were debriefed regularly upon landing, no matter what time this might be, in the early morning hours. One of the younger members of the Met staff would walk over from the Control Tower, just below my office, to the Briefing Room in the operations block for this job. That particular night, Rutherford, a young Met Assistant of the RAF, was on duty. When the last plane had landed he left the Met Office to go over and debrief the crew. He did not return to the Office, but it was late and so it was assumed that when he went off duty, he had gone straight to bed. Yet that particular crew was never met by a debriefing Met Officer. After they had been waiting for some time in the Briefing Room, the Operations Officer in charge sent them to bed, assuming that the Met Office had not bothered to send someone over because it was so late. Thus it was not until a day or two later that his absence was noted. His girlfriend inquired about him, and it was discovered that he had not reported for duty the previous day. An unproductive investigation was made in his home town, but it was decided that he was not the type to go AWOL, and his footsteps prior to his disappearance were traced from the Met Office to the Control Tower to the Debriefing Room in the operations building. Directly on the path a twenty-by-twenty-foot concrete water reservoir for emergency fire-fighting, with sloping concrete walls, had been set into the ground. They dragged the pool and pulled out Rutherford's body. Barraclough, the Senior Met Officer, took Rutherford's body back to his home for burial in accordance with the custom of an officer accompanying the body back to the place of the funeral. Fifty dollars was usually given to the relatives toward the cost of the funeral.

On October 25 my medical board at the RAF hospital in Halton took place, the only result again being that I was to remain grounded. I returned to Snaith to take up my work as Duty Pilot, hoping that soon I would be back in the air. In accordance with this hope I could be found in my rare leisure hours occupied in one of two "pastimes"— inhaling balsam at the station hospital or making spore traps for sampling the air from a *Wellington*. Most of the time I was kept busy with ops, as F/L Brown was once more on leave—the whole responsibility fell on my shoulders again. I spent a great deal of November 8th tidying up the Control Office, as the Inspector General, Air Chief Marshal Sir Edgar Ludlow-Hewitt, was to visit us the following day. He pronounced himself quite pleased with our efficiency.

On Tuesday, November 11 it was back to Halton hospital. I took the opportunity for another visit to the Beaver Club for pancakes on the way through London, then went on to Halton, where I was put in Ward 7. The ENT (ear, nose, and throat ward) was filled, and Ward 7 was the one from which RAF men were given their medical discharges, though I didn't know that at the time. The men there were having quite a time discussing the various reasons for their discharges—some were "putting it on" and exaggerating their actual ailments. "What are you getting out for?" came the inevitable question.

"I'm not being discharged," I replied. "I'm here for treatment and a possible operation. They can't discharge me here—I'm a Canadian."

They laughed. "Everyone from this ward gets a discharge."

This worried me no little, and I was definitely relieved the next day when I was transferred into the ENT, Ward 1. In the evening I played checkers with other patients and chatted with a sergeant recovering from serious burns. He had been on the deck of an aircraft carrier in the Mediterranean when a plane crashed on takeoff. Burning high-octane fuel had splashed over him, and he had been badly burned, especially on his back. He was still unable to wear a greatcoat, because it weighed too much. Another sergeant was in for ear trouble, like myself. He had come from Limavady in Northern Ireland and had already had several unsuccessful operations.

Later the next day I went up for treatment—more Eustachian tube cauterizations, which were thoroughly unpleasant. The treatment, given by a Squadron Leader Fraser, was finally completed, and I was immediately off to see Group Captain Dickerson. My ear trouble was not yet remedied, but I asked for the chance to fly again, at least in some capacity. He considered for a moment or two; "May recommend you for low-level flying, Instructor, or Coastal Command." I was jubilant. A medical consultation with Wing Commander Simpson followed, and I formally requested a transfer to Coastal Command, provided my health permitted.

I returned to Snaith from the hospital on November 27. The Wing Commander had gone to Prestwick to fetch back two more of the four-engine *Liberator* bombers that were arriving from the United States. There was already one on the station, and the pilots were taking a conversion course on them. These were lovely planes with quiet engines, comfortably upholstered inside, and even containing ash trays; one could smoke in them. This did not really affect me personally, as I have never taken up the habit, but for many airmen it was a pleasant change. On ops we were usually only allowed to smoke, unofficially, in the rear turret where there was no danger of fire.

I saw the Winco on his return on November 29, and he promised to recommend a transfer for me to Coastal Command. Meanwhile, I was back as Duty Pilot until further notice, taking over as F/L Brown was again on leave. Bob Dale had been awarded his Commission and was away in London picking up his new uniform.

In early December I visited 405 Squadron, RCAF, at Pocklington. This Canadian unit was flying the new Mk II *Merlin*-engined *Wellington*. I visited their Control Tower to observe their performance. Later, Bob Dale, Barraclough the Met Officer, and I went for our weekly entertainment into Doncaster for a leg show. The trip was always awkward, because the show lasted until 2230 hours, and our last train for Heck left at precisely the same time. So we three, who always sat the front row of the vaudeville theatre, would stand up and walk out just before the finale. The showgirls did not appreciate our exodus, but at one of the performances we explained our predicament to them, and they became forgivingly sympathetic.

Sunday, December 7, 1941—Japan attacked Pearl Harbor; the United States and Japan were at war. We grouped around the radio at Snaith to hear Roosevelt's war declaration speech. It was, for some of us at least, an unexpected and exciting turn of events.

I now started to do some local flying on the airtests, and was relieved to find that my ear wasn't giving me too much trouble. On a similar test a Sergeant Lewis had difficulty locating the runway. He overshot and crashed his *Wimpy,* breaking his collar bone and receiving various cuts and bruises.

As 1941 drew to a close 150 Squadron was warned to begin a continuous standby. The guns were supplied with "daylight" ammunition, which had a higher proportion of tracer rounds in the belts than that used at night. Apparently the *Luftwaffe* was becoming more active in our area. For our part, there were ops to Brest on the 17th, with all aircraft returning safely, and a few days later to Dusseldorf. On the latter operation the aircraft piloted by Sgt. Eastwood was shot up; his second pilot, Sgt. Purdy, was killed, and the rear gunner was injured. Sgt. Eastwood was awarded an immediate DFM.

Although I wasn't allowed to go on any operations, my services at the Control Tower and some test flying kept me hopping, especially as F/L Brown was sick. But I found time to see the Huddersfield variety show, the "Whiz Bangs", when it came to the station on December 21, and I enjoyed myself thoroughly.

On Christmas Day I was Duty Pilot all day and night, though I managed to get over to the buffet dinner in the mess. A "present" arrived a few days later in the form of acceptance by the University of London to take me as an external student. I also received some less pleasant news that day; my good friend Bob Dale would be leaving on January 29 to go to Canada for his navigation course.

For a New Year's Eve celebration Sergeant-Observer Skrender, an English navigator, invited me to join him, his fiancee, and her girlfriend for the Hogmanay dance at the Majestic Hotel in Harrowgate. We started off in a fog in his little Triumph, whizzing along through the narrow lanes and streets. We picked up the girls in Leeds, somehow managing to pack everyone into the tiny car, and went on to the Majestic Hotel. The nearest rank to our own seemed to be a Group Captain, and Generals and Air Vice-Marshals were thick on the ground. As a sergeant observer and a sergeant pilot we didn't quite fit in, but we nevertheless enjoyed ourselves. We didn't return until 0330 hours. The New Year's message of King George VI was a very moving one, and I remember it well:

> I said to the man who stood at the gate of the year
> 'Give me a light that I may tread safely into the unknown.'
> and he replied: 'Go out into the darkness and put your hand into
> the hand of God. That shall be to you better than light and safer
> than the known way.'

And thus the old year ended and a new one began.

New Year's Day, 1942—after my late night, I missed breakfast and slept until 0900. We then had gas drill, wearing our uncomfortable respirators for half an hour. Ops were on and then scrubbed. The projected target had been the U-boat pens at St. Nazaire on the Biscay coast of France. The squadron had started daylight formation flying, and I wondered what was up. I did not look forward to these daylight ops with any relish, picturing the returning aircraft full of holes. Brown was again in poor health, and I was given no time to rest at the Control Office, despite my celebrations of the previous night. This, unfortunately, was not to be one of the days when I was able to pass my "duty" hours at the Watch Office catching up on my sleep.

The New Year brought me good news early. Wing Commander Miller told me that he had spoken to the Air Vice-Marshal. My new posting would either be with Coastal Command or as an Instructor, and I was to get some leave before being posted out.

On Sunday, January 11, my leave underway, I went to a Beaver Club dance in London. A fellow RCAF sergeant and myself found two delightful girls to share our hamburgers with, and we later saw them home to their residence behind the Cathedral near the Houses of Parliament. I went on to Horsham and then to Partridge Green the next day to see George, going back to stay at the King's Hotel in Horsham for the night. On Tuesday I went to Brighton to watch George playing on the Canadian hockey team, and afterward we went to his billet for tea. He then took me to the Officers' Mess, where I met the Brigadier, even though I was but a Sergeant Pilot. On my return trip through London I looked up Mary, the girl I had met at the Beaver Club a few days previously, and we went to a show together. She spoke with a most becoming Irish accent, for she hailed from Northern Ireland near Londonderry. Many Irish girls could not find jobs at home and consequently came to England seeking employment—Mary worked for the Post Office in London. I was quite taken with my attractive young companion, and I ended up spending much of the rest of my leave with her. I did manage to tear myself away long enough to complete my registration at the University, but by the evening I was once again with Mary, this time at a dance in Covent Garden. While twirling around the floor with my lovely partner, I suddenly heard a loud shout.

"Don! Don Fraser! What are you doing here?"

I stopped and looked around. Lo and behold, it was Clark Adams, a lad I had taught some four years before in Sunday School. He was now a pilot flying *Spitfires* on his way to North Africa. We practically threw our arms around each other in the middle of the dance floor, then turned and walked off the floor together. Only then did I remember my dancing partner: "Oh no, what have we done?" Fortunately, our two girls hadn't taken our forgetfulness amiss, and were cheerfully following behind us talking to each other. We excused our rudeness and the four of us went together for some refreshments. Clark was his usual buoyant self. We retraced our steps for one another; he had just finished his OTU course and had not yet flown on operations. This was the last time I would see him; he left for Africa a few days later, returned due to illness, and then became an instructor in Scotland. There he was killed when his plane developed engine trouble and crashed.

Friday, January 23, 1942 was my 24th birthday. The day passed with a variety of minor activities; the only birthday present I received was my pay of six pounds twelve shillings. There was a stand-down in the afternoon, as it was raining with sleet mixed in, which gave me the chance to have the arm of my reading glasses soldered. That evening I did some Morse code exercises. The stand-down lifted and three freshers were on to Emden. This made me recall an earlier briefing when the operations officer asked the crews to choose their own target in Germany that night. Many chose Emden, for it was lightly defended and not too far away, so there was a good chance of returning from such an operational sortie. Bob Dale phoned to tell me that he was leaving for Canada. Life went on with the usual comings and goings. I had begun studying navigation in the afternoon and Lepidoptera— butterflies and moths—in Zoology at night.

Tuesday, February 3, I was once again off to Halton hospital. A very heavy snowfall the previous night slowed the journey considerably. They stopped the express train for me at Heck at 0930 hours, but I didn't get to Halton until early evening. The Medical Board finally okayed me for flying, much to my relief, and recommended me for flying boats. Events proceeded remarkably quickly after that. On the day following my return to Snaith I received a posting to 1417 Flight of 19 Group in Coastal Command, at RAF Station Chivenor, in North Devon. The Winco told me that 1417 was flying *Ansons* and *Blenheims* and that there was also an OTU there. As I was getting my clearance from Snaith a huge glider landed; the Americans were taking our *Liberators* away. Now that the United States was in the war, they needed these aircraft themselves. And so 150 Squadron went back to *Wimpys* just as I was leaving. I was issued a lot of webbing, a useless gun holster without a pistol, and a water bottle, and was off on the 1230 train to London, where I arrived that evening. I found it difficult to get a room for the night, but finally found one near Waterloo. The next day brought the long, slow trip to Chivenor.

Chapter Six
172 Squadron and the Searchlight Wimpy

IT WAS LATE AT NIGHT when the train puffed into Wrafton, the local railway station two miles from RAF station Chivenor. Although it was pitch-black, red and green lights could be seen overhead indicating night flying. Suddenly there was a flash in the hills to the north, and glowing flames began to flicker. This could mean one thing only—a bomber had crashed into the hillside. It was not an auspicious introduction to my new station.

The RAF van, for once, was waiting for me. I piled in my gear and sat dejectedly on our ride to the station thinking of the poor types who had bought it a few moments before. Soon I was climbing into bed, dead tired, to be awakened only a few minutes later, it seemed, by a batman knocking at the door. The mess was a welcome sight; it wasn't too crowded, as the aircrew who had been night flying were still asleep.

During breakfast I learned that this was an OTU for twin-engined *Beaufort* torpedo-bombers. My heart sank. These aircraft did not have an enviable reputation. They were reported to suffer the dual handicaps of being prone to engine failure and being well-nigh impossible to fly on one engine. I checked in at the Orderly Room expecting the worst. So far, little had encouraged me to think I would like the posting.

"1417 Flight," the WAAF Corporal repeated. "Oh, that's in our 'Hush-Hush' group in D hangar, right at the very end." She pointed out the window to the long line of hangars.

I walked slowly, watching the *Beauforts* landing at what seemed a dangerously high speed. At D hangar I showed the guard my posting orders and he took me into the 1417 Flight Office. Squadron Leader Geoffrey Greswell, an RAF type, greeted me.

"You're the first of our new arrivals; I believe you've got lots of time on *Wimpys*. You'll be able to show us a bit." With that, he ushered me through the back door of the Flight Office and into the big hangar. I almost fell over. There, in all its ponderous glory, squatted a *Wimpy*, not in the familiar, black, Bomber Command colour scheme, but in the gleaming white of Coastal Command. My fears and misgivings all fell away as I walked around the *Wellington,* pleased as punch that I would be dealing with an old friend.

Over the next few days I became quite impressed with our Flight Commander, S/L Greswell, and the high opinion that I formed stays with me to this day. A thin, wiry man with a small moustache and a crop of black hair, he was a veteran of Coastal Command, a pre-war pilot who seemed to know what he was doing. Greswell survived the war with an enviable record and ended his Air Force career as an Air Commodore. When we visited him in 1971 at his country home near Picket Post, Southampton, I recognized him immediately after almost thirty years. We discussed the contribution of Commonwealth pilots to the RAF and some of the "personalities" among the first pilots to join 1417 Flight.

In my new group I was probably the one with the most experience in flying *Wellingtons,* though I had never flown the new searchlight *Wimpys,* a ropey lot, which needed considerable servicing. I got a dual machine to check some of the pilots out on flying it, but the engines were duff, cancelling that idea.

Author's girlfriend, Mary, in Kew Gardens, London, June 1943.

On Friday, February 13 we learned that the German battlecruisers *Scharnhorst* and *Gneisenau* had escaped up the Channel to Heligoland. It was reported that the RAF lost 42 planes in trying to stop them. Now I realized why 150 Squadron at Snaith had been practising daylight formation flying and had been issued with daylight ammunition—they must have been expecting the breakout of the German battlecruisers. I wondered if the Squadron had lost any planes, but I never heard. All my friends from there were by now dead, missing, or posted away.

The searchlight *Wellingtons* were checked for their final installment at RAF Station St. Athan's in South Wales. Trips were made not only there but also to an old CCDU Station across the Bristol Channel at Carew Cheriton. On one of these trips the exhaust ring on an engine of my *Wimpy* cracked in the air, but, with a pounding heart and dry throat, I managed to make a safe landing. After this I wasn't too upset to learn there was no more flying that day. I flew in an *Anson,* a twin-engined trainer, for the first time on the following day. I had trained on single-engined *Harvards* in Canada and had not flown an *Anson* before. This was not an auspicious first flight; we were practising low-level bombing when the port engine started missing. But, again, thankfully, we landed safely.

When all of the aircrew had finally been posted in, Squadron Leader Greswell explained the purpose of 1417 Flight. Britain was having a lot of trouble getting supplies from the New World. The U-boats were sinking ships faster than they could be built. Now, in early 1942, with the United States in the war, but not running their ships in convoy, the German U-boats were having their second "Happy Time" sailing to attack and sink ships off the American coast. The U-boats would run submerged during the day at about five knots, and run on the surface at night at sixteen knots, charging their batteries at the same time. In this manner they would cross the area most dangerous for them, the Bay of Biscay, and head across the Atlantic Ocean. The RAF *Sunderland* flying boats, together with the land-based *Whitleys* and *Hudsons,* were patrolling the Bay of Biscay, and even with their primitive radar they could keep the U-boats submerged during the day. But there was no way to find them at night, and the enemy vessels took advantage of that weakness. It was just prior to this that Squadron Leader Humphrey de Verde Leigh, DFC, an RNAS pilot in the First World War, who was now Personnel Officer in charge of postings at Coastal Command Headquarters, showed his great inventive genius and persistent nature. I saw him in those days at Chivenor when he would nip down from Headquarters near London to supervise the final adjustments to the large, moveable, 125-million candle-power searchlight which fitted into a special support where the old mid-under turret of the *Wellington* bomber was located.

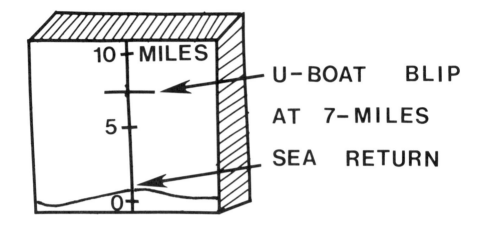

AIR TO SURFACE VESSEL (ASV)

RADAR SCREEN IN PLANE

Air-to-Surface Vessel (ASV) Radar Screen in plane.

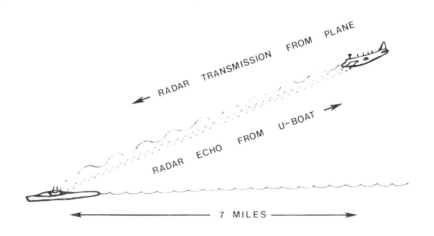

SURFACED U-BOAT DETECTED ON RADAR OF LEIGH LIGHT WELLINGTON

Surfaced U-boat detected on Radar of Leigh Light *Wellington*.

The originator of the Leigh Light, the retractable, swivelling search-light that turned our *Wellingtons* into new weapons against enemy submarines, was born in Aldershot, Hants, in 1897, the son of Canon John de Verde Leigh. After his education in the Old Ride Preparatory School and Cheltenham College, he passed the City Guild Engineering Examination in 1914 and went on to Vickers Ltd. as an engineering student. The following spring he received a commission in the Royal Naval Air Service as a Probationary Flight Sub-Lieutenant and was posted to the Grahame-White School, Hendon, to learn to fly. On the 13th of June, 1915, one month after receiving his commission, he took the Royal Aero Club Certificate No. 1321 in a Grahame-White "Box Kite" aeroplane. In September 1915 his rank of Flight Sub-Lieutenant was confirmed.

S/L (Later Air Commodore) J.H. Greswell, 1943. C/O of 1417 Flight, and Pilot of Leigh Light *Wellington* that drew "first blood" on the *Luigi Torelli*, June 3/4, 1942.

From October to December 1915, Leigh was in France flying on anti-submarine patrols from Dunkirk. From January to July 1916 he was one of those dropping food to besieged troops of General Townsend in Kut el Amara, Mesopotamia, flying Short seaplanes off the Tigris. In June 1916 he was promoted Flight Lieutenant and for the following two years flew on anti-U-boat patrols, and reconnaissance and bombing in Palestine. For his efforts he was Mentioned in Dispatches, awarded the DFC, and promoted first to Flight Commander, then to Squadron Commander (equivalent to Major in the RAF).

Leigh left the service in December 1919 and spent most of the time between the wars as manager of a cotton plantation in the Sudan with the Sudan Plantations Syndicate. He did not marry until 1935.

In 1939 Leigh returned to the RAF via the Emergency Reserve and was posted to the Personnel Branch of Coastal Command HQ, under Air Chief Marshal Sir Frederick Bowhill, who had been his Squadron Commander in Mesopotamia. Up until June 1st, 1941, Coastal Command aircraft had sighted 233 U-boats and made 164 attacks, but had only one confirmed sinking. There were several reasons for this lack of success. The destructive power of the anti-submarine bombs used by Coastal Command was almost negligible, and existing depth charges could not be set to explode at less than 100 feet, not very effective against submerging U-boats sighted by the aircraft. Another weakness in the anti-U-boat war was the lack of means to detect a surfaced U-boat from a distance. By 1940 airborne radar installed in Coastal Command aircraft alleviated the latter problem to some degree, but unfortunately, it was limited in effectiveness, especially at night. For the last mile of approach the target blip was lost in the "sea return" showing on the radar screen.

In early 1940 Leigh was in the Officers' Mess when a newly-arrived officer, Squadron Leader Lugg, sat down beside him for coffee. Lugg was supposedly on a "hush-hush" assignment, but he openly discussed with Leigh his task of fitting radar on the aircraft. Their conversation set Leigh to thinking about how the problem might be solved.

On October 13, 1940, Leigh placed before Sir Frederick Bowhill a proposal to install a naval searchlight in an aircraft, to be used in conjunction with ASV (Air to Surface Vessel radar) for the detection of and final attack on U-boats. With the full support of his Commanding Officer, Leigh energetically pushed ahead with the development of his idea. A *Wellington* was adapted for the installation of a moveable, swivelling searchlight in the mid-under machine-gun turret position. Initial trials carried out in early 1941 indicated the project to be a successful proposition. Unfortunately, Bowhill was transferred from Coastal Command on June 15, 1941, to take over the newly-formed Ferry Command at Dorval airport, Montreal, Canada. With the change of command, Leigh lost support for the development of his invention. Bowhill's successor, Sir Philip Joubert, favoured the Turbinlite developed by Group Captain W. Helmore, a trained engineer associated with a research laboratory in Cambridge.

Helmore's Turbinlite was originally fitted into the nose of a twin-engined Boston *Havoc* night-fighter, and its adaptation to submarine warfare seemed highly probable at the time. But what was to have been

Count Augusto Migliorini, Captain of the *Luigi Torelli* on the night of June 3/4, 1942 when she was attacked by Leigh Light *Wellington* skippered by S/L J.H. Greswell of 172 Squadron.

the advantage of the Turbinlite, its widely-diffused, high-intensity beam located in the aircraft's nose in front of the pilot, turned out to be the reason for its failure. The bright light was reflected by the moist air back into the cockpit, blinding the pilot rather than increasing his field of vision. Helmore's specialized technical knowledge just couldn't match Leigh's experience and inborn inventiveness. Leigh knew from his own air-to-sea experiences during the First World War that optics through the moisture-laden atmosphere above the sea vary greatly from those encountered under land conditions.

S/L H. deV. "Searchlight Sam" Leigh, inventor of the Leigh Light, 1942.   (Imperial War Museum)

Although Leigh had been ordered by Joubert to discontinue his searchlight research, he had approached Vickers Aircraft and the Fraser-Nash turret manufacturers to push on with the development of his invention. He had been confident that his design was the one that would work, and he had persuaded the manufacturers to support his secret efforts. When, some months later, Sir Philip Joubert found that he had backed the wrong horse, for the Turbinlite was a flop as far as anti-U-boat operations were concerned, he called in Leigh to inform him that his research would get full official support from then on.

The Battle of the Atlantic was reaching a crucial stage, and Churchill was after Joubert to increase the efficiency of his Coastal Command aircraft. It is to Joubert's credit that, when he realized his mistake, he was ready to admit it and offer his support to Leigh.

Joubert asked Leigh how long it would take to prepare a working prototype of his searchlight. Rather than replying directly, Leigh asked his Commanding Officer to join him on a visit to Vickers. There, in the hangar, was a *Wellington* with an installed prototype searchlight.

"Who gave you permission to go on with this work?" demanded Joubert.

"Nobody, Sir."

Joubert realized that Leigh had not only disobeyed orders, but also, as Personnel Officer, had been posting qualified officers to work on his invention. Yet nothing more was said, and Leigh's work continued with official approval. (Later, in 1980, Leigh was to tell me how he and his wife had crawled under the bed with a matchbox to represent the U-boat and a flashlight as the searchlight *Wimpy* to ascertain the effectiveness of his invention.) And so it was that Leigh had established No. 1417 Flight at Chivenor in early February 1942, when I joined this fascinating and challenging group.

Training continued throughout February, March, April, and May of 1942. Squadron Leader Greswell appreciated the value and scarcity of the searchlight *Wimpys* and realized how foolish it would be to train new crews on these valuable aircraft. He therefore got in touch with Coastal Command Headquarters and managed to get some ropey Bomber Command *Wimpys* released for local training. It must be remembered that most of the pilots in the unit were only experienced on Coastal Command aircraft and had never flown a *Wimpy*. I was supposed to be one of the fortunate ones who knew the *Wimpy* forward and backward, its strengths and its weaknesses.

I flew with Southall and Blackie on February 20 to Cranwell, where Southall picked up an old Bomber Command *Wimpy*, and I flew back with Blackie in another one, acting as navigator. Southall flew out on a Cranwell-bound *Wimpy* the next day also, but returned to Chivenor when a heavy fog closed in. We sergeants had our problems. One of us was caught in bed one Saturday morning, and as a result, the Group Captain had all sergeants on parade Sunday morning at 0900 hours. Later that day I flew with Pilot Officer Syer for three and a half hours on his familiarization flights. Syer, an Australian, had the record time for flying a *Hudson* bomber over the Atlantic with Ferry Command.

Wing Commander H. deV. Leigh (centre), the inventor of the Leigh Light, with Squadron Leader Terry Bullock (right) who is now a commercial pilot. Squadron Leader Bullock sank four U-boats while flying a Leigh-Light *Liberator* during the war. With them is Professor D.A. Fraser (left).

I was not forgotten by the folks back home. Every week I received more letters and parcels: from Mother, neighbours, schools, and friends. One of the parcels was from Class 4E of my old high school, North Toronto Collegiate, and another was from our next door neighbour, Mrs. Webster. The arrival of each message made the time pass more quickly, as did my French lectures on Tuesday and Thursday evenings. These were arranged by the Education Officer on the station and given by a winsome WAAF of Swiss origin. I thought that an understanding of the language would be immeasurably valuable should I be shot down some day over France.

On Friday, February 27 I was called in to see the Commanding Officer. He relayed orders for me to report the next day to Squadron Leader Mathews at RCAF Headquarters in London. I saw S/L Mathews in the morning; he was an amiable chap. It appeared that I might be taken off ops with a posting to instruct at an Elementary Flying Training School or on Beam Approach and Blind Flying back in Canada. I let him know that I was at an interesting stage in the development of the searchlight *Wellington* and would much prefer to carry out operational flights with this machine, once all the quirks were ironed out and a sufficient number of aircraft were available. I found it exciting to be taking part in the experimentation of a new anti-submarine device.

I was back on flying at Chivenor Monday. A lot of the boys were killing time in the pubs and cinema halls of Barnstaple as the service-ability of the planes was none too great, nor was the weather the best. Wednesday saw us on defence drill. I always took an active part in this drill because of my pre-war COTC experience with the Vickers machine-gun, with which the pill boxes around the station were equipped.

I hadn't much luck with flying that week. On one day I had been up for only five minutes when the starboard engine decided to get a bit ropey and refused to rev up properly. Then on the 6th I took off to practice single-engine flying and ended up with the real thing when the ring cowl of one engine came off in mid-air. I landed safely, but was satisfied with merely doing simulated instrument flying later on the Link trainer.

At last we were able to get in some cross-country flying on March 7 to the Scilly Islands off Lands End in Cornwall. When we reached this turning point, a *Hurricane* fighter intercepted us. I told the navigator to fire our identification cartridges, but several moments later nothing had yet happened, and I was becoming distinctly nervous about the fighter's reactions. Turning around to peer down the inside of the fuselage, I saw that my navigator had dropped the astrodome and was poking his head through the opening into the slipstream showing "thumbs up" to the *Hurricane.* The Verey pistol was apparently not working. The *Hurricane* flew in formation with us for a few minutes and then whizzed off, probably back to St. Mary's aerodrome on the Scilly Islands. After the few minutes of excitement we had just settled down again, when, heading up overland parallel to the coast, the gunner shouted, "*Spits* at 5000 feet in front of us to starboard, Skipper."

I looked up to the right. We were just at 1000 feet, and there they were above us, three *Spitfires* in formation, just starting to peel off and come down on us. Envisioning the mincemeat they could make of us, I yelled, terrified, "Don't touch our guns!" I then attempted to make us look as innocent as possible, dropping our wheels, putting on some flap, slowing down, waggling the wings, and flying straight and level, hoping for the best. We had a black training *Wimpy* and the *Spitfire* pilots probably wondered what it was doing over the southwest coast of Cornwall in the middle of the day. Whatever they thought, they must have recognized us, for they veered off. After carrying out a number of simulated attacks, while we sweated and trembled, they passed over us again and zoomed away. Intensely relieved, we all began to breathe normally again, but our eyes were peeled for the approach of any more "friendly" aircraft. Two scares in a matter of a few minutes were two too many. On the way back I practised single-engine flying, thinking that the way things were going, I just might need it in the future.

And the training went on: I practised ground controlled flying and landing. More packages arrived, one from the Department of Botany at the University of Toronto. We listened to lectures on the ASV and began to appreciate its possibilities. A few of us saw Orson Welles in *Citizen Kane* one evening in Barnstaple—an intriguing film, but one that few in the audience seemed to appreciate.

Tuesday, March 10, 1942—the five-year diary that my classmate from high school, Douglas Horniblow, had given me just prior to my departure for overseas, now had one year of entries. A great many of us had begun keeping diaries during our service days, something we might have scorned in peacetime. Perhaps it was a sub-conscious attempt to maintain our individuality in the great wheels of the war machine. As it turned out, I used my diary regularly for almost another four years, but never had the pleasure of discussing it with Douglas. He joined the Royal Canadian Army Service Corps, and reported sick one weekend while on duty in Halifax. A few days after his admittance to the hospital he died with a ruptured appendix.

I started to learn more wireless and flew a few ground controlled approaches with Pilot Officers Syer and Russ, an Australian and a Canadian. It was often quite misty, so this training was essential. I went to Iifracombe one evening and had one of the few paid dancing lessons of my life. It was an amusing evening, but despite the protestations of my partner, I don't think she was too pleased with my progress. Not long afterward I received a cigarette lighter from Mother and 300 Wings cigarettes from Mrs. Sifton, the wife of my old Professor of Botany. At about this time a bad case of diarrhoea was keeping me on the run, so to speak, but my misery was lessened by the knowledge that everyone in my bunk was suffering from the same ailment. There must have been saltpetre in our soup—and it would have to be on the weekend too!

I started giving lectures on the Vickers machine-gun, in defence training. Only the Armament Officer and myself were genned up on this machine-gun, because the only guns the Air Force had used previously were the Browning and the old Lewis MG.

I had mapped out the route to St. Eval aerodrome in Cornwall, and one afternoon we flew there and back. On landing I was notified that I had been promoted to Warrant Officer First Class. (It would not be until years later, on January 22, 1963, that I actually received my Warrant, signed by the current Canadian Defence Minister, Douglas Harkness. It appointed me Warrant Officer, First Class, effective April 1, 1942.) This rank was as high as one could go without receiving a commission as a Pilot Officer. I was still eating in the Sergeants' Mess after that, but was on a senior level—oh, the privileges of rank!

Leigh Light *Wellington* with searchlight extened.

(H. deV. Leigh)

Flight Lieutenant Squires arrived on the station in March, and we could not have had a better instructor. He taught a course on astro-navigation to the navigators and gave a few lectures on the subject to the pilots. Because I knew the *Wimpy* well, I started to give instruction on the petrol system: the nacelle tanks, how to switch them on by pulling a wire next to the main spar, how the cross-over feed switch worked, the position of the overload petrol tank, and so on. Also in March, we began airborne ASV radar work on Helwick light vessel in the Bristol Channel. On one of these flights the flaps on my *Wimpy* went unserviceable, and as a result we had an exceedingly rapid landing.

Leigh Light in an old shadow factory south of London, July 1971. Later moved to the RAF Museum Hendon.

Skeleton framework of the Turbinlite on display in the London Science Museum, 1971.

(Photo by S.D. Fraser)

As we came sailing in over the high hills around Chivenor aerodrome, I noticed the runway was soaking from a recent rainstorm—more bad luck. The *Wimpy* touched down going like a bat out of hell. I saw the end of the runway coming up fast, much too fast—no flaps, and the brakes were none too good either. About one hundred yards before the end of the runway, I applied the left rudder; we swung off the runway onto the wet grass and went sliding sideways, then backwards across the grass. It was a wonder that the undercarriage did not collapse. The plane stopped just on the edge of the level part of the aerodrome. Thanking my lucky stars, I taxied slowly back to tell the mechanics what was up and to put the machine unserviceable.

The next day I went as co-pilot on a three-hour cross-country flight with Sergeant Bramwell. We were part way down the coast over the sea, off Cornwall, flying at about 500 feet, Bramwell was in the cockpit, and I was back checking with the ASV operator when, abruptly, both engines stopped. I realized immediately what was happening: the engines were somehow out of gas. I scrambled hurriedly back to the main spar and pulled the wires to turn on the wing nacelle tanks. We were skimming uncomfortably close to the surface of the sea before the engines picked up and we climbed back to 1000 feet. It was fortunate that Bramwell had not panicked, but kept the plane straight and level, easing back on the control column so that our forward speed would keep the plane airborne as long as possible. It was perhaps even more fortunate that I had had considerable experience with the *Wimpy* and knew immediately what the trouble was. An SOS had been sent out by the wireless operator on his own instigation as soon as the engines cut. I cancelled it when we began climbing again. Everybody was in a sweat, thinking how close we had come to a dunking. What had happened? Operational machines carried an additional 140 gallons of gas in the overload tank in one of the bomb bays. That supply lasted for about two hours flying, after which the crew would switch onto the wing tanks. Because there was no gas gauge for the overload, we had to estimate the time when the tank would have emptied. The overload tank was used first, so that in case of ditching it would at least be partially empty, and would provide some flotation. The gas in the wing tanks could always be jettisoned, should the plane have engine trouble and it became necessary to land in the ocean; there was usually not enough power in a single engine to keep the plane airborne. Following this disturbing episode I always did a special check on the overload tank prior to takeoff. Opening the bomb doors under the plane, I would tap the overload tank to make sure, by the sound, that it was full. The episode off the Cornwall coast happened when a mechanic neglected to fill the tank, but still signed it up as full on the inspection sheet. Both of our engines cut after only half an hour of flying, because they were both fed from the more than half-empty overload tank. I wondered if many other missing planes had gone down for this very same reason; an unfilled overload tank that failed at low altitude.

Wednesday, March 18 was a typical day for me at that time. We had the usual Wednesday anti-invasion exercises around the aerodrome. A lecturer gave us gen on the Lewis machine-gun. I took some Astro star shots with the bubble sextant at night. That afternoon I turned in my Sergeant's stripes at the station clothing store for the badges of Warrant Officer Class I rank. With the promotion I was able to increase my pay assignment to my mother to $60 per month. Another day we practised visual signals with the Aldis lamp. The Navy was really hot on visual signals, for they did not give their position away to the enemy as radio transmissions might. Thus it was necessary for us to improve our efficiency with it. After some experimentation on our part we were warned by Southall to keep our visual signals "clean". The Group Captain's daughter, who lived within sight, apparently understood the visual Morse code quite well.

The Boston Havoc twin engine night fighter with Turbinlite in the nose. Old photograph on display in the London Science Museum.

(Photo by S.D. Fraser)

A submarine illuminated at night by a Leigh Light *Wellington*.
(Imperial War Museum)

After dinghy procedures on March 21 with Flight Lieutenant Southall, who had been promoted to that rank from Flying Officer, a group of us went to Barnstaple. We spent a pleasant evening watching *Riders of the Purple Sage* from Zane Grey's western novel and *Sun Valley Serenade* with Glenn Miller, the orchestra leader who was to go missing two years later on a flight across the Channel.

The next day I took off on a navigation trip with Pilot Officer Spencer Watkins as navigator. His brother, who flew with 150 Squadron in Bomber Command, was well known because of his pet dachshund, which drank beer by the mugful. When the dachshund was drunk, it would try to walk sideways, much to the amusement of the flight crews. On our nav trip we went thirty miles out toward the Scilly Islands and returned through poor visibility and bad weather.

On Monday I worked on the Dalton computer for navigation and then spent a relaxing afternoon at Ilfracombe on the Bristol Channel, where I collected sea shells on the beach. I was able to take life easy on Tuesday as well, when a flight to Exeter did not come off. I went to Bideford across the mouth of the nearby River Taw for some sightseeing. My tourist-like activities included a viewing of the statue of Charles Kingsley, author of *Westward Ho,* and I also bought two small teak elephants for luck. I always bought small elephants as souvenirs wherever available, but their trunks had to be turned up. This was after an old belief that, when the end of an elephant's trunk was turned up, the good luck associated with elephants would not "run out" as it might if the end were turned down. Aircrews have always been a somewhat superstitious lot. They even created a type of leprechaun, the gremlin, to whom they attributed many unexplained events, both good and bad, that occur when flying.

I took the Defence parade the following day as senior Warrant Officer, then flew three hours cross-country afterward. I almost went up to Limavady in Northern Ireland, but Bramwell took the trip while I was chasing up keys for the defence posts, cement bunkers at various points around the stations camouflaged with straw and containing Vickers machine-guns. Up till then nobody had bothered to look inside them, except perhaps the armament officer. By this time we had finally been given a squadron number, 172; the squadron had been formed from the nucleus of 1417 Flight of Coastal Command Development Unit.

March 28 I took off on an Isle of Man trip, but returned after three hours with an unserviceable starboard propeller pitch control. Weather was duff again on April 1, but I managed to do some Lorenz blind approach landings. We received news that the German ships *Scharnhorst* and *Gneisenau,* which had escaped from Brest in February, were at Kiel and Wilhelmshaven. I had a good navigation trip the next day and for the first time saw Southern Ireland from the air.

Sgt. John Smith, "Smitty", my faithful Wireless Operator/Air Gunner who stuck to his set sending out S.O.S.'s when our *Wimpy* was going down. He is listed as missing.

On Friday, April 3 I missed pay parade; I was off on bombing practice in "J for Johnnie" when the aileron controls on the plane failed. I made an emergency landing, having dropped only eight bombs. And so it went: poor weather, training flights, frequent trouble with the machines, parcels from home.

On April 5 I flew to Cranwell with Squadron Leader Greswell, Flight Lieutenant Heale, and Flight Sergeant Bramwell. We ferried back three new kites, then I practised bombing again. We usually practised with our old machines to save the specially adapted searchlight ASV *Wimpys.* Later in the week I flew to St. Athans aerodrome in South Wales to bring back a modified *Wimpy*. While waiting for it I saw a twin-engine plane in the hangar. I was not familiar with the type, which had a single tail fin like a German *Heinkel* bomber. A groundcrew erk noticed the direction of my curious gaze and explained, "Oh, that's the new secret machine, the De Havilland *Mosquito* fighter-bomber."

Members of my crew going on leave from Wick when I was on my way to London to purchase a Pilot Officer's uniform. Smitty was on compassionate leave at the time because of his mother's sickness. Left to right: "Red" McGrath (whom we could not later rescue from our dinghy in the North Atlantic), my rear gunner; Len "Hutch" Hutchinson, my ASV operator and gunner; the author; and Len Thompson, my second pilot and search-light operator. September 1942.

I moved closer to it. It had two good Rolls Royce *Merlin* engines, and looked sleek, but when I tapped it I found it was made of wood. "Oh, oh," I thought. "The *Wimpy* is covered with fabric, but at least the body is of metal. Things are really getting tough if they're making planes out of wood!" As it turned out, of course, the *Mosquito* was one of the best, if not the best, aircraft the RAF used to carry the air war into Germany.

Our training intensified, and on Sunday, April 13, a wet, misty day, Pilot Officer Russ flew off to St. Eval aerodrome in Cornwall in "B for Beer". At 1600 hours he was posted as missing. I was practising low-level bombing in "P for Peter" at the time, and joined Flight Lieutenant Heale in a futile search for "B".

We were gradually getting more lectures on the electronic side, ASV jamming, intelligence, and so on. Night flying was often laid on in those days, but almost as often was cancelled due to unserviceability. The night flying included operation-like sorties, homing in on the Helwick light vessel in the Bristol Channel with the ASV radar, lowering the searchlight, and illuminating the vessel in the dark hours of the night. One day an autogyro landed at the aerodrome, to be immediately surrounded by a crowd of fascinated airmen. We were all quite excited with its potential. It was really the predecessor of the helicopter.

Operational status was growing near when I was given a 48-hour pass on April 20. I hopped aboard the 1238 train for London and went on to Littlehampton on the Channel coast to find that my brother George was away on a scheme. I never did get to see him, and returned to London to stay at the West Central Hotel, deciding that a leave spent with Mary was far from wasted. I had pancakes again at the Beaver Club and then went with Mary to a dance at Covent Garden. I spent the next day at Madame Tussaud's Wax Museum before returning to Chivenor.

During my absence "B for Beer" had been found on the cliffs near Hartland Point. Pilot Officer Russ and crew had all been killed in the crash and their bodies burnt in the resulting fire. The crew members were P/O Lebon, P/O E.A. Blair, 2nd Pilot, RNZAF, F/O L. Noble, Observer, RAF, and Sgt G.T. Daniel, WO/AG, RAF. The *Wellington* (Z8731) had been found at 2100 hours on April 21 at Beckland Bay, half-way between Clovelly and Hartland Point. It had not been possible to investigate it closely as night was coming on, but the next day five burnt and crushed bodies had been hauled up from the site of the crash and identified as P/O Russ and his crew. An inquest, held April 23 at Station Sick Quarters, brought the unsurprising verdict of accidental death due to the crash of the aircraft. All the deceased were interred on Saturday, April 25 at the local cemetery with full military honours. The relatives of P/O Lebon, P/O Noble, and Sgt Daniel attended. It was a sad affair.

Immediately following the short funeral service, several of us had to prepare our planes for yet another search. Two *Whitley* twin-engine bombers had gone missing from St. Eval. The search was scrubbed as we were taxiing out, so we decided to practise flying again instead. Blackie overshot and ran into a steamroller parked near the extension of the runway, then under construction. No real damage was done, but we had to walk back from the end of the runway, leaving the plane to be towed back the next morning.

Graves of Hughie Grant and fellow airmen at Stanforham cemetery near Newcastle. Hughie was a Sunday School student of the author. He was killed in a *Spitfire* accident in 1942.

When I heard that Pilot Officer Russ was missing and presumed dead, I realized that P/O Blackmore had lost his second pilot. Blackie was an old CCDU pilot assigned one of the first four searchlight *Wimpys*. These scarce machines were assigned to Wing Commander Russell, Squadron Leader Greswell, Flight Lieutenant Southall, and Pilot Officer Blackmore. I immediately volunteered to fly with Blackie as his second pilot until a searchlight *Wimpy* for my own crew was available. Blackie agreed. Thus I was able to get in double time, with my own crew and with Blackie's, until mid-July, when I was assigned my own machine, "N for Nuts".

Being a Warrant Officer First Class, I was entitled to wear a trench-coat similar to that the commissioned officers wore. Unfortunately, these coats were not automatically handed out by the RAF, and the necessary clothing coupons were not issued to Warrant Officers or lower ranks. As a WOI I would be issued a tailor-made uniform of blue barathea material, similar to a commissioned officer's uniform, except that the trousers had an almost indiscernible vertical side seam sown to the outside rather than the inside. On the lower outside end of the sleeves was the coat of arms, or "cats", instead of the circular rings that denoted various commissioned officer ranks. My good uniform that I had brought from Canada was far better quality than the usual RAF airman's uniform, and I regretted having to turn it into the clothing stores in exchange for my new one. Among the groundcrew was a Canadian sergeant in RAF administration with whom I was on good terms. He asked if I might give him my well-kept sergeant's uniform of Canadian origin and turn in one of his old RAF uniforms instead. To this I agreed readily, and the exchange was made. The Canadian airman's unifrom kept a press very well, while the one made of RAF material did not. In fact, when an airman was questioned about his appearance by a Canadian officer, the usual query was, "Are you RAF or did you sleep in that uniform?"

I had become accustomed to attending the local village church in nearby Braunton, the largest village in the United Kingdom. The organist, Hesketh Scoyne, usually invited me to his home for tea after the Sunday services. My wife and I enjoyed the Scoyne hospitality again when we visited them in 1954. In 1971, when I went with my whole family which by then included two children, we stayed in the village, but dropped in for an evening. Mrs. Scoyne welcomed us, saying that Hesketh would be in later. We chatted over some refreshments, then I sat down at the piano I used to play many years before. I had barely started on "The Robin's Return" when the door opened and a hearty voice boomed out, "This must be Don Fraser!" Mr. Scoyne had recognized me by the tune that had been my favourite all those years.

During the war years, Mr. Scoyne, in spite of a bad limp, was a great hiker. He proudly showed me all the local sights during our many walks together and also introduced me to the Ramblers, a group of young people from the church who had regular Saturday hikes. I got to know some of them very well—it was a relief to have some sort of social life outside the squadron. Mr. Scoyne was also the owner of the local haberdashery, and it was he who finally arranged my order for a trench-coat, a major enterprise in wartime Britain. Nevertheless, I still had to carry out some brisk trading to get the necessary clothing coupons. Twenty-seven were needed, making the transaction particularly complex.

At about this time an interesting story was circulating about one of the pilots, who had gone on leave and did not return when expected. The rumours about what had happened to him were rather intriguing. He always seemed to be flush with money, and usually spent his leave in extravagant but happy dissipation in London. Apparently this time he went to a certain night club several times to see his newest lady love. One day there was a tap at his hotel-room door; a Scotland Yard detective and a member of the Security Police introduced themselves when the airman answered. Apparently his latest girlfriend was suspected of espionage. Our searchlight squadron was on the secret "hush hush" list, and the girl may have known of his involvement with it. Accordingly, her relations with him were motivated by more than friendship. The Security types supposedly arranged for this fellow's leave to be extended, gave him extra cash to spend on the woman, and also suggested certain false information to be passed on to her. The thrill of possible espionage lent excitement to our daily routine. Yet the attempts to keep our activities "hush hush" were not as successful as the men at the top might have wished. 172 Squadron's American pilot, Wiley Howell, was drinking beer with his crew at a local Braunton pub when one of them dropped a shilling. While he was on the floor under the table looking for it, the barmaid sauntered over to remark, "You searchlight boys shouldn't have any trouble finding it!"

On Monday, April 27, I did a bit of work on the new battery storage unit before taking my pre-operational leave, during which our aircraft would get a major inspection. My first stop was at Newcastle on the northeast coast of England. I had received word from Mrs. Grant of our church in Toronto that their only son, Hughie, had been killed flying *Spitfires* and was buried at Stanforham cemetery in Newcastle. I had last seen Hughie on guard duty at RCAF Station Debert, Nova Scotia, in 1941, just as I was leaving Canada. Hughie had already had engine trouble once before, when the glycol coolant in his *Spitfire's* engine had leaked out, but on that occasion he had managed to force land in a field. He was not so lucky the second time, and while attempting to force land his *Spitfire* he ran into a stone fence, pushing the engine back on top of him. I visited his grave at the little churchyard and took some pictures of it to send home to his mother, hoping they could be some consolation in her loss.

The rest of my leave was spent hopping around from one place to another. I was trying to visit as many people as possible before beginning operations, for although I, like many others, tried to avoid thinking about it, I knew that an airman's lifespan was often brief. From Hughie's graveside I went on to Edinburgh, where I stopped for a few hours to talk with Dr. Marian, my old biochemistry professor, and Dr. Gus Graham, a Canadian working with him. Then it was on to Midcalder, between Edinburgh and Glasgow, to make a promised visit with the sister of my old Sunday School teacher and her daughter, a nurse. They invited me to inspect their local secondary school. The principal gave me an interesting tour of this omnibus school, a combination collegiate and vocational training establishment. I finished off my Midcalder stay that evening at a whist drive. In Glasgow the next day I dropped by the Police Headquarters, not to admit to some heinous crime, but to meet my father's old friend James Inglis of the Glasgow Police. Inglis's son was also on the force, and I was given the grand tour of the Headquarters and the detectives' department. By late afternoon of the next day I was sitting down to tea with Wilson Argo's family at Newmacher on the other side of Aberdeen. Argo was my mother's cousin and the father of a friend of mine, George Argo of Thistletown, near Toronto. The customary "sheet signals" had the neighbours visiting us before tea was over. In the evening I went back to Aberdeen for an old-time dance, and the next day I saw my Aunt Jeannie and Great-Aunt Kate. A final foray through London to Littlehampton and the 48th Highlanders completed my busy leave. Unfortunately, George was away on course, but I passed the time there quite pleasantly with Lieutenant Bill "Dusty" Miller of Toronto. On Tuesday, April 5, at 1700 hours, I returned to Barnstaple, my week of leave over.

A buzz of animated conversation rippled through the mess at breakfast the next morning. A German twin-engine bomber, a *Junkers 88*, had landed at Chivenor. Some of our new crews had been practising takeoffs and landings on their night flying. The usual procedure during such practice was to retract the undercarriage after takeoff, then the flaps, and then adjust the engine power and propeller pitch to climbing settings. After circling around at 1500 feet, or just below the cloud base if that was lower, the plane would fly the downwind leg, check for permission to land, and the aerodrome Control Pilot would flash a green light in the letters of the aircraft that had requested permission to land. The aircraft would then fly across wind, with the wheels lowered and engines adjusted, swing into the wind, and land. While one of the crews was taking its turn a second aircraft joined the circuit, flashed its identification light, and came in for a smooth landing. The Duty Control Pilot couldn't figure out who the newcomer was, so he sent a ground-crew member out with a flashlight. The erk didn't recognize the black twin-engine machine, but thought it must be a *Whitley*. He began walking around the aircraft to investigate, and, directing his flashlight on the plane, was shocked to discover a black cross on the fuselage and a swastika emblem on the tail fin. His heart suddenly in his mouth, the erk dropped the flashlight and ran pell mell back to the Control Tower. The Duty Pilot was as startled as the groundcrew man by the news, but took it all in stride. "Crank up the armoured car," he shouted, and within minutes the car had been driven out in front of the *Ju 88*. By that time the enemy aircraft had started to taxi out again to takeoff position, as the crew members were, naturally enough, becoming suspicious about where they had landed. With the armoured car in its path the plane was forced to halt, and a temporary stalemate developed until a spray of Lewis machine-gun fire from the armoured car burst over the top of the plane. Recognizing defeat, the German pilot shut down the engines and the four *Luftwaffe* aircrew climbed out of their machine. Whatever might have happened to them after they left Chivenor, their initial evening at our base was far from harsh. Welcomed to the mess, they were given food and drink to ease their first hours as POWs. They had been on an anti-shipping strike against convoys off Ireland and were returning up the Bristol Channel with Wales on one side and Devon on the other, thinking it was England to port and France to starboard. Short of petrol and unable to stay airborne much longer, they landed at the first aerodrome they saw in "France". Much to their surprise and chagrin, the "French" aerodrome turned out to be none other than Chivenor in North Devon, England. Their story didn't quite end there. In the very early hours of the following morning, while the *Luftwaffe* crew was still being entertained in the mess, one of the station's RAF types returned from a night of celebration in Barnstaple. The first thing he noticed were the German aircrew members at the bar, and without stopping to ask any questions, he turned and ran, first to his billet and then to the armoury to find a Sten gun. He returned ready to open fire, and was only prevented from doing so by the exertions of his alarmed squadron mates. As he expressed it later, "The Germans can capture *anything* but the bar."

On my way to the Flight Office later that morning I spotted the unfamiliar aircraft parked on the grass, and headed over to see what kind of plane the enemy was flying. It was deadly looking, with its two engines protruding from the wings and a single tail fin. A horrible smell surrounded the menacing machine, apparently originating in the engines. I touched an oil smear and brought my greasy finger near my nose—that was the culprit. The lubricating oil seemed to be synthetic, or perhaps of some unusual vegetable origin. It could almost literally be said that you could "smell the enemy a mile away".

A special pilot came in from Farnborough and flew the *Ju 88* away after the Nazi emblems had been replaced by RAF roundels. It was used later for fighter affiliation with our *Wimpys* and *Beaufighters*, which were running into *Ju 88* fighter patrols over the Bay of Biscay.

The *Beaufort* Operational Training Unit left Chivenor on Wednesday, May 6, which was a good thing as 172 Squadron was by this time taking up most of the available space on the station. I flew a few hours with Blackie that day on a practice run with the ASV radar. Our wireless operator, Flight Sergeant Brown, was away on leave but with his return the next day our crew was complete, and we carried out more flying, this time with a full bomb load of four Torpex depth charges. Several nights of flying practice with the ASV and searchlight on Helwick light vessel in the Bristol Channel followed. The weather was misty and foggy most of the time—that is, when it wasn't raining.

The next Wednesday we had our usual defence drill, then took off on a seven-and-one-half-hour night navigation trip with complete war load. This was much longer than we had been used to, but everything went smoothly and we arrived back at the aerodrome at 0840 in the morning to sleep all day. A great surprise was waiting for me when I awoke; George had sent me eighteen clothing coupons for my trench coat. I walked to Scoyne's store to see if the coat had arrived, and to give him the coupons. Later that week I moved into Warrant Officer's quarters.

A few days later my Warrant Officer's uniform was ready in clothing stores, and Sergeant Lees was finally able to have my old Canadian uniform. While at stores I picked up a hat for the armament officer and shoes for the medical officer which they were buying on "repayment", that is, on installment through pay deduction—one way of getting everybody clothed and happy.

I was still studying Botany as an *in absentia* University of London student, and occasionally taught Mathematics in the special evening classes at the station when the regular instructor was sick. My French having reached what I felt was an acceptable level I was now taking German lessons from a Swiss girl in the WAAF. You could never tell when you might want to know more German; one could be forced down in the Bay of Biscay, for instance, and picked up by the enemy.

On Saturday, May 23, Squadron Leader Greswell assigned me a crew: Navigator Sgt. Ronnie Davies from Manchester, Wireless Operator Sgt. John "Smitty" Smith from Bury St. Edmunds in Cambridgeshire, Sgt. Len Hutchison from Saskatoon, Saskatchewan, and Sgt. James "Red" McGrath as my rear gunner. No second pilots or searchlight operators were available as yet.

One day I learned that there was a squash court at the station. It was located in a cement building in the middle of a field, at least eighty yards from the nearest office. I railroaded Flying Officer Abrahams, the Sports Officer, into playing a game with me, and we picked up squash rackets and a ball in the gym and headed for the court in our gym clothes. The cement walls of the court stretched upward for twenty feet, with narrow slits for windows just under the roof. We entered the building from a small anteroom, closed the door, and began our game. Despite the cold weather and absence of heat on the court, it wasn't long before we had worked up a hearty sweat. At the end of an hour or so we were totally burned out, and decided to call it a day, knowing that it was the best exercise we had had for some time.

Abrahams turned to open the door, and the sunken latch used to spring the lock broke off in his hand. After a few moments spent struggling with the latch he announced that the door was locked fast and there was no way to open it. We looked with despair at the cold cement walls and the lock, but after ten minutes and several broken fingernails, we were still locked in. Our sweaty bodies were rapidly becoming chilled, and I had visions of our skeletons being found many weeks later. We were the first to use the court in months, and we had not told anybody where we were going. I imagined the scene as the station security police scoured the countryside for us. There wasn't even a light in the court to draw attention, as the switch was outside in the anteroom.

We looked around for something, anything, we could use, but to no avail. My fear and despair must have worked some magic then, for suddenly the long-forgotten memory of an eight-year-old boy watching his father spring a lock came back. I took off the buckle from the belt around my shorts and worked it into the lock, just as I had seen my father do once in an "emergency". (The police band had been locked out of their practice room above No. 2 Police Station on Dundas Street, Toronto.) I persisted, chilly sweat dripping from my brow, until I finally managed to spring the lock. Rarely had I felt such relief. We both heaved enormous sighs, grabbed our sweatshirts in the anteroom, for by now we were nearly frozen, and ran quickly back to our billets. It had been a close call, at least in our estimation.

Monday, May 25: a *Stirling* four-engined bomber and a twin-engine *Hudson* bomber lobbed down last night from an operational sortie and I paid these kites a visit. After my inspection of the bombers I spent the day inside going over schoolbooks and mail, which included more chocolates from my brother Douglas. It was encouraging to receive the many parcels and letters sent me from family, friends, and groups back home. It took one's mind away from the many minor annoyances of station life, such as the current shortage of tap water in the camp. Heaven only knew why there was any scarcity, for it was raining all day. This rain meant that night flying was cancelled, of course, so in the evening I worked again on the battery storage for the searchlight *Wimpy*. Next day I flew at 1800 hours, expecting to be sent on a trial flight to search for and light up a British submarine off Plymouth, but the flight was scrubbed when the engine on the sub packed up.

On Wednesday I took my crew on a navigational flight to the Scilly Islands and we ran into bad weather, having been late taking off due to water in the engine oil. Despite all these problems we managed to finish our flight. The next day I had an interview with a Canadian liaison officer from RCAF Headquarters in London, who informed me that, as a Warrant Officer I, my pay was now $5.70 a day and I had more English back pay coming to me. It was still not as much as that of a Pilot Officer, who received $6.25 a day.

I was with Blackie's crew on Saturday, May 30 for a practice searchlight operation on the British submarine off Plymouth. On our way there we passed through a thunderstorm over Cornwall, and experienced the phenomenon known as St. Elmo's fire. The propellers turned an eerie blue as sparks of electricity discharged into the atmosphere. When we reached the area of operation we started a "square search" flight pattern in a hunt for the submarine N34. On the second time round we picked up a blip on the ASV and lowered the searchlight. I turned on the light at a calculated distance of one mile from the target and picked up the submarine without difficulty. Blackie brought the *Wimpy* screaming down on the sub's conning tower. I believe that our little demonstration quite convinced any skeptics who might have been watching that our modified *Wellington* was quite capable of finding and attacking a submarine on the surface at night.

The next day a group of eight new pilots from Rhodesia arrived, none of whom had ever been in a *Wimpy* before. Four months had passed since the formation of 1417 Flight in February 1942. The time had been spent in intensive training to perfect methods in the pursuit and combat of U-boats with the searchlight *Wellington*. Long after the end of the war I compared notes on training procedures with German submarine Captains Klaus Scholtz and Henry Baldus, and it was interesting to learn that it also took four months for our adversaries to train in the art of submarine warfare.

It might be apropos to review the sequence of events that led to the operational readiness of 172 Squadron. At the beginning of 1942 the German U-boats were very near the apex of their success. Surface vessels were still the only effective U-boat hunters. Aircraft were but a minor threat to submarines; in the daytime the subs could remain submerged and at night they could surface to recharge their batteries, secure in the knowledge that the aeroplanes had no way to locate them. The introduction of ASV radar offered some hope. Yet, although this equipment could detect surfaced U-boats from a distance of about seven miles, the crucial last mile was still without guidance because of sea-return interference on the ASV radar screen. A visual contact facilitated by direct illumination of the target was the only answer, and thus the Leigh Light came into existence. The searchlight was operated by controls mounted in the nose of the aircraft. It was lowered beneath the fuselage when ASV contact was made, and swung back and forth, up and down, until the object of the blips was detected. The Helwick light vessel in the Bristol Channel served for practice detection at night. Bombing was practised during the day against a floating target off the steep cliffs of North Devon. In the bomb run the aircraft would approach from the land, then dive toward the floating target to simulate an attack on a surfaced U-boat from an altitude of 1000 feet and a distance of one mile. On one occasion a *Wellington* with a full crew plus several passengers, including 2nd Lieutenant D.H. Kaufman, USAAC, homed in on a blip thought to be the Helwick light vessel. Unfortunately, the blip was an American tanker, the *Gulf of Mexico,* steaming up the Bristol Channel. Its alert crew opened fire—the burning *Wellington* fell into the sea. There were no survivors.

Originally there was only one Leigh Light *Wellington* available for training purposes. As this was clearly insufficient, S/L Greswell sent a signal to Group Headquarters: "Request some operationally-tired *Wimpys* from Bomber Command to familiarize our pilots with flying the *Wimpy* and to perfect their low-level bombing technique." Gradually more Leigh Light *Wellingtons* (six in the first batch) became available—but slowly, ever so slowly. Their assignment priority was obvious: the first to Wing Commander J.B. Russell; the next two to the Flight Commanders, S/L J.H. Greswell and F/L A.W. Southall; and the fourth to P/O F. Blackmore, an experienced CCDU pilot. Warrant Officer Fraser, naturally, was much further down the list.

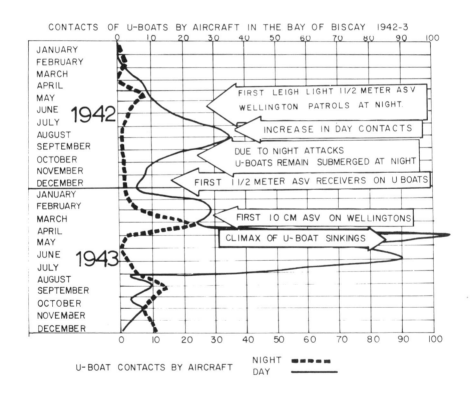

U-boat contacts by aircraft.

116

With the *Wimpy's* all-up weight of 33,000 pounds, its two 980-hp Bristol *Pegasus* engines were severely tested. In Bomber Command the same aircraft had an all-up weight with full bomb load of only 29,000 pounds. The unfavourable power/weight ratio affected the single-engine flying characteristics of the aircraft. This was eventually rectified when we received later marks of the *Wellingtons* in which 1425-hp *Hercules* powerplants replaced the old *Pegasus* engines.

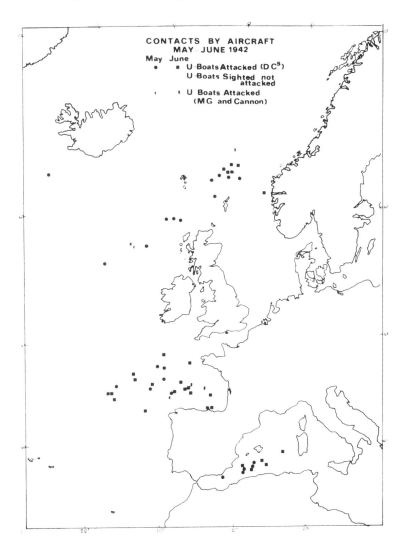

Contacts by aircraft, May - June 1942.

U-995 in Kiel, West Germany, 1980.

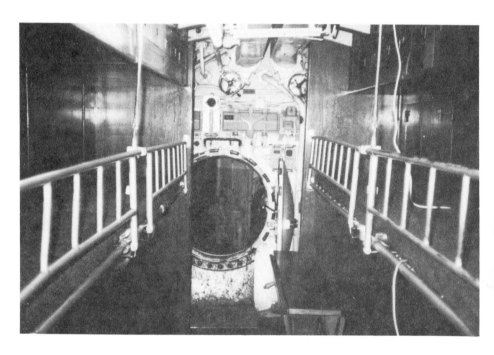

Torpedo tube between bunks in the U-995, 1980.

Controlling wheels inside the U-995, 1980.

It had taken four months—perhaps not really long under the circumstances—but by early June 1942 the Leigh Light *Wellingtons* and their crews were ready to be tested in battle. There had originally been six aircraft, but P/O Russ crashed in one of them, and shortly before the squadron became operational a groundcrew member accidentally ran a tractor into "A for Apple". Yet the critical situation at sea precluded any further wait for more machines.

On June 2, 1942, the long-awaited news arrived. 172 Squadron was operational. A slight let-down followed, as ops were cancelled that night. But the crews of the four serviceable Leigh Light *Wellingtons* were warned to stand by for the next night. The pilots were Wing Commander J.B. Russell, S/L J. Greswell, F/L A. Southall, and P/O F. Blackmore, with whom I flew as second pilot and searchlight operator. This would be the testing of the first "weapons system", long before the term was to be coined, in the Second World War.

Air Vice Marshal G.R. Bromet was the special guest at the operational briefing for these initial four Leigh Light *Wellington* sorties on June 3. The first aircraft to take off was to be P/O Blackmore's at 2035; the others were to follow at five-minute intervals. The weather looked favourable, with some clouds making, on the whole, for a very dark night. The briefing ended with the usual, "Any questions?"

"Won't we be sitting ducks when the searchlight is turned on?" queried one gunner.

There was a momentary, but deep silence before the Operations Officer answered brightly, "Open up with all your front guns. That will make the U-boat's crew keep their heads down."

The gunner was not satisfied. "Please, Sir, we don't have any front guns."

The embarrassed Operations Officer paused for just a few seconds, then rose to the occasion and replied resourcefully, "Keep the light in their eyes; that will blind them." A ripple of laughter ran through the room, and the tension was broken, to be replaced with an atmosphere of high excitement.

The last slivers of daylight were slipping over the horizon when the four *Wimpys* taxied to the very end of the runway, revved up their engines, and surged forward, one after the other. In our heavy machines we needed every inch of runway on that calm summer's evening, but taking a chance was the rule of the day: overloaded planes, short runways, and hills far too close for comfort were the norm, as grimly attested by the cemeteries close by.

Blackie, the captain of our aircraft "B for Beer", was a pilot I trusted absolutely. He had been born in Morocco of French-British parents, and Greswell told me that he spoke many languages, but none without an accent. Blackie was a permanent RAF type with considerable flying experience, especially with the CCDU, and I felt completely safe with him in the pilot's seat, or at least, as safe as one could ever feel in a heavy kite in wartime.

Our crew climbed into the machine through the opening under the nose—Blackie took his place first in the pilot's seat on the left side of the plane; there were no dual controls in the operational kites. The rear gunner, Sgt Wadsworth, went in next to wend his way down the fuselage to his position, and the ASV operator, F/Sgt Brown, took his place in front of the radar set near the main spar. F/L Barnett, the navigator, climbed in with his bag of charts, followed by Sgt Collindine, the wireless operator. Finally, yours truly got in, pulling the front door down into a locked position and standing beside Blackie as the engines were run up. I checked that the escape hatch above Blackie's head was firmly locked into position and that the searchlight controls appeared normal. I always waited until the plane was airborne before I took my place, as it was at the very front of the machine, in the perspex nose behind the searchlight controls. In the case of a tire blowing or some other accident during takeoff, anyone in the nose would be smashed into hamburger.

It was always breathtaking to stand in the cockpit as the aircraft rushed down the runway. "B for Beer" started a slow climb—ever so slow—straight out to sea—then a gradual turn toward the south, the Scilly Islands, and Bishop's Rock, from where we would strike a track directly for the coast of Spain. I looked around but did not see any of the other three planes; we were on our own. Blackie set "George", the automatic pilot, so he could relax for a while. We had the Farnborough RAF type which turned by applying rudder only, so the aircraft always skidded around the turn, not like the Sperry George, which applied bank for its turns in the correct aerodynamic fashion. But beggars can't be choosers, and the Farnborough George was a godsend, for we were flying on a minimum nine-hour trip, and some trips took up to thirteen hours, if there were a U-boat encounter.

Night came quickly—it was pitch black except for the occasional twinkle of a star. A sporadic shower of meteors burned itself up in the earth's atmosphere, momentarily frightening us with is unexpectedness. I sat patiently in the nose of the aircraft behind the searchlight controls. For a number of hours I had been humming a tune that kept coming back into my head, and I unconsciously and softly sang out: "Toronto, Toronto, is our university. Fight, oh, fight, men of every faculty. *Velut Arbor,* may she ever thrive; Oh, God, forever save our Alma Mater."

Suddenly the ASV operator shouted over the intercom, "Blip coming up five miles ahead, Skipper; five degrees to port." The plane turned slightly to port as "Action Stations" alerted the crew.

My eyes began to feel as though they were stretching out of their sockets as I strained to discern the object of our ASV blip. The searchlight had been lowered, and the navigator had scrambled up beside the pilot. I put the searchlight through a practice run with the light off, adjusting the searchlight controls up and down and from side to side as shown on the indicators in front of me; the index finger of my right hand toyed with the on/off switch for the searchlight beam. The ASV operator counted off the distance to our hunted object. "Five miles— four and a half miles—four miles—three and a half miles—three miles— left a little more, Skipper—two and a half miles—two and a quarter miles—two miles." The tension mounted.

"Are the bomb doors open?" I yelled.

"Bomb doors open," replied Blackie.

"One and a half miles—one and one quarter miles—one mile."

Instantly Blackie shouted, "Light on!" and I switched on the searchlight and started to swing it across the path of our flight. Amost immediately we focussed on the object of our search—a U-boat? No, a tunny-fishing boat.

We were down to less than one hundred feet, skimming over the surface of the dark water. As soon as Blackie realized the object was not a U-boat, he ordered, "Light off—light up—bomb doors closed." The engines whined as he opened the throttle and the *Wimpy* climbed slowly to its patrol height of a thousand feet. Burnett, the navigator, was not amused—he was the one who had to hand-pump the searchlight back into its retracted position—a laborious job. Then he returned to his navigation to adjust for the deviation from our authorized course.

Barnett had just given Blackie a new course when the ASV operator shouted out a second blip warning—ten degrees to starboard, six miles. The operation with the light was repeated, and once again we encountered only a tunnyman. This was to be the norm for most patrols. Some excitement occurred when, at the end of the outbound leg, the coast of Spain was sighted, and the lights of its cities brightly reflected a country at peace. The crews of Wing Commander Russell and Flight Lieutenant Southall experienced similar encounters with tunnymen on this first operational sortie, but S/L Greswell had more luck. As he neared the Spanish coast on the outward leg of his search, his radar operator picked up a blip at seven miles. It turned out to be a big Italian submarine, the *Luigi Torelli.*

The presence of an Italian submarine in the Bay of Biscay was not surprising. When Italy entered the war Mussolini had sent a number of submarines around to French ports, from whence they operated, with a varying degree of success, against the Atlantic convoys.

The historic encounter between Greswell's searchlight *Wellington* and the *Luigi Torelli,* commanded by Captain Augusto Migliorini, an Italian Count, is probably best narrated as it is recorded in Migliorini's log. The *Luigi Torelli* was Migliorini's first submarine command, although he had followed a naval career since 1928, when he had entered the Italian Naval Academy in Livorno. After five years in the academy he had served on the cruisers *Zara* and *Bari,* and in 1937 was sent on a submarine warfare course. He then joined the submarine *Ferraris,* and shortly afterward became the second-in-command on the *Tembien* for 1938-1939, and on the *Nereide* in the Atlantic for 1941-1942. Migliorini was finally given command of the *Luigi Torelli* in mid-1942. At 0227 on the night of June 3/4, 1942, he was proceeding at a northerly course at a speed of nine knots, a few miles off the Biscay coast of Spain, when he was surprised by the first Leigh Light *Wellington* sortie.

A huge searchlight on a low-flying plane suddenly illuminated an area about 300 metres to the right of his bow, then swung across to the centre of the submarine. The officer on duty immediately gave the order to increase speed to full ahead and turn to port. The plane continued to follow them and, after another direct illumination, switched off its light. The night was very dark with no moon, but there was much phosphorescence on the sea. As soon as the light had been switched off Captain Migliorini reduced his speed to a minimum, thinking that the aeroplane was detecting him by his phosphorescent wake, and prepared to dive.

Before the sub could begin its dive, the searchlight of Greswell's plane again lit up the right side of the stern from approximately 300 metres, focussing on the conning tower of the *Luigi Torelli*. The Captain ordered a turn to starboard and shouted to open fire with the anti-aircraft guns. The plane passed very low over the submarine, firing rapid bursts from the rear turret. Greswell turned off the searchlight again, but Captain Migliorini could still follow him for a few seconds. Then, when he thought that the plane had lost him because of his small wake, he again gave orders for a rapid dive.

Yet once again the *Luigi Torelli* was brilliantly illuminated, this time from a very close range and while Captain Migliorini still had his head out the hatch. The bosun had already given the hooter signal to dive when the Captain ordered another turn to port, and just a few seconds later the submarine was rocked by a series of explosions under its hull. The submarine, surrounded by columns of water, jerked violently, and sank slightly by the bow. As the concussion hit the *Torelli,* the lid of the hatch freed itself from its hook and slammed over the Captain's head. A strong decompression was created before the diesel engines could be stopped. The Captain had to introduce air into the chambers with the watertight doors near the bow to equalize the air pressure, so he could again open the hatch to let in the bosun, trapped on the outside.

Damage to the *Luigi Torelli* as a result of Greswell's attack was severe: there was a complete loss of electrical power; fire had broken out in two battery chambers, accompanied by strong smoke; many of the battery elements had been smashed and were leaking acid so that small pockets of chlorine gas were developing; numerous fixtures were broken.

The *Luigi Torelli* made way for the nearest port on the Spanish coast, Jean de Luz, and throughout the night her men battled the flames. Even after the blaze was extinguished at dawn, her troubles were far from over. In a dense fog the submarine grounded on rocks off the Spanish coast, damaging her hull. After emergency repairs the *Torelli* continued her journey, despite being attacked by *Sunderlands* on two separate occasions. Finally forced to put in at a Spanish harbour, the *Luigi Torelli* was interned. Two weeks later the Italian crew over-powered the Spanish prize crew, put them in a rubber dinghy, and sailed out of the harbour and back to France. The *Torelli* was later converted to a transport sub by the Italians and used on runs to the Far East, being taken over by the Japanese in 1943 upon Italy's surrender. It was captured by the Americans in late 1945 and sunk in their Pacific tests.

As Squadron Leader Greswell homed in on the *Luigi Torelli* he, too, experienced some difficulties. First he overshot the Italian submarine because the altimeter gave a falsely high reading due to changing barometric pressures. On his second run, the *Luigi Torelli* shot what appeared to be recognition signals into the air. Could it be a British submarine? It was a horrible thought, but then Greswell recalled that British submarines never shot up recognition signals, burning flares on the surface instead. The submarine's anti-aircraft gun abruptly opened fire, and as the tracers spewed upward to his plane, Greswell dived in to attack. The Leigh Light kept the submarine in sight, and also helped Greswell to judge the surface level accurately. Bomb doors were opened and the depth charges set to explode at a depth of 25 feet. Greswell swung low over the *Luigi Torelli* and dropped a stick of four Torpex depth charges 35 feet apart from a height of fifty feet. Three of them exploded, one on the starboard quarter about five yards from the hull, and the other two on the port side.

After the *Luigi Torelli* had dived, Greswell located a second U-boat about twelve miles away. With his depth charges totally expended, Greswell attacked the sub from about 150 feet with machine-gun fire, scoring hits on the hull and the conning tower. Greswell was of the opinion that the second U-boat may never have seen him, as it was already submerging when he spotted it with his ASV and searchlight. What saved both these submarines was the failure of the attacks to signal the other *Wellingtons* on patrol in the area, and home them to the battle.

At 0520 hours on June 4 we landed back at Chivenor after that historic first operational Leigh Light sortie. As I slept till 1230, the only thing I did that day worth noting was to buy a Webley .45 revolver from Flight Sergeant Carter for three pounds. It was a prized possession until it went down with my plane some five months afterward.

We were off again that night on ops. Many blips were visible on the ASV radar, and correspondingly there were many shouts of "Action Stations!" In each instance I scrambled over the batteries into the searchlight operator position in the "greenhouse" nose of the aircraft. Flying Officer Barnett would literally drop the searchlight (once the catch was released the light would sink down from its own weight), and Blackie would peer over his control column, keeping watch both on his instruments and the windscreen. It was pouring rain that night, and we had a chance to use our new windscreen wipers, which proved a boon to visibility. After lowering the light Barnett would take his place beside Blackie and search for the target with large Navy binoculars, at the same time cocking his Leica for a picture. I checked the azimuth and elevation dials for the searchlight and fingered the on/off switch, ready to turn on the light as soon as Blackie gave the order, usually when the ASV operator said on the intercom, "Blip at one mile, dead ahead". Then there was the steady sweep of the cone of piercing light to pick up objects just under one mile ahead. Invariably that night we would see a white sail billowing out over a small fishing vessel, a tunnyman, probably from Spain, maybe from France, or possibly Ireland. Each time, sweeping near to it, we investigated from startlingly close to zero height. Then light off. Barnett would move back to the main spar to pump the searchlight back into the cabin position, Blackie would increase the revs on the propellers and the boost on the engines, and we would climb slowly back to 1000 feet to resume our patrol. It was something like fishing. Every blip on the ASV was a strike, but the real question was whether it would be a "big fish", a U-boat, or a "little fish", a tunnyman. Later, when our patrols took us out into the Atlantic Ocean, we sometimes "caught" one of our own Allied merchant ships or Navy vessels.

The next day, to our intense relief, we had a stand-down. All of us were exhausted, for our patrols ran for at least nine hours, sometimes eleven or twelve, and occasionally even thirteen hours. I received more parcels from home, and took a trip into Barnstaple to price a bicycle.

Saturday, June 6 was rather misty, and I spent the morning plotting aerodrome locations on a map. I tried unsuccessfully to get some sleep in the afternoon, because ops were on again that night. Takeoff was at 1020 hours. As we approached the Spanish coast I spotted a long patch of light off to starboard. The ASV had not picked anything up, and simultaneously Blackie and I expressed a horrible thought; could it be a coastguard beacon from shore? Would we crash into the high hills behind the Spanish coast? As I took my place at the searchlight controls, Blackie swung around sharply. No coastline was in sight, but suddenly the mysterious light was explained when we spotted a U-boat going like a bat out of hell. It had submerged by the time our plane swung over its position again. It was midmorning by the time we returned to base, and, after debriefing, we stumbled to our beds.

The following day a fellow Torontonian, Pilot Officer O'Gorman, joined the squadron. The weather was fair at last, so ops were on again. We took off at 2230 hours, and half an hour later the starboard engine abruptly cut out—stopped dead. None of us dared voice the black thoughts which immediately stormed into our minds, but Blackie quickly jettisoned the depth charges and I scrambled back from the searchlight position in the nose. Calling for us to take up our dinghy positions, Blackie swung the plane to port in an effort to reach land, a manoeuvre in no way assisted by the loss of the starboard engine. Just as the turn was being completed the recalcitrant engine coughed, sputtered, and slowly picked up again. Blackie brought the plane over land at Cornwall, and we landed at the closest aerodrome, St. Eval, just before midnight. With our nerves still tingling from our close call, it was some time before any of us could get to sleep in our borrowed beds. The next morning mechanics swarmed over "B for Beer", trying to find the cause of the problem. Naturally, the engines ran perfectly, and finally the mechanics decided it was but another job of those mischievous gremlins, whose chief delight was scaring aircrew. The engines were still purring smoothly when tested the next day back at Chivenor, and we practised on another British submarine, the *N-74*, off Start Point near Eddystone in the evening.

We slept all day after our night flying, and the next day went to White Waltham, an aerodrome near London, to demonstrate the new battery storage we had designed and constructed. In the evening, I took time out to see the show *Weekend in Havana* in Maidenhead. On Saturday I went to Barnstaple and bought myself a *Hercules* for just ten pounds—no, not the aircraft, a *Hercules* bicycle. It had both a hand brake and a rear wheel brake, highly advanced technology for those days. It had been made for export to Canada, thus my purchase was, to some extent, appropriate.

Allies Flag Day was June 14. We practised some astro sights and I explained the cockpit of a *Wellington* to O'Gorman. Then I walked to the church on the hill with Sergeant Lewis, a quiet, friendly Welshman who was a wireless operator/air gunner with the squadron. Lewis had brought his wife with him to live in the nearby village of Braunton, where they rented a room from my friend Hesketh Scoyne. Lewis' tale has a sad ending, for near the end of the summer his plane did not return from an operation. He was posted as missing, and nothing was ever heard from him again. The Scoynes helped Lewis' wife dismantle her room and arranged for her to move back with her parents in Wales.

The next day I spent some time in the ops building; ops were on, but our kite was unserviceable while the radio-altimeter was being fitted. Finally deciding to wait around no longer, I rode my new bicycle to Saunton Sands for a spot of sightseeing. The machine was still unserviceable the next day, so I went into Barnstaple with Davies and Bramwell to see the show *Dive Bomber*.

The mechanics were still working on our machine on Wednesday, June 12 when Squadron Leader Greswell strode into the flight room. "Anyone here flown *Tiger Moths*?" I waved a hand. "Come into my office," he said. "The local maintenance unit on the other side of the aerodrome wants to borrow a parachute for their pilot to test a rebuilt plane. I told them I'd send over one of our own pilots to test it."

Picking up my parachute, I asked Smitty, my wireless operator, if he wanted a flip in a *Tiger Moth*. He was game, grabbed a chute, and we took a truck over to the maintenance unit. I reported to their foreman.

There's the machine sitting out on the grass," he said. "Take it up for a test; I think we've rebuilt it okay."

I walked over to the *Moth* with a mechanic. Smitty climbed into the rear cockpit, and, after walking around the plane for an outside check, I climbed into the front. The pitot tube was uncovered and there were no restraining bars on the controls. As soon as I had signed the Daily Inspection sheet, the mechanic shouted, "Switches off."

"Switches off," I repeated.

After turning the propeller around a few times to pull the gas into the carburetor and cylinders, the mechanic yelled, "Switches on."

"Switches on."

The mechanic gave the prop a quick spin and jumped back as the engine roared to life. While the *Moth* warmed up I tested both magnetos and made sure the cockpit harness was strapped on, a rather important step, to put it mildly, when flying an open cockpit aircraft. I checked that Smitty was also strapped in, then waved to the mechanic, who pulled away the wheel chocks. Revving up the engine I taxiied out slowly. There was no tail wheel as in the Canadian *Tiger Moth*, but there was a tail skid, so we kept on the grass for as long as possible. The light *Tiger Moth* felt like quite a different kite from the lumbering, truck-like *Wimpy*.

I climbed into the blue sky, out over the water, and turned in over the River Taw. Everything was clear as we rose to 5000 feet, and we could see the countryside for miles. It was a beautiful day, but I was there to test the plane, not sight-see. I tried a few steep turns, first one way, then another, cutting back the engine and holding the nose up. The speed fell rapidly from cruising at 80 mph, to 70, then 60 . . . 50 . . . 40 . . . and all of a sudden the wing started to drop and the plane began an incipient spin. I caught it with opposite rudder and some engine, then climbed up again. "How would you like a loop?" I asked Smitty. He nodded assent. After checking for other aircraft in the vicinity, I put the plane into a shallow dive. The speed built up; at 125 I eased back on the control column and opened up the engine to full power. The nose tilted ever more sharply upward until we were on our backs. I throttled back on the engine and we continued the rest of the loop, diving straight down, and finally levelling out again. The plane had handled well; there was no need to worry. I flew over Barnstaple, circled the green fields and hills, then came back over the aerodrome to land on the grass next to the runway. Cutting the engine I heaved a short, happy sigh. It cheered me to know I could still fly *Tiger Moths* after being away from them for almost two years.

Thirty-three years later I was reminded of this test flight when I drove out to Granby, Quebec, to examine their water reservoir, sadly depleted after a dry summer. I rented a light plane to take me over the reservoir for pictures. The regular pilot was not available to take me around, but when the Chief Instructor discovered that I was an old Air Force pilot, he said he would take me up. He taxied out to the runway, ran through the cockpit check, and then announced, "You can take it up." There was no time to say no, but I wouldn't have anyway. I lined the plane up with the runway, opened the throttle, and the plane surged forward. We built up speed and I wondered how fast I should be going for takeoff. Deciding that this speed wouldn't be much different from that of the old *Tiger Moth*, I allowed ten miles per hour extra just to be on the safe side, lifted the plane around on a left hand turn, ascended to 1500 feet, and headed for the Granby reservoir. Then I remembered that I had come up to take pictures, not to fly the plane. Returning control to the CFI, I switched to my self-appointed task of photographing the reservoir and the surroundings of Granby. But it had felt good to do a bit of flying again after all those years.

Back at the Repair Depot at Chivenor I told the foreman his plane had checked out perfectly. Smitty had enjoyed the ride too. Altogether it had been a thoroughly refreshing experience.

That evening I tested the radio-altimeter on our regular machine, "B for Beer". It was finally behaving itself so we were on ops again that night. "A for Apple" and "D for Donald" experienced engine trouble during the mission, but everyone returned to base safely.

I slept until 1600 hours the next day, and awoke to find a letter from Mother; my deferred assigned pay, I was happy to hear, was reaching her. Rumours were circulating that we might return to Canada. Apparently the U-boats were having a heyday off the US coast, and an RAF squadron was to be posted to the Bahamas to help the Americans ward off the subs. We kept our fingers crossed. Oh, what I would have given to fly a *Wimpy* over Yonge Street in Toronto, or even off Halifax. But we really should have known better than even to hope for such a turn of events. We later heard that a *Hudson* squadron had been posted to keep an anti-submarine patrol in that area.

Years later, in 1963, when I visited Nassau in the Bahamas, I made it a point to visit the wartime cemetery behind the old aerodrome near the statue of the late Sir Harry Oakes. Outside the cemetery wall grew a mass of brambles, a tangled vegetation that could only develop so quickly in a sub-tropical climate. I pushed my way along the overgrown path to the cemetery entrance and passed inside near the two trees planted there by Princess Margaret at an earlier time. Wandering among the reasonably well-kept graves, I noted a number of stones marking RAF and RCAF aircrew killed in crashes on the islands. Of course, many who went missing in the area on wartime ops would have found an unknown watery grave. There, but for the grace of God, could have been my position—six feet under.

Chapter Seven
Enemy Encounters: Germans and Gremlins

JUNE 19, 1942 BEGAN MUCH THE SAME as any other day that summer. The air was warm and clear, air and groundcrew moved about the station, a few rushing around with papers or clipboards in their hands, but most with the somnolent pace of early morning. The hours slipped by slowly, the only novelty in my day being a visit from Jack Deacon, a Staff Sergeant with the 48th Highlanders. In exchange for a letter from my brother, I gave him a brief tour of the station. At last it was evening, and I was off again on a patrol. It was to be the longest sortie of my tour, just ten minutes under thirteen hours.

Our takeoff was as uneventful as any takeoff can be in an under-powered *Wimpy* about two tons overweight. After half an hour we were cruising at about 1000 feet; the engines, for a change, were purring nicely; the propellers were synchronized to an even hum. The rpm of the propellers and engines were cut back as far as possible to give a better gas consumption. This practice was harder on the engine, which was normally run with a high boost, and was probably one reason why we so often had the sticky exhaust valves that gave us so much trouble. We flew down past the Scilly Islands and set course for the Spanish coast from Bishop's Rock lighthouse off the southwest tip of the Scillys.

"Blip coming up," reported the ASV operator.

"Action Stations."

I scrambled forward to the searchlight controls. Blackie peered with squinted eyes through the perspex windscreen. The navigator, Flying Officer Barnett, moved forward with his night glasses and camera. The blip was coming closer, slightly to starboard. We turned to the right a bit, and gently lowered the light. With muscles tensed, we silently went through the countdown—three miles . . . two and one half miles . . . two . . . one and one half . . . one and one quarter . . . one mile. Light on. I swept the beam back and forth. On the first sweep I picked up the tunny-fishing boat responsible for the blip. I think we all felt mingled relief and frustration as the navigator pumped up the light and I switched it off. Blackie increased the boost to climbing settings and we staggered up to 1000 feet. After several false alarms, we neared the Spanish coast —"Action Stations." Again we made our approach, switching on the light at one mile. Once more I caught the object in the beam in the first sweep, but this time it was . . . a U-boat! Unlike our previous trips when we had passed high over the U-boat, this time our ASV operator brought us dead on. We sped directly toward it, rapidly losing height. A second or two after I picked out the U-boat with the light I saw machine-gun tracers and rapid fire, probably from 20-mm guns, spurting up toward me. I felt very lonely and naked sitting out in the greenhouse at the front of the plane. I had not yet started to shake, that would come later. The shells appeared to be bursting to starboard. Were they hitting the wing? I couldn't tell. All I knew was that they were coming closer and closer. Blackie brought the *Wimpy* low over the water, and I elevated the light to keep the U-boat's conning tower in the beam. The shells continued to burst around us as Blackie brought the plane even nearer to the sub.

"Are the bomb doors open?" I shouted. Hearing no reply, I repeated it over the intercom. There was still no reply, but I was too occupied with the light and the shells to ask again, as I carried out my job of holding the light on target. We swept over the conning tower at what seemed like zero feet, although it was actually ten or twenty. I could see one of the U-boat sailors clearly—I can still see him as if it were yesterday, with his bulky, white turtleneck sweater. He was manning one of the guns, but as he looked up at us he seemed suddenly to panic. As we swept over their boat he turned and jumped behind the conning tower, or perhaps into the sea. We pulled up after we passed the U-boat, and I switched off the searchlight.

At that moment I heard Barnett shout, "The right engine is on fire!" At our low altitude it would take but a few seconds to crash into the sea, and if that happened I would be smashed into mincemeat. But we didn't appear to be losing height, so after a moment I relaxed. Our rear gunner's machine-guns were chattering away, going like blazes. He shouted to the Skipper that the depth charges had not gone off, but Blackie did not reply. I scrambled back over the batteries to the second pilot's position, fearing that Blackie had been hit by gunfire and I would have to take over flying the machine. On my way back I glanced at the right engine; there were no flames to be seen. Either Barnett had imagined it after seeing so much flak exploding nearby, or I had misheard

him. Blackie, unharmed after all, glanced up when I appeared next to him and told me that the bomb doors had not opened. What had happened? A moment of forgetfulness? A jammed control? We would never know. Scrambling back to my nose position, I realized with relief that I had done the job I was trained for and had not even flinched, at least not externally. The plane swung around in the darkness in a mile-long extended circle, I turned on the light again, although the ASV operator had not picked up anything. The searchlight swept the surface of the sea, illuminating the swirl of dark water where the U-boat had submerged. We had lost our quarry. They had probably lost one crew member, and others may have been nicked by our machine-gun fire, but the sub itself was unharmed. Our Captain was greatly upset, if not downright angry. He circled again. Having missed our chance to make a successful attack on the U-boat, he was not to be put off easily, and continued a creeping, line-ahead search. For hours and hours we searched the area, taking into account the forward speed of the U-boat, but all to no avail. Just as we were deciding that Blackie was definitely becoming unbalanced by it all, and that we would end up swimming home, we turned to base. Creeping up the Cornish coast, we picked up the ASV beacon for the Scilly Islands. The wing tank indicator wavered on empty. We had long since used all the petrol in the overload tank, as well as the 56 gallons in each of the engine nacelle tanks. It was with relief that we came in over the Chivenor aerodrome to land at 1130. We had been in the air just ten minutes less than thirteen hours, and our usual scheduled time of flight was nine hours; we were almost four hours overdue. There were only a few drops of petrol left in our tanks, but our consumption had been about 58 gallons per hour for both engines, out of this world for fuel economy. Blackie had run the engines with low revs and high boost, a good combination for energy efficiency, although less beneficial for the life of the engine.

On our return flight at 0821 hours we had received a wireless message that *Wellington* "A for Apple" was in distress. We had set course for the estimated position of the aircraft, but saw nothing along its given track. Later that day we learned that "A" had gone down in the drink from engine trouble some 180 miles off the Scilly Islands. Our plane was not assigned to the search, so I went swimming that evening with Ronnie Davies, my observer, at Saunton Sands, and later we had chips in Barnstaple; my bicycle was proving its worth.

On Sunday, June 21 the crew of "A" was spotted in their dinghy and a *Sunderland* flying boat was sent to their rescue. Fortunately, the ditching of the *Wellington* had been successful. All crew members had safely boarded their dinghy and were eventually picked up by a motor launch at 2200 hours on the 21st. The crew included F/S I.C. Virgo, F/S J.R. Marshall, F/S D.J.G. Norton, Sgt E.T. Deacon, Sgt L.P. Bellamy, and Sgt N.R. Vardy, all RAF types.

Two new Leigh Light *Wimpys* arrived on the 21st as replacements and to increase 172's operational strength.

On Monday, June 22, another aircraft, a *Whitley* twin-engine bomber, went down at sea. Ops were scrubbed that evening, so once again I made use of my bicycle, one of the best investments I had ever made. I heard that Tobruk in North Africa had fallen; Rommel was advancing through Libya toward Egypt. The next day I received a letter from home informing me that Doug Horniblow, my old North Toronto Collegiate pal and neighbour, was in the Army. We were on ops again that night, but this time for only nine hours. We landed at 0600 hours on June 24, having seen Spain. It had given us an unexpected pleasure to coast along the Spanish shoreline near Santander and Bilboa and see the lights of the cities glowing throughout the night, free of blackout regulations.

Air Vice-Marshall John Russell with the author at the author's residence, Town of Mount Royal, P.Q., 1972.

The author (second from the right) and fellow aircrew on a cycling trip to John O'Groats from Wick, October 1942.

Tunneyman fishing boat illuminated with Leigh Light. Bay of Biscay, 1942.   (Imperial War Museum)

I slept all that day and stood by for 502 Squadron *Whitleys* all night, but we were not called out. I learned in another letter from home that the Police Department was not exempt from military service in Canada. My younger brother, Douglas, a policeman, was to join the Navy. He later served on the Canadian frigate, HMCS *Grou,* on the Murmansk run escorting convoys to Russia.

Ops were on again the next night. For this uneventful trip we had a Squadron Leader from Coastal Headquarters with us. In the early hours of the morning he crawled up to my lonely position, and I explained all the searchlight controls as we buzzed over the Bay of Biscay. In return he told me of an RAF night fighter pilot who was a unique sort of ace; he had shot down the required five planes, but all had been British—two *Wimpys,* one *Lancaster,* one *Stirling,* and a *Whitley.* The bombers had been struggling back from raids on Germany, all shot up and with the IFF (Identification Friend or Foe) "black box" inoperative. When they accidentally flew over London, a forbidden area, the British night fighters were directed by radar on to these apparently hostile aircraft. This one particular night fighter pilot became a nervous wreck, understandably, and had to be taken off ops.

I heard via the grapevine that they were trying to break up my crew, that is, the one I was going to captain as soon as another searchlight *Wimpy* became available. We had put in a lot of time training together, and my crew objected, as I did, to the possibility. I decided to put in a bit of time chasing down the rumour, as there could be nothing worse than to have a false tale break up the morale of my crew. I never did find the source of the story, but I had a brief reprieve from my worries when I went to a dance that evening. The next few days were rather uneventful, with ops on again/off again as the weather deteriorated throughout each day. By this time my non-commissioned status had begun to rankle. I was the senior NCO of the squadron as a Warrant Officer Class I. After the command of Wing Commander Russell to "Fall out the officers; remainder carry on," I was left alone to assign and supervise drill and defence exercises all afternoon. A ludicrous situation. One aspect of the difference in rank, as I recalled from my Military Law course, was that commissioned officers had their pay continued when taken prisoner-of-war, whereas non-commissioned officers and other ranks did not. Also, a commissioned Pilot Officer received $6.25 per day, and a Flying Officer $7 a day, compared to a Warrant Officer Class I's pay of $5.20 a day. I had never actually applied for a commission except when I first put in my application to the RCAF for pilot training in the fall of 1939, but I thought it was now high time to try again. I felt that my achievements had warranted it even though I was certain that "taking the bull by the horns" more than a year previously, when I wrote to the Hon. Vincent Massey about the unwarranted deduction of income tax from the Canadian service-men's pay, had not endeared me to the RAF. I brought up the matter with the Wing Commander when we were discussing defence exercises in his office.

"How about a commission, Sir?"

He looked at me closely. "Well," he replied after a moment, "I really don't have much to do with you Canadians."

"Couldn't you even recommend me for a commission?"

"Oh, if you just want a recommendation, certainly." He pressed a buzzer and the Adjutant came into the office. "See that Fraser fills out the application for a commission. I'll sign it and get it off to Head-quarters." My mind was now more at ease; at least I had tried.

By Wednesday, July 1, Dominion Day, I had put in the completed form for a commission. It had been okayed by the Winco, the Education Officer, and the Medical Officer, and I was to have an interview with the Group Captain the following day. The interview went smoothly; the Group Captain seemed quite pleased and said that he would forward my application to RCAF Headquarters in London.

Within the first month of active operations, more pilots and their crews as well as additional aircraft had joined the squadron. In some cases experienced second pilots and searchlight operators were only waiting for their aircraft. In other instances the new crews were arriving fresh from the Coastal Command Operational Training Unit at Cranwell.

F/O G.V. Syer was one of the new men. An Englishman, Syer had been a minister working in Australia when war broke out. (Greswell repeatedly joked that Syer kept his "dog collar" in his flying clothing locker.) Syer promptly joined the Royal Australian Air Force, trained in Canada, and flew across the Atlantic in a *Hudson,* breaking the speed record in doing so. Posted to 172 Squadron, he took his crew on their first operation in a Leigh Light *Wellington* in July 1942. He was awarded the Distinguished Flying Cross for his valiant efforts. Then, unfort-unately, Syer fell ill.

The RAF had scrubbed regular medical examinations for the duration of the war, and only gave them after illness or when an airman was recommended for a commission. Apparently, when Syer was given his examination, the Medical Officer discovered his eyes had packed up. They were so bad he was no longer permitted to fly. The Australians wanted to post him back to Australia, but instead he resigned his commission with the RAAF and joined the RAF as a padre. It was unique to have a padre with wings and a DFC.

The first of our pilots to get a confirmed U-boat sinking was Pilot Officer Wiley Howell, an American pilot with the RAF. Howell was posted to 172 Squadron on June 25, 1942. Two days later he flew as a passenger—an "extra body"—with S/L Greswell on an operational sortie over the Bay of Biscay. On the morning of July 5th he flew a practice bombing mission with me, and that night Howell went on his first operational trip as a Captain. It may seem an anomaly that Howell should get a searchlight *Wimpy* before me, but there were several points in his favour. As a volunteer American pilot with the RAF he had refused posting to the Eagle Fighter Squadron on *Spitfires* and, instead, was the first American to volunteer for bombers. He completed a navigation course at Squire's Gate near Blackpool and did his conversion to *Wimpys* at Cranwell, where he was teamed up with a full crew including a second pilot. Hence, he arrived at Chivenor with a complete crew. I myself had no second pilot as yet; these, like the Leigh Light *Wimpys,* were in short supply at Chivenor.

On his first operational trip Howell spotted and attacked a fully surfaced U-boat with depth charges; it was not until some years later that it was identified as the *U-502,* a submarine that never returned to base. His luck held, for exactly one week later he made his second successful attack. His debriefing on his second attack was as follows:

Left base [Chivenor] 2215 hours 12.7.42. At 0100 in position 46.42N 04.55W one U-boat was sighted and attacked. "H" was flying at 1,000 ft on Course 136° T when a S.E. contact was obtained on homing aerials dead ahead at 7 miles range. Aircraft homed and when ¾ mile on course of 100 (T) at 300 ft, L/LT was exposed illuminating a U-boat fully surfaced on course 090° (T). The U-boat opened up with fire as the L/LT was switched on. At 0104 hours four Torpex filled depth charges were released from 100 ft across U-boat from one point on port quarter to one point on starboard bow. The explosions obscured the target and made it difficult to observe results.

The rear gunner fired 400 rounds into the explosion and a red glow appeared through the water thrown up. A search was carried out in the area with both aerials for two hours four minutes, and though some S/E contacts were obtained, nothing was seen of the U-boat. About 8-10 minutes after the attack flashes were seen in the distance which probably resulted from flak fired at aircraft "K" of 172 Squadron. H/172 returned to base at 0635 hours on 13.7.42.

It is interesting to compare Howell's report with the German version of the attack:

0102/13.7 *Kapitanleutnant* Witte was proceeding on the surface, when the aircraft came swooping in from port beam, illuminating the U-boat with the searchlight. In spite of accurate fire from the U-boat's 2cm, the aircraft did not diverge from the attack. Three d/cs had very little delay action setting and the boat got the whole effect of the blast. A great deal of damage was caused, some of it very serious. 59 battery cells were fractured. *U.159* made an emergency dive. Efforts were made to effect some repairs. Then at 0618, Witte took his boat to the surface. The battery was fully exhausted so that the boat was no longer able to dive. About noon, the escort was met and *U.159* entered Lorient in the early afternoon.

U.159 was a Type IXc boat returning to Lorient after her first operational patrol in the Caribbean.

Capt. Wiley Howell, D.F.C., U.S.N. Skipper of the American Aircraft Carrier *Bennington*, in 1969. Wiley was, in 1942, a Pilot Officer
in the RAF with 172 Leigh Light Squadron. He flew with the author
on a practice bombing mission, July 5, 1949, the day before he
sank the U-502.

Wiley Howell was born in Prairie City, Oregon, in 1921 and had
wanted to fly for as long as he could remember. He was a flying instructor
at a civilian flying school in early 1941, and was assigned to teach six of
the ten women who were fledgling pilots at the school; he wasn't
particularly keen on this aspect of his work. During a cross-country
flight from Pornfollo, Idaho to Spokane, Washington, he and his female
student encountered bad weather and were forced to stay overnight in
Spokane. While there, Howell was approached by an individual who
represented the Knight Committee. This Committee was associated

with the American Lafayette Escadrille—American pilots who had served with the French in the First World War. Howell was offered a chance to fly heavy aircraft and to have a commercial pilot's medical examination. He jumped at the chance, for the package was worth $100 and he would be able to have his flying license, or "ticket", renewed at no cost to himself.

Shortly thereafter Howell filled out the necessary forms. It was not long before he received a phone call one afternoon. "If you are interested in flying with the RAF, be on the plane tomorrow morning at 0900 hours for Chicago and Ottawa." He spoke to the Chief Flying Instructor about it, and the next morning was on his way.

Capt. Wiley Howell USN (Retd.) 1980, formerly Pilot Officer RAF in 1942. He got the first confirmed U-boat sinking with Leigh Light *Wellington*, July 5/6, 1942.

In Chicago he met sixteen other Americans, all recruited in the same unusual way, and they flew together in a DC-3 to Ottawa. From there they proceeded to the Spartan School of Aeronautics at Tulsa, Oklahoma, where they were given a six-week refresher course. Dressed as civilians, they were flown back to Ottawa and then travelled by train to Halifax. Here their luck ran out. No one seemed to know anything about them, but they were put up in a good hotel nevertheless. After four days spent waiting for instructions, the pilots made their way on their own around the harbour, looking for a ship to take them to the United Kingdom. Howell and five of his colleagues managed to get aboard the passenger ship *Madura,* when six of the booked passengers did not show up. The other eleven pilots found transportation on another ship. This latter group encountered tragedy when their ship was torpedoed—two of the pilots drowned and a third slipped off the side of the sinking ship and had his leg sliced off by the turning propeller. The six American pilots on the *Madura* were more fortunate. They were even "adopted" by an English lady who was returning to London. The only one in the group to whom she did not give the telephone number and picture of her "niece" in London was Wiley.

In London the RAF marched the American pilots, still in civilian clothes, into Moss Brothers, where they were outfitted in RAF Pilot Officers' uniforms. Wiley was sent on a general reconnaissance course during September and October 1941, and then went on to the Coastal Command Operational Training Unit at Cranwell on *Wellingtons.*

Although Wiley had not been given any address, he made it a point to look up the "niece" of the English lady aboard the *Madura.* Within three weeks of meeting the young lady, Patricia "Paddy" O'Sullivan, he was walking down the aisle with her. One minor difficulty did arise—he was two weeks short of 21 and had to get special permission from his Commanding Officer to be married.

The American in the RAF, Pilot Officer Wiley Howell, marries Miss Patricia O'Sullivan of London, two weeks before his 21st birthday, April 1942.

Wiley was awarded the Distinguished Flying Cross later in 1942. He had applied for a transfer to the American forces when the United States entered the war. The American Air Force offered him a senior rank, Major, but would do nothing for his wife as far as passage to the United States was concerned. The American Navy, on the other hand, said that they would literally put his wife on the next boat to the US, but could only offer him the rank of Lieutenant, junior grade, equivalent to his present Pilot Officer rank in the RAF. Howell accepted the offer from the Navy, and early in 1943 he and his young wife were both on the *Queen Elizabeth* en route to the USA. They were assigned a private cabin, a luxury not generally associated with such a junior rank. Wiley later explained that the privilege really belonged to the high priority, secret design he carried for a modified, nacelle-type Leigh Light suitable for *Catalinas* and *Liberators*. In the future he would work in liaison with the General Electric Company for the manufacture of the modified searchlight and its installation on American aircraft.

After the war Howell realized that his choice of transfer from the RAF to the American Navy, which had primarily been to get his London-born wife immediate passage to the USA, may have inadvertently saved his life. Most of his fellow American pilots had transferred from the RAF to the American Air Force, and many of them, even those with senior ranks, had been killed in daylight bombing and fighter raids over Germany. I contacted Wiley through the Pentagon in early 1980. Imagine his wife's consternation when the Pentagon phoned him—she thought he was being called back into the Navy from his retirement!

The Pentagon caller calmed her fears. "No, no—nothing like that. It's only an old fellow RAF type, Don Fraser, who wants to get in touch with your husband."

I found an invitation waiting when I returned from Europe in April, and was literally on the next plane to pay him a visit--38 years after we had last seen each other. In addition to being an excellent pilot, Wiley has many athletic accomplishments to his credit. These are now being recognized by the Idaho State University, Pocatello, Idaho where he played football and boxed in 1938, 1939, and 1940. In November 1980 he was inducted into their Athletic Hall of Fame.

The battle over the Bay of Biscay was coming to a boil, as evinced by increased enemy air activity in addition to more effective U-boat opposition. Adverse weather and problems with the *Pegasus* engines of the *Wellingtons* added to 172 Squadron's difficulties. Doenitz, head of the German U-boat arm, had complained to Hitler of the serious opposition his U-boats were encountering from the Leigh Light *Wellingtons* and had been assigned 24 *Ju 88* long-range fighters to fly offensive patrols over the Bay. In addition, Doenitz was allotted *Arado 196s*, floatplanes armed with both 20-mm cannon and machine-guns. It was not long before the *Wellingtons* of 172 Squadron met up with these new foes.

On July 14, 1942, P/O Blackmore, P/O Syer, and P/O Dixon, with normal crews, took off on operations. F/L Sander, the Station Intelligence Officer, was a passenger with P/O Dixon's crew. At 0645 hours the next morning, "J", captained by P/O Dixon, was on the homeward track 100 miles off the Scilly Islands and flying at 300 feet, when two *Arado 196s* were sighted 800 yards astern at sea level. The enemy aircraft apparently saw "J" at the same time; they immediately carried out climbing turns, crossed over, and attacked "J" from the starboard and port quarters. These developed into attacks from above and head-on at very close range. Outnumbered and taking hits, P/O Dixon jettisoned his depth charges and returned fire before diving to sea level with the starboard aileron control shot away and considerable damage to the port aileron. The intercom had been put out of action in the opening attack and the wireless operator had been wounded in the leg. The enemy aircraft ended their attack when one *Arado 196* fell away, flames and black smoke billowing out behind. The other *196* broke off to investigate and "J" was again alone. Several signals were sent by "J" and navigational aid was obtained. The trim of the aircraft was out of control, necessitating extreme left rudder to maintain direction. Only one leg of the undercarriage was operational and the aircraft developed a violent swing to port when Dixon crash landed at Portreath at 0835 hours on July 15. The aircraft sustained considerable damage, and P/O Dixon, P/O Lambarth, F/L Sander, and Sgt Gerett were injured in the crash. Sgt Connon, the wounded wireless operator, also received further injuries. P/O Lambarth and Sgt Connon subsequently died as a result of their wounds.

On Tuesday, July 7, at long last, my kite, "N for Nuts", arrived from the factory. For the next few weeks I was working both day and night getting "N" and my crew into operational status, while continuing operations as second pilot and searchlight operator for Blackie in "B for Beer". The day "N" arrived I took off on night ops with Blackie. As usual, we intercepted a number of tunnymen and little else. In the early morning, while we were flying just off the Spanish coast, a blip appeared on the ASV. "Action Stations". We started to home in. The searchlight was lowered; the engines were throttled back. We were closing for the attack when the starboard engine grumbled ominously, shot out a series of sparks, and stopped dead. All thoughts of the blip vanished as the plane swung violently, frighteningly, to the right before Blackie could compensate with the left rudder. I scrambled back from the searchlight operator's seat as we plunged lower, and two of us rushed to get the searchlight cranked up to reduce the drag on the slipstream. Blackie jettisoned the depth charges and the rest of us prepared to throw the machine-guns overboard—the rear gunner had already started dumping his extra ammunition through the opening behind his turret doors. About half our gas had already been used, so we had to keep the remainder to get home—that is, if we stayed airborne. The plane sank lower and lower, as did our spirits; the port engine was screaming with the propeller pitch in fine and boost at full power. "B" levelled out a few feet above the water. With panic and prayers we sent out an SOS, and were at dinghy stations awaiting what seemed the inevitable, when a most welcome sound was heard; the starboard engine was growling back to life. Blackie eased the throttle lever slightly forward; more power developed. We began climbing again; the port engine was gradually throttled back as the starboard engine improved. We slowly gained height—200 feet, 300 feet, 500, 1000, 2000! Up we climbed with our nose turned homeward. Wildly relieved, we were just beginning to cheer when the starboard engine suddenly began throwing sparks out the exhaust manifold again, and the power diminished. 1200 feet, 1000, 800, 500. But once again the starboard engine kicked to life, and we started another climb. We probably had sticky exhaust valves on the starboard engine. When the engine then shut down, it began to cool off, and the exhaust valves would start working again so we could once more get power from the engine. Thus it went, up and down, all the way back. We finally reached base and came in for a perfect landing. Feet firmly on the ground once more, we all thanked Lady Luck for bringing us home safely. I thought I deserved my long sleep that day.

On Thursday it was confirmed that "N for Nuts" was ours. I looked on it with loving eyes and checked it over carefully, more than glad to be released from "B" and its wonky engines. My luck held out that afternoon: at sports I threw the javelin 128½ feet, and later our medical officer, Dr. W.S. Noble, let me know I could use his microscope whenever I needed one for my own experiments. He had had his personal one sent down from his office on Harley Street in London. Now I would be able to examine what I was collecting in my airborne sampling trap, and carry on my studies for the University of London. For most of my time the next few days, I concentrated on "N", inspecting it, chasing up a part for it, finding it torches or flashlights. On Monday the 13th I learned that the following day I was to go to Headquarters of 19 Group, Coastal Command, in Plymouth for my commission interview. I could only hope that Lady Luck hadn't deserted me yet. That day I also received a bundle of *LIFE* magazines from my brother, Douglas, and several *Toronto Star Weeklies* from my mother. As I was out of touch with some of the more domestic incidents of Toronto and Canada, these magazines and papers pleasantly filled many long hours in the days ahead.

On July 14th I was up early, as I had to be at Plymouth for my interview by 1400 hours. Flight Lieutenant Southall, on the Winco's suggestion, offered to take the Group Captain's *Tiger Moth* down to Roborough aerodrome near Plymouth later in the afternoon and fly me back to Chivenor after the interview. Arriving by train in plenty of time for my appointment, I sat nervously in an outer room for several moments before being ushered into the presence of Air Vice Marshal G.R. Bromet, OBE, DSO. He motioned me to sit down after I stepped in smartly and saluted. My papers lay on the desk before him. Scarcely looking at me, he read through the papers, obviously for the first time, hemming and hawing throughout. "WOI Fraser . . . hmmm . . . a degree in Honour Science from the University of Toronto . . . hmmm . . . qualified as Lieutenant in machine-guns in the COTC . . . yes, yes . . . hmmm . . . flew with 150 Squadron in Bomber Command, and now you're in our hush-hush Squadron." Finally he looked up, but I wasn't asked to say more than a few words. I briefly expressed my enthusiasm for Leigh Light operations, described my efforts at working up my own aircraft and my crew to operational efficiency, mentioned my eagerness to contribute to the war. The AVM then concluded the interview by saying, "Fraser, good Scots name; you'll have no trouble." In other words, he implied, "Commission granted." As I stood up to leave he nodded and said for a second time, "Fraser, good Scots name."

A staff car was waiting outside Headquarters to drive me out to Roborough aerodrome, where I arrived to see Southall and the *Tiger Moth* just landing. It had scarcely stopped before I climbed up and strapped myself in. We were back at Chivenor in 35 minutes, a much faster trip than the train ride that morning. We landed and I dashed over to the Operations' Room in time for briefing with Blackie's crew. After supper, a few minutes rest to read the mail, and a quick change into battledress, it was back to the Flight Office. We took off at dusk.

Again the gremlins pursued us, as our engines continued to act up. But we were beginning to get used to it, as much as that was possible, anyway. We struggled back to base after a nine-hour operational sortie and landed at 0700 hours. As our plane circled to land I looked down. The usual Wednesday defence exercises had begun. Almost the whole station had been up since 0400 hours, before dawn. We taxied up and went for debriefing, coffee, and breakfast. As I wearily prepared for sleep I glanced out the window and saw the poor erks crouching with their rifles on the defence exercises. We aircrew were a privileged few. After being on ops against the enemy all night, there was no need for us to practice defence exercises. But there was to be little sleep for me; I found a telegram on my bed—George was coming in for a visit at 1030 hours. I welcomed him sleepily when he arrived. He cut quite a figure in his new officer's uniform. We had been indulging in a friendly competition to see who would be commissioned first, and he had won. I did not resent it; after all, he was the older.

We were standing by for ops again that night, but the engines of "B" were even more uncooperative than usual. The mechanics were unable to immediately locate the trouble, so our sortie was cancelled. I took advantage of the extra time by taking George to Barnstaple, where we saw the film *Married Bachelor*.

The next day I had the batteries put in "N for Nuts"; we swung the compass for deviation and the loop aerial, then took an air test. She flew as smooth as glass. George went into town for some entertainment, and when ops were scrubbed at 2130 hours I also went into Barnstaple, but could not find him. The next day I continued working on "N", though I took time out in the afternoon to visit with George, and, incidentally, to withdraw five pounds from the bank to lend him. I was on Blackie's patrol that night as operations were on again. Although I did not realize it at the time, it was my last trip with Blackie.

On July 19 at 0005 hours, Flight Officer Syer saw two star-shaped, green and yellow lights above his aircraft, "A for Apple", at about 2000 feet. At 0253 hours "A" received a message from base reporting the position and course of a U-boat. This was the first time, to my knowledge, that the specific location of a U-boat was wired to a Leigh Light *Wimpy*. The capture the previous year of *U-570*, with its grid chart and Enigma cypher machine, by a *Hudson* from Iceland had helped British Intelligence break the German naval code and made it possible to interpret U-boat signals. Of course, the Germans had also broken British naval codes by this time, and were plotting the sailing and location of British convoys.

On the 19th I took "N" up on an air test. It was in good form and I did an air swing on the compass. A few days later I did an ASV run on the Helwick light vessel in the Bristol Channel, but a big ship convoy was there so I sheered off and returned to Chivenor. That day a rash of promotions were announced. S/L Greswell was promoted to the rank of Wing Commander and posted to Headquarters, Coastal Command for Operations Plans Tactics duties. F/O Southall was promoted to Flight Lieutenant and P/O Blackmore and P/O Dixon were made Flying Officers. The following day I ran another flight on Helwick to train my crew on ASV homing, then a training flight that night with the searchlight, but low stratus clouds blew in and we were recalled.

On the 22nd I took "N" for her first long navigation trip for fuel consumption testing. In over four hours twenty minutes we went from Chivenor to the Scilly Islands, to Fastnet Rock off South Wales, and then home. At last we were ready to make our first operational sortie, but the weather was poor that night so all ops were off. As a consolation my crew and I went into Braunton to see the film *Dangerous Moonlight*. It was a real Second World War tearjerker, with various passions and pitfalls between a Polish pilot/composer/piano player and a rich American industrialist's daughter who was also a reporter. It was rather loosely based on Richard Adinsell's *Warsaw Concerto.* Coincidentally, just a few days before I wrote this page in November 1975, I turned on the television set and saw a rerun of this 1941 movie.

On July 23rd my crew and I went on our first operation, along with the crews of F/O Syer, F/O Blackmore, F/O Triggs, and F/S Bramwell. We were out nine hours, ten minutes. Weather was poor over the Bay of Biscay, and to complicate matters, during one of our first ASV investigations the searchlight controls went unserviceable and the beam could not be elevated. What luck! It was just as well we did not run into any U-boats that night.

We slept most of the next day—I even missed pay parade! Two nights later we went on ops again. Everything began well; the members of my crew worked smoothly together. But something had to go wrong, and this time on our first ASV contact the beam of the searchlight would not depress at all. Bad luck again! The gremlins were with us still, but at least they were not bringing us any danger. Ops were scrubbed the next night due to a heavy rain, so I had supper at the Scoynes after the Braunton church service.

On Monday, July 27 we took "N" up for testing. This time the ASV literally blew up, with lots of smoke for effect. The searchlight control still refused to depress. The only good thing about the whole affair was that we were not on ops when it happened. Handing "N" (and she *was* "nuts") over to the mechanics, we attempted to drown our sorrows with a swim at Saunton Sands. Then, while our *Wimpy* was taken in for a forty-hour inspection, our entire crew received a 48-hour pass. I received several letters from home, and another stack of *Star Weeklies* from Douglas. He had been given a five-month exemption from the draft and was taking Mother up to Sparrow Lake in Muskoka, north of Toronto, for holidays. Longing to be able to join them in that peaceful setting, I instead visited Jack O'Bryant in the base hospital, then went on a ramble with the Scoynes and some of the young church group; it was quite pleasant, but still a far cry from Sparrow Lake and family.

While I was cursing my ill luck for being grounded with an unserviceable aircraft, the other crews were encountering engine trouble during their flights. Triggs, while flying in "F for Freddie" on July 25/26, had part of the exhaust pipe of the No. 8 cylinder fall off the starboard engine at 0200 hours. Syer, flying "A" on July 29/30, had the air intake on one engine come adrift shortly after becoming airborne. He jettisoned 150 gallons of petrol and returned to base.

All in all the month of July had been a fiasco for me and my crew. Everything possible had gone wrong with "N for Nuts". Not only were the searchlight and the ASV being repaired, but "George", the automatic pilot, was also unserviceable. This resulted in a rather disappointing flight record. The rest of the squadron, with rarely more than three planes operational on any one night, had their ups and downs as well.

On the 1st of August the port motor on "N" went unserviceable. Later on in the afternoon we were told that the searchlight was still not working. Taffy, the mechanic from the Frazer-Nash turret people, came down to the aerodrome to fix it, but by the next day he had still met with no success. The mechanics decided to put in a new valve box, and a few extra parts were ordered.

By the 4th the Winco decided that with "N" still unserviceable we should take "L for London" on ops, although it had experienced some engine trouble when flying the previous night. The Flight Commander suggested we take an extra passenger along on operations to give him some experience. With no time wasted for politeness I replied that I'd rather take along an extra 1000 rounds of ammunition for the machine-guns. He didn't suggest a passenger again. That day new orders came through: any fishing boats sighted in the Bay of Biscay were to be shot up with the machine-guns. I thought of the many times I had looked down the cone of the searchlight as we homed in on what turned out to be fishing boats. It was undoubtedly true that some of them had wireless equipment to signal our position to the Germans, others may have had machine-guns, and a very few were proven to be camouflaged German reconnaissance craft. Some members of our squadron had shot up these boats, and had collected a few bullets from them for their pains. As for myself, as soon as I realized that the vessel illuminated by the Leigh Light was not a U-boat, I peeled off to one side. With the engines as unreliable as they were, it wouldn't take many bullets to put my crew and me in a dinghy in the middle of the Bay of Biscay. In any case, I didn't think my conscience would stand for me to shoot up fishing boats with my machine-guns, unless, of course, they fired first. Most of the tunnymen were honest, hard-working fishermen, who undoubtedly needed the fish they caught to keep life and limb together for their families. I made a personal decision not to shoot up any of the fishing boats. Even our Winco and Operations officer apparently found it difficult to make up their minds. We received the orders to machine-gun the fishing boats in the pre-flight briefing, only to have the order rescinded at the end of the runway before takeoff. Then the order came back again to definitely machine-gun the boats. This was not for me; I had already made up my mind—I was after Germans and U-boats, not fishermen and fishing boats.

Thirty years later, while I was searching through war records, I found a note: "Blackmore, Riding, Bramwell, and Russell carry out instructions. Fraser veers off after homing in on the fishing vessels. Fraser has decided not to shoot up the fishing vessels unless they open fire on him first, indicating that they are German rather than French, Spanish, or Irish boats seeking a living from the sea." Crew members of the submarines faced a similar moral dilemma when they were ordered not to waste their time picking up all survivors from their torpedo attacks, only the captains and first mates.

On August 5, while work continued on "N", I received more parcels from Canada, including a box of chocolates from my brother and a letter from Douglas Horniblow, who was in the Royal Canadian Army Service Corps. I went for a bike ride to the lighthouse at Croyde Point in the evening. The next day, unable to tolerate the lack of an aircraft any longer, I suggested that I use "D for Donald" until our "N" was repaired. "D" was Southall's personal machine, but he was away on leave. "D", along with Blackie's "B", had the batteries in the nose and was therefore a better machine to fly, because it was not so tail heavy. After all my trouble I didn't go on ops that night, but "C" and "B" had engine trouble and "L" and "K" were diverted to Exeter aerodrome, so the following day I was ordered to test "D" as soon as the weather cleared. The test was smooth and trouble free, to my intense relief.

I received two parcels that day, one from the Siftons and one from the University of London, some books for my studies. With all my unwanted spare time, I should be able to make good use of them. That night I stood by with my crew on "D", but with a plane finally usable, ops were scrubbed due to bad weather. The rotating surface joint on the searchlight controls of "N" was finally replaced the next day, making the aircraft serviceable again at last. Ops were on again that night, and as I taxied out "N" and started surging down the runway with a full bomb load, plus the overload of petrol, I discovered a new problem—no brakes. The end of the runway was approaching quickly, and our speed had increased almost to the takeoff level, but with no other choice I cut back the engines and swung the plane around with the rudder. I suppose I could have taken off without brakes and controlled the swing with the engines; I certainly felt like doing just that, since we had had so much other trouble trying to take "N" on operations, but what would I have done nine hours later? It would have jeopardized the lives of my crew. Instead, I swung the plane off the runway into the soft grass and closed down the engines. The crew climbed dejectedly out of the plane, agreeing with me that with no air pressure in the pneumatic brakes, I had no choice.

It was a far more hair-raising story on Monday night, the 10th. I tested the brakes and, as they seemed to be in fine working order, we took off. We flew over the Bay of Biscay, a bumpy but otherwise uneventful trip. Yet by the time we returned the brakes had gone unserviceable again. We all held our breath as I attempted to gently and cautiously land the plane. Somehow I managed to avoid smashing anything. Exhausted by all our troubles, I slept right through most of the daylight hours, and awakened to the news that the brakes on "N" had been fixed and we were on ops again that night. Two nights in a row—maybe we could make up for lost time. I also learned that my commission was through, at last, and had been backdated to July 1, 1942.

On the trip that night we again saw Spain with its lighted cities, an almost nostalgic sight for us. Tunnymen were sighted frequently, but no U-boats were to be seen. We ran into some meteorite showers coming back, something which is quite familiar in modern space movies, but which in 1942, in the skies over the English Channel, was infrequent. dangerous, and a bit frightening. Later I was taken off my guard when, off to starboard, I thought I saw another brief flash of light—more meteorites? No one else had noticed, and although I kept my eyes peeled, the sight was not repeated. We returned safely to hear that F/O Triggs had taken up "D for Donald", Southall's machine, as his own was unserviceable, and that now he was down in the drink with a *Sunderland* out looking for him. The lights I had seen could have belonged to Triggs's machine.

Wing Commander Middleton, RAF Captain of the ill-fated Sunderland that crashed while trying to pick up F/O Triggs' crew from a dinghy, August 13, 1942.

(Imperial War Museum)

148

I learned the full story of Triggs's ditching later. At 2030 hours on August 11, F/O A.W.R. Triggs and crew took off for operations, at the same time as myself and F/S Bramwell and our crews. At 0355 hours Triggs's tail gunner reported that far too many sparks were passing him and trailing like a cluster of stars for about one hundred yards behind the aircraft. Almost before he had the words out of his mouth, the oil pressure fell to zero, and the aircraft began to lose height rapidly. The first wireless operator/air gunner started to send out an SOS on Group frequency, while the aircraft fell from 1200 to 1000 feet. Within a few tense minutes the *Wimpy* had ditched, the bump being lighter than a belly landing on a runway. All forward motion stopped abruptly, and the second wireless op/gunner was flung forward, receiving a slight cut over one eye. Triggs quickly unbuckled his safety harness and began to make his way, with the other crewmen, to the escape hatch. As he took his first step he stumbled over the second pilot, who was on his face below water. Triggs lifted the unconscious airman and pushed him halfway through the escape hatch, then, having climbed out himself, pulled the second pilot out onto the wing, where he began to cough and splutter as he recovered consciousness. The aircraft was sinking slowly, but it could only be a matter of minutes before it was completely submerged. For some reason the automatic emergency dinghy had not released itself. Pounding desperately at the release catch as the aircraft gradually slipped deeper into the water, Triggs finally managed to pry the lid from the dinghy storage with his hands. The dinghy inflated properly once it was on the water, and the crew, thankfully all alive, climbed aboard. They were beginning to get settled when it was realized that the packet of emergency supplies had been left behind. Undaunted, Triggs swam to the almost submerged *Wellington,* secured the packet, and handed it to the crew members. He then pushed the dinghy along till it was well clear of the aircraft to prevent it from getting fouled in any wires. The sea was very rough, and waves continually washed over the edges of the dinghy, spraying the men with water as they sat waiting for rescue.

At 1037 hours the next day, as no message had been received from Triggs and his crew, a search was instigated by 19 Group. A *Whitley* from 77 Squadron with an escort of three *Beaufighters* carried out a special reconnaissance in the area where I had seen the unexplained flash of light. At 1440 hours the *Whitley* sent a message that a dinghy believed to contain five aircrew had been sighted. A *Sunderland,* escorted by *Beaufighter* "B" of 235 Squadron, was sent to pick up the downed aircrew, and at 1953 hours the *Sunderland* was over the dinghy and preparing to alight on the sea's surface.

Early in the war a *Sunderland* had landed in the mid-Atlantic to successfully pick up survivors in a dinghy. Ever since, it had been assumed that the flying boats could land in the open sea with ease. But that first *Sunderland* had been lucky; others to follow were less fortunate. The one attempting to pick up Triggs and his crew flew low over the dinghy and began a long, low landing run. Just as it touched down, a wing float caught in a swell on the rough sea. The pilot gunned the engines too late, and the tip of the starboard wing broke off. The starboard engine screamed agonizingly and burst into flames. The flying boat nosed over into the sea, and with horrifying speed sank from sight. It had gone down several thousand yards away, but Triggs and his crew saw a dinghy appear and assumed that the eleven-man crew had escaped. It was not until a few days later that they were able to contact the second dinghy. There was only one survivor. Triggs's crew began their second long night on the sea, while a fifteen to twenty knot wind agitated the waters about them. Hungry, sunburned, and cold, the men tried to rest. Deepening water around their feet alerted them suddenly to a small hole in the floor of the dinghy, and a few anxious moments were spent trying to plug it. After this the crew gradually settled into a fitful sleep; two men were ill, one had an injured ankle, and all were exhausted and miserable.

The next morning the downed airmen saw various aircraft, but they waved and shouted in vain. Finally a *Whitley* appeared over the horizon, and this time their frantically waving arms brought notice. The *Whitley* dropped a Lindholme dinghy, a large life-saving raft with emergency supplies. Unfortunately, the dinghy was not dropped close enough, and the weary airmen could only watch numbly while the *Whitley* itself was shot down by three *Arados.*

Later that day a large tunnyman appeared downwind of Triggs's dinghy and passed within 400 yards to their north. The airmen made no signal; knowing that it could belong to enemy sympathizers, they had decided that unless he saw them, they would let him pass. In any case, they were sure they would be rescued soon, as many other aircraft had flown overhead during the day. They could not know, of course, that none of these aircraft had spotted the dinghy.

On the morning of the fourth day at sea, the 15th, Triggs's crew had their first meal, consisting of a biscuit, a malted milk tablet, a square of chocolate, and a small mouthful of water. Despite their days of fasting none of them felt hungry any longer, but they knew they must keep up their flagging strength. Fog had closed in around the area and no aircraft had been sent out to search that day. All the ditched crew saw, other than the sea stretching out endlessly around them, was the large fin of a basking shark. As the shark cruised toward the dinghy, Triggs loaded the Verey pistol. Even if the shark made no attempt to attack, its rough skin, brushing against the dinghy, could cut the rubber. But the shark kept its distance and after about two minutes it swam away. The

150

incident served to revive some of the vigor of the men on the raft. They discovered a way to lessen the growing, insidious sense of helplessness. Breaking the telescopic mast in two, they improvised a sail out of the mast pieces and their flag. Sailing before the wind their speed was increased by nearly three-quarters of a knot, a great improvement over their aimless drifting of the previous three days. At dusk, after another "meal", the crew settled down for another night at sea.

Saturday the 16th was the crew's fifth day on the water, and it was much the same as the fourth. Fog and rain still prevented any aircraft searches, so Triggs and his crew saw no aircraft. That evening they shared a special meal, a can of tomato juice. During the night the first wireless op/air gunner saw two dark blobs at the far end of the dinghy. For a few excited moments he thought they had drifted into a river or harbour and that the "blobs" were bollards. He was disappointed to realize they were the heads of his fellow crew members, silhouetted indistinctly by the cloud-covered moon. Torrential rain began suddenly and continued until daybreak, adding to the misery of the airmen.

Dawn on the 17th brought clear blue skies. The search for the airmen began again, and at about 1200 hours a *Beaufighter* spotted the dinghy and responded to its signals. A *Wellington* crew sighted a second dinghy, that of the downed *Sunderland,* in the distance. The *Beaufighter* signalled to Triggs that an MTB (British motor torpedo boat) was on its way, and in the meantime they were to attempt to contact the other dinghy. The crew began to paddle in the direction indicated by the *Beaufighter* overhead. Five hours and 1000 yards later, the *Sunderland* dinghy was within hailing distance. In reply to Triggs's inquiry, the lone survivor yelled, "I feel fine, thanks", though he looked cold, unhappy, and weak. Finally pulling up beside the second raft, Triggs's crew hauled the airman aboard their dinghy. They quickly stripped him, rubbed him down with their sleeping suit packing material to bring back his circulation, wrapped him in a waterproof sleeping suit, and fed him a malted milk tablet, two biscuits, some sweet chocolate, and half a tin of tomato juice. After a cigarette and some rest, the crewman felt much better. Four *Focke-Wulfs* flew low over the dinghy, but did not attack.

At dawn on the 18th three *Hudsons* and two *Beaufighters* appeared. While circling the dinghy, one of the *Beaufighters* signalled, "It won't be long now", and five minutes later Trigg sighted what he took to be a destroyer headed straight for them. The "destroyer" turned out to be a Royal Navy motor launch. The dinghy crew was rapidly taken aboard and given hot tea and blankets. At 1740 hours the boat arrived at the Newlyn harbour, and the airmen were rushed to the Royal West Cornwall Hospital at Penzance. The next day Group Captain T.P.D. Gracroft, AFC, and Squadron Leader G.H. Henderson picked up the crew and brought them back to base, just over a week after they had taken off.

On Thursday, August 13, with the search just starting for Triggs and his crew, I took up "N" with my crew for an hour's air test. Upon landing I taxied over near the Flight Office, so the plane could be bombed up for the night's operations. The Flight Commander walked over to the plane as I shut down the engines and poked his head though the entrance/escape hatch at my feet. While I looked down at him, he said, "Fraser, I've three or four things to tell you."

I rather wondered if it couldn't have waited till I was out of my *Wimpy,* but merely asked, "What's up?"

"Well, your Commission is through."

I knew this already, but nonetheless replied, "That's good news."

He seemed surprised that I had taken it so calmly, but said no more about it and continued, "Your leave's cancelled."

"That's bad," I said with a frown. My crew would not be too happy; they had been looking forward to a few days' relaxation.

The Flight Commander concluded with, "Ops are cancelled again tonight, but you leave for Wick tomorrow on detachment."

"Well," I said, "that's so-so." "N" had finally been performing well and the crew was ready for more "fishing" in the Bay of Biscay. Yet I wasn't averse to seeing a bit more of Scotland. I believed this would be a short-term detachment, similar to one a couple of months earlier when Southall flew up to Wick to observe the German Navy (the *Tirpitz* had been making her way from Germany through Norwegian waters to break out into the Atlantic). How wrong can you be! I would not return to Chivenor again, except on leave or for a short trip to pick up spare parts for the *Wimpys.*

Several of us flew north to Wick the next day, arriving in the early evening of August 17. We had had a pleasant trip, flying across land to the North Sea Coast, then up the coast, across to Aberdeen, and on to Wick. A hearty supper was waiting when we landed.

I spent the following day getting organized. Wick had a nice pre-war aerodrome adjacent to the town itself. It had comfortable hangars, flight offices, met office, and operations room. The aerodrome also provided billets for RAF personnel, and it was easy to walk from the aerodrome into town. This proximity wasn't quite as pleasant for the townspeople, especially when the station was bombed by *He 111* and *Ju 88* bombers operating from Norway in 1941. The runways at Wick were considered a bit on the short side for takeoff in a fully loaded Leigh Light *Wellington,* but we discovered that it could be accomplished by starting at the very beginning of the runway, accelerating as rapidly as possible, and having everyone hold their breath, speed up their heart-rate, and grit their teeth until the *Wimpy* was airborne.

Skitten, some fifteen miles to the west, had been under construction when I first arrived at Wick. It was built both to increase the distance between the town and the enemy's bombing target, should the Germans choose to strike again, and to provide runways more suitable for the heavily loaded bombers. As soon as this satellite aerodrome was completed, a new procedure for operations came into effect. Our crews would fly the planes without a bomb load and only partly gassed up to Skitten. We then returned by truck to the Wick Ops Room for briefing, then went back to Skitten for takeoff. On our return, some nine hours later and five thousand pounds lighter, we were able to land on the shorter runways at Wick, where we would have our debriefing. We continued to sleep in our comfortable billets at Wick, so by landing there after each operation, usually at 0400 or 0500 hours, we saved ourselves a long truck ride from Skitten before debriefing and sleeping.

On Wednesday the 19th we had the usual standdown, so I went into Wick to see the show *Banana Ridge.* The people at Wick were always hospitable, and airmen could count on a warm welcome at any social event. My pleasant evening was overshadowed by news the following morning that "M for Mother" had been shot down near Chivenor. Ten crew members had been on board, including the Station Navigation Officer and the Station Wireless Operator plus the usual crew. The kite had been on ASV practice homing on the Helwick light vessel and came too close to an American tanker, which shot it down as an enemy aircraft. There were no survivors. This was not the end of the episode. One of the pilot officers who had flown with me to Wick had had several close friends in the aircrew team shot down in this *Wimpy.* A few weeks later he wrote to some friends back home, and in no uncertain terms expressed his opinion of the gunners on the American tanker their aircraft identification knowledge. He did not know at the time that all mail was censored. The censors passed his mail over to the authorities, and he was put on trial and nearly courtmartialled for saying unfriendly things about British allies. I believe he eventually got off with a reprimand and the loss of seniority. In the long run it mattered little for him, as he was later shot down by a U-boat while operating with 179 Squadron at Gibraltar. In such a manner were so many of the bureaucratic niceties of war mocked—it seemed a hard irony that this man, upbraided by authorities for expressing his natural grief and outrage at the useless death of a friend, should subsequently give his own life for his country and those which fought with her.

On Thursday we went back to Skitten to test our kite and do an air swing on the magnetic compass. That night we were standing by for ops that were scrubbed, so I went to a dance at the Sergeants' Mess instead. The music at that evening's dance consisted mostly of Scottish reels. As they were making up foursomes for one reel a call went out for participation from members of our newly arrived detachment of 172 Squadron. My pals pushed me forward; after all, they insisted, with a name like Fraser, I should be well up on my Scottish dancing. And, as it turned out, I didn't disgrace the Squadron too badly, for I had danced some of the reels at the Cairngorm Club in Toronto and had also attended many dances of the 48th Highlanders there. It was an invigorating evening to say the least, in no way less so for being well-populated with pretty Scottish lasses. I was particularly enamoured with my young partner, who steered me expertly around the Eightsome Reel. I danced with her most of the evening, and saw her home to Wick afterward. One of the "older" lads in the Mess took me to one side before I left with her: "Be careful," he warned. "She's lost two husbands already from the RAF, both missing in action. She's a bit of a jinx." I had a lot of sympathy for her—it couldn't have been easy losing *two* husbands already from the RAF—but all the same I avoided her after that evening. All aircrew tend to be a bit superstitious, and this word to the wise was sufficient to discourage future interest.

The next day I went to the ops room with my crew to collect maps for the night's operation, but then ops were scrubbed; it was, as usual, raining and foggy. It was still cloudy the next day. A *Hudson* bomber sat forlornly near the end of the runway. It had pulled up its undercarriage too soon when taking off, pranged, and bent its propellers. Despite the clouds, ops were on; we did a trip straight west for nine hours, ten minutes. The engines were running a bit rough, but we returned safely after an uneventful trip.

I spent most of Sunday the 23rd in bed, but woke in the afternoon to go to church in Wick with Ronnie, my navigator, Len, my second pilot, and Smitty, my wireless operator. On our return I wrote some letters. Three kites, "O", "P", and "Q", were on ops that night; three aircraft were usually our maximum effort on any one night.

On Tuesday Smitty received a telegram that his mother was very ill; he left the next day on compassionate leave. With Smitty away, the rest of my crew and I hoped to be granted leave as well, but no such luck, though for all the work we accomplished we might as well have been on leave. Almost every night for the remainder of the week we were standing by for ops, which were invariably cancelled. The weather was as miserable as it could be, cold and windy with rain or heavy mist. "L" went unserviceable with a fault in the reduction gears of the propeller. It reminded me of a problem that frequently turned up while I was with 150 Squadron, in Bomber Command. The reduction gears of the propeller housing would wear, become loose, and rub against the housing, thereby wearing still further. On several occasions, as a result, a propeller would fly off while the aircraft was in flight, leaving the pilot to get home on one engine—an unnecessary danger that should have been easily avoidable.

Later that week we learned that the Duke of Kent had been killed with fifteen others in a *Sunderland* flying boat. He had been on his way to Iceland for a tour. Apparently they had been cutting across Scotland under the clouds and following one of the valleys. The valley turned, they tried to climb, but hit a mountainside just a few feet below the peak.

We finally had ops on Saturday, August 29, despite the rainy, chilly weather. I climbed into the kite with my crew and started up the engines; or tried to, for the port engine was balky. It finally started, but then, like an old truck, the entire aircraft vibrated noisily. I could not get up sufficient revolutions per minute on the propeller, and the indicator was unserviceable, so, for us, operations were scrubbed. Sunday night, "N" was still out of service; the reduction gear was giving us trouble. That would account for the vibration. I took "S for Sugar", Southall's machine, on an air test from Wick to Skitten, where it was bombed up.

On one occasion at about that time, the van that was taking our three crews from briefing at Wick to takeoff position at Skitten ran out of gas. We were on an isolated, rarely travelled road, and we could have been there for hours, far too late for takeoff. We were about four miles by road from Skitten but only two miles cross-country, so I told the crews that I would jog across the fields and bring back transport. It was a warm evening, and running cross-country was harder than I had thought it would be, with numerous rabbit holes, uneven ground, and, when I reached the limits of the aerodrome, stretches of barbed wire around its perimeter. I managed to squirm my way through, ripping one leg of my trousers in the process, and finally puffed into the transport room to tell them of our predicament. "Oh," said one fellow, "a truck on a special run already came across the stranded crews on the road—they've been in for nearly half an hour." They must have been found just after I left. Still puffing, I crawled into the Mess to get my pre-takeoff meal. The crews I had so gallantly set out to "rescue" were relaxing over the end of their dinners. They all had a good laugh at my expense.

A somewhat bigger piece of carelessness than letting a van run out of gas took place during an opertion around this time. One crew sighted a U-boat and made a bang-on approach and attack, but the rear gunner suddenly exclaimed, "No explosions, Skipper!" The problem was found when they landed. When depth charges were dropped, the safety pins were designed to latch onto the bomb racks, so the bombs fell away with their firing pins set to explode. No safety pins had been left on the racks in this case, so the captain of that kite must have dropped his depth charges in the "safe" position. A courtmartial followed!

There were always various SNAFUS (Situation Normal, All "Fouled" Up). I was generally briefed for ops at Wick with two other crews, usually those of Ronnie Riding and Ron Bramwell. One day the weather looked quite poor, and at the briefing it was a new Met lad who stood up and went over to the weather map. He told us that a low front was moving in bringing fog, and he concluded, "When you return in the morning at about 0500 you won't be able to land because of the thick fog, and will probably have to bail out." The Winco was furious; we all laughed, but of course we did realize the seriousness, as it was closely linked with our future span of life. The Winco asked the Met lad if he could change his forecast, but no dice. Nonetheless, the Winco had the last word, so we were off on ops. I was flying a borrowed kite, "S", with a borrowed wireless operator, Sgt. Roberts; he was a good lad, but was not like old Smitty, who was still on leave because of his mother's illness. This patrol was known as a *Flora*. We went north, past the Orkney Islands where the big naval base at Scapa Flow was located, up past the Shetland Islands, and still further north yet—almost to the North Pole, we joked. The weather was simply lousy. As we passed the Shetlands and headed up into the Arctic, I told Roberts to keep his ears glued to the set listening for a BBA, or recall to base. I was almost certain that a recall would be sent, considering that we would be unable to land when we returned at the end of a full sortie. The nearest diversionary aerodrome was Benbecula in the Hebrides, and we would not have enough gas to reach it by the end of the operation. We had heard of mistakes before, as in a raid on Berlin in July 1941. Head winds of some sixty to seventy knots were met on the return trip and only one kite landed back at Snaith. The others were all over the place. Over sixty bombers went missing that July night from Bomber Command. Most were out of gas over Germany, some were down in the drink, others crash landed with no gas around England.

Suddenly it came: "BBA, BBA." Our crew let up a little shout, and a sigh of relief. Although we had not expressed our fears to one another, we had all worried about the return trip. I whipped the plane around on a reciprocal course almost before the wireless op had the words out of his mouth, and called to Ronnie Davies for any course corrections. We landed back at Wick after three and a half hours in the air, just as the weather was closing down on the base. We barely managed to land in the decreasing visibility, and were deeply indebted to the ASV, which had enabled us to pick up first the coast, and then the Wick aerodrome itself. The next morning I peeked out the window of my room. It was impossible to see more than ten feet ahead, the fog was so thick. The Met lad had been right after all. Shortly after I got up, the squadron leader called me in to his office to let me know that my whole crew had been given leave at long last. I was able to get travel warrants for us because in the RAF one was given free travel to one's home anywhere in the UK while on leave. This was alright for the British types, but we Canadians . . . well, being a geographer as well as a pilot, I asked for a travel warrant to Lands End in southwest England, so that I could tour the country as I pleased. When at Chivenor I had always asked for a travel warrant to at least as far north as Inverness in northern Scotland.

A telegram arrived from my mother later that day, congratulating me on my promotion to Pilot Officer. The groundcrew of my squadron looked on my promotion almost as a demotion. Most of the pilots arriving from Canada were already Pilot Officers, but only operational aircrew who had been in the United Kingdom for at least a year had reached the rank of Warrant Officer Class I. I had no hesitation about my new rank, as it paved the way for further promotion, and, if one were qualified, more responsibility. In the RAF when WOIs were commissioned they became Flying Officers. The RCAF was a bit different. The promotion from WOI was only to Pilot Officer. It would be another six months before I was promoted to a higher rank.

I was paid eight pounds in "subsistence" allowance, then packed up and went to an evening dance in Wick to celebrate. I caught the 0820 train from Wick the next morning with my crew and arrived in London at 1000 hours on the morning of Wednesday, September 2nd. On the train between Inverness and London our compartment was packed. Along with my crew there were two gals who had been on holidays in the Highlands. I slipped in beside one of them when I found out that she was from Oxford and the university. Liz was the daughter of a university professor, a blood specialist, and was herself a medical student. Recognizing her surname, I asked if her father were the one involved with the development of the sampling apparatus for the oxygen content in blood, which I had used at the University of Toronto. As it turned out, it had been her father, and the miles passed quickly as we continued our conversation, though it no doubt would have carried less fascination for anyone not interested in biology. The two girls prepared to change trains for Oxford before we reached London. I had half a mind to join them and follow them home. Indeed, Liz, half jokingly I suppose, invited me to come along with them. I almost weakened, but then I remembered that I was on my way to see George. It was possible that the 48th Highlanders had taken part in the Dieppe raid, which, I had heard, had been a fiasco. Though I was certain I would have heard if George had been injured, I nonetheless wanted to make sure personally that all was well, so I stayed on the train. In London, after booking a room at the West Central Hotel, I was fitted for a Pilot Officer's uniform at Austin Reed's of Regent Street. Then I hotfooted it over to Lloyds' Bank to collect a chequebook. As a commissioned officer I could have my pay put directly into the bank and just write a cheque whenever I needed money, and as I was just beginning leave, I would want that chequebook! I took in a "leg show" at the Windmill Theatre, and later went to a dance at Covent Garden with Mary.

The next day I left early to visit George, and arrived in East Hoathly in time for lunch at the Officers' mess of the 48th Highlanders. Asking Captain Cato where I might find George, I was shocked to learn that he was in the hospital at Lingfield, but my fears concerning Dieppe were hastily relieved. George had dislocated a shoulder during a military scheme, when the truck he was riding in had an accident. I once again caught the local train, and arrived at Lingfield at 1915 hours. After walking a mile to the military hospital, I had a very pleasant reception. There were some Canadian nurses on duty, and it was a treat to hear their lovely voices, free of the English accent. I was getting used to English gals, and had forgotten the pleasures of hearing a Canadian girl speak. They seemed delighted to see me as well; perhaps George had been right when he said that after the Battle of Britain the Air Force pilots were the glamour boys. I was ushered into a ward where I found George, with his arm in a special sling, reading a book. He quickly got over his initial surprise, and we went for a cup of tea. I met several other officers in the ward, but by far the most pleasant of my new acquaintances were the nurses, with whom George seemed to be on excellent terms. By the time my evening's visit drew to a close it was quite late. My room in London was waiting for me, yet I had no way to get back at that late hour. The sympathetic Canadian matron took care of the problem—winking, she showed me a room with another bed. Her solution: "We'll just book you in as another patient and wheel this bed into your brother's room. You can sleep there."

Well on the road to recovery, George was released from the hospital the next day. He returned to his unit immediately to get a 48-hour pass, giving us time to visit both Brighton and London, where we stayed at the Cumberland Hotel, near Marble Arch. That first night we went to see *The Goose Steps Out,* a film mimicking the German army—the soldiers goose-stepped forward and then backward to the music. It was followed by *The Doctor's Dilemma* with Vivian Leigh, a marvelous play. Sunday, a warm, beautiful day, we ate a huge breakfast before checking out of the Cumberland. George and I hadn't had this much time together since he left Canada. We spent most of the day at the famous Kew Gardens, then had another massive meal, our "tea", before George had to catch his train back to Lewes. Some friends of a Toronto neighbour were next on my list, and at last I went round to Covent Garden to again meet Mary. The next morning, after the by now standard pancakes and maple syrup at the Beaver Club, I bought a trunk with the remainder of my officer's clothing allowance and spent the rest of the day as a typical tourist might. "Join the Air Force and see the World!" Well, I might not be seeing the world, but I was certainly getting to know London well.

On Tuesday I continued my travels and went down to Stafford, where I found Auntie Mary and Uncle Horace looking well. I wasn't quite as healthy, as my left upper tooth, which had been giving me trouble off and on for several weeks, was aching again. I spent the evening quietly, taking a walk with my uncle. On Wednesday I had arranged to lunch with Dr. Donald Gunn of the Biology Department of the University of Birmingham. I had worked on cockroach behaviour in various experiments at the University of Toronto before the war. My studies were based on some of Dr. Gunn's work on the influence of relative humidity on their behaviour patterns.

I returned to Stafford at 1800 hours—fog was beginning to fill the valleys and hollows in the surrounding fields. The next day, having fixed the handle of my suitcase, I arranged to leave that night for Aberdeen for a stay with Auntie Jeanie, then spent the afternoon with Great Aunt Kate. There were lots of relatives for me to visit in the UK, some of whom I had not even known existed.

On Wednesday, September 16, I left Aberdeen at 0435 hours and did not arrive at Wick until 2030 hours that evening, stiff and grimy from my long trip. In the Officers' Mess I met Squadron Leader Wilson, our new Flight Commander. All too soon it was back to work, when I took over as Duty Officer the following morning. Lord Trenchard, the "founder of the RAF", was to be at Wick that evening for Mess dinner, and everyone was rushing around in a flurried panic of preparation. Being on duty, I was the only one in the Mess in battledress, but on the other hand, I was almost alone at the time as I ate well before the main dinner. I had to get over to the control tower to check on the ops, even though there was only one machine in the air.

The weather continued to deteriorate. There was a widespread sea fog over the whole area on September 19 when Virgo, John, and I went on patrol. Our briefing officer made no mention of naval ships or convoys in the area, and we assumed that any convoys had been informed that they might be lit up by searchlight *Wellingtons*. But with a dangerous lack of foresight, on this occasion as on many others, the Navy had been told nothing of our operation. These omissions would later have disastrous results. On this particular night, Virgo sighted two naval units that flashed incorrect challenge letters. Another unidentified vessel was also illuminated. I sighted one destroyer and one cruiser, and illuminated one small, two-masted sailing vessel and a merchant vessel of about 2000 tons. John homed in on an ASV contact and found he was over a convoy of nine merchant ships at 300 feet. No warning of this convoy had been given during the briefing, and his aircraft could have easily been shot down by the ships, as some of our planes already had been.

After putting up once again with a severe toothache for several days, I finally went to the dentist. A quick look at my swollen jaw was all he needed before pulling out the offending tooth. The nerve had been septic. Despite my puffed cheeks, I went on an eight-hour operation the next day in an endless rainshower. Our targets knew better—we didn't see a single U-boat, or even a tunnyman. We had the next day off, and I spent most of it catching up on lost sleep and hoping my "chipmunk" look would disappear.

On Monday, September 21 the whole squadron packed up and moved to Skitten. Several of us were immediately sent off on ops from our new base at 1800 hours, but because of severe icing conditions we returned early.

By that Friday I had moved some furniture into my room, and it was beginning to look a bit more tolerable. I was a bit more tolerable myself, as my cheeks had returned to their usual lean handsomeness. Despite the good effect this had on my personality, I still wasn't very popular that weekend, as I started to practise the chanter I had bought in Inverness. This is the musical instrument one must master before graduating to the bagpipes, something which, as a "Scotsman", I was anxious to learn.

Even though we had more planes than pilots right then, I brought a new machine back from Wick that weekend. My crew moved our kites, parachutes, and maps to "O for Orange", which was to be our machine for a while. "N" was still not operational. Its serviceability record was abominable, with the aircraft unfit for operations almost half of the time. We were all glad to be assigned to another aircraft, even if only temporarily. We went on ops north of the Shetland Islands that Saturday night. The weather was miserable—driving rain and low cloud, and very high sea return on the ASV radar. The weather made it unlikely that we would pick up a U-boat, and sure enough we landed nine hours later after an uneventful trip. The next day we woke to discover that Flight Sergeant Hodgson had taken "O", with all our parachutes, to Chivenor. Naturally enough, we didn't go on ops that night, .

Monday the 28th was slightly warmer. I received letters from George, the Scoynes, and Jenny Gray, the daughter of my Sunday school teacher's sister at Midcalder, near Edinburgh. By evening it was pouring rain, so ops were cancelled. Low cloud and fog the next day again meant no flying, so I visited my dentist's home in Wick. After all my tooth problems, Dr. Grant and I were by now almost old cronies. He was a native of this quaint village, and he invited me out to visit some of his friends in town that evening. We had a great time, and at one home we saw coloured slides of the local area, including pictures of the "Herring Queen", the pin-up girl of Wick's fishing fleet.

On Thursday, October 1, Flight Sergeant Hodgson finally returned from Chivenor in "O" with our equipment. It was about time, as we were scheduled to visit Chivenor on the following day to bring back all our personal gear along with instructional equipment; Skitten was to become our new base as we formed the nucleus of 179 (Searchlight *Wellington*) Squadron.

We took off in "N" at 1250 hours on Friday with five extra passengers, personnel who were going on leave. At that time it took almost a full day to get out to Wick by surface travel, so there was usually a line-up of lads waiting to get a lift on any plane heading in their direction. Most of them wanted to go to London, but I wasn't going to divert "N" that far off my flight path to Chivenor and risk repeating the episode of over a year and a half earlier when I force landed at Northolt in London during an air-raid alert. Instead, I sent a signal ahead that I would put down at Snaith, my old Bomber Command station. It was on the main railway line from Edinburgh to London and the lads could catch a train there, while we hopped straight west to Blackpool and down the Irish Sea to Chivenor. As we passed from Scotland to England the weather started to deteriorate. We had gone over Middlesboro, a great steel manufacturing city with towers belching a rusty red smoke, and were down along the coast when we received a wireless signal to divert to Elsham aerodrome near Hull because Snaith had been closed down due to bad weather. Elsham was the home of 103 Squadron where Kozlowski, an ex-squadron mate of mine, had been posted over a year earlier. But the prospect of seeing a familiar face didn't make me forget that the balloons from Hull frequently occupied the air space from the north. Indeed, one of our 150 kites had gone off course and had run into the balloons. Because the wire cable damaged the cable cutters on the wing, the aircraft was forced down into the river. I was loath to take a chance on ending up in a similar situation and, because our wireless operator could raise neither Elsham nor Snaith, wheeled the plane around on an opposite course. I was only a few hundred feet up and the weather was by this time deteriorating rapidly, so I went back up the coast to land at Thornaby aerodrome. Next to my parked aircraft sat a strange-looking *Wimpy* with no nose turret and a partially blacked-out cockpit. I wandered over curiously to meet Sergeant Innocent, who had been with me on Bomber Command and who was now testing this Blind Bomber—a special modification of the *Wellington* with the top-secret target-identifying radar.

The next day I took off from Thornaby minus my five passengers, who had ungratefully decided it would be faster to take the train. I began flying west toward Blackpool—my conscientious navigator, Ron Davies, was exactly on track. As we ploughed along just under the overcast at about nine hundred feet, I suddenly saw the Blackpool Tower poking its spire up through the misty skies only a few hundred yards in front of me. I literally lifted one wing to fly around the tower.

Soon we were out over the water and cruising down the Irish Sea to

Chivenor. It was like coming home. How I loved Chivenor for its better, or at least warmer, weather compared to cold and windy Wick. Ops at Wick were so often cancelled because of the bad weather that my gunner Hutch used to say, "Bring your knittin' to Skitten."

Once at Chivenor I visited the Scoynes to say goodbye, and began to collect my books, bicycle, and other belongings. But the following day it was raining cats and dogs, so my crew and I were given a brief respite before having to return to Skitten, "our knittin'", and the new 179 (Searchlight) Squadron.

Professor D.A. Fraser (left) discussing the Leigh Light Wellington with Sir Barnes Wallis, the designer of the Wellington at the latter's home in Effingham, England, July, 1971.

Chapter Eight
Chance, and Death, and Mutability

THE WEATHER DID NOT IMPROVE until Tuesday, October 6, and even then our takeoff was delayed because a *Beaufighter* had crashed on the runway and blocked it for a few hours. We finally got airborne at 1500 hours. Because weather conditions at Wick were, as usual, poor, I decided to land at Dyce aerodrome near Aberdeen, thus giving my crew a short, but much needed break. There were several *Beaufighters* parked at Dyce, probably from the RCAF's 404 Squadron that was based with us at Wick. Shortly after arriving I caught the bus into Aberdeen to surprise my Aunties Kate and Jeanie. I stayed with them overnight, but at 1000 hours was back at Dyce taking off. We landed at Wick an hour later, and found seventeen more kites had arrived along with our new Wing Commander, W/C Combe. A gale had already begun to blow.

The groundcrew looked at us in amazement as we taxied up to the hangar. "But you're missing!" they exclaimed. Apparently, the signal from Thornaby that we had landed there instead of at Snaith or the suggested diversion aerodrome of Elsham did not get back to Wick directly, and for some time our plane had been listed as missing. The rumour had spread around the base quickly: "Poor Fraser, and with all those poor blokes with him going on leave." A signal from Wick later revealed our safety to a select few, but the rumour of our demise was not completely dispelled for some time.

On Friday I ran up the engines of "N" on the ground; they seemed okay. Our operations were scrubbed again because of duff weather, but the next night we were finally sent up for a late takeoff at 2200 hours. We were only part way out on patrol when we ran into severe icing. It was piling up on the windshield and wings, and all controls on the *Wimpy* began reacting very sluggishly. We finally had to cut the patrol short and head back for base, where we landed safely.

An ENSA show came to the base on the following Tuesday evening. It was a welcome break from routine, and to show our appreciation we entertained the cast in the mess afterward. Around this time I was given censorship duties. I had to read all mail written by squadron groundcrew before it was forwarded to the post office. I learned a lot about the personalities of the men, but I always felt like I was spying into their private lives, though of course they knew their mail would be censored. Whenever they mentioned our kites, the searchlight, or the Torpex depth charges, I pulled out the scissors and cut the lines out of the letter.

On October 14 a gale with winds over sixty miles per hour blew up unexpectedly around midnight. As a result, the Aussie pilot who was on as Duty Officer that night, later went up for a courtmartial. The Met people woke him up at about 0500 in the morning to tell him that winds of gale force were blowing. He asked how long it had been going on, and when they replied, "Since about 0100 hours," he decided that any damage to the aircraft must have already been done, and went back to sleep. The next morning none of the *Whitleys* on the station were serviceable—all the control cables had been strained. Fortunately, the *Wimpys* had been securely tied down. Inexplicably, the Duty Officer was given nothing more than a reprimand.

I had been getting a thorough and unpleasant taste of North Atlantic weather; wet, cold, and blowy. This, together with the poor service-ability of our machines, kept us from flying at least half the time. Rumour had it that the Royal Canadian Air force was at last to run its own show and would be posting Canadian aircrew to several all-Canadian squadrons. I saw the Winco and asked for a posting to one of these new RCAF squadrons, should the rumour prove to be correct.

In the meantime, I travelled to Wick to do some glass blowing with the equipment I had borrowed from Mr. Scott, a science teacher at Wick High School. While in town I also managed to make some more spore traps for my airborne micro-organism samples. I had found bits of mesophyll—tissues from leaves—floating about 1000 feet up in the sky, a fascinating discovery.

On October 20 I carried out an airtest in "P for Peter". Apparently the mechanics found it impossible to get all the bugs out of "N" so it was relegated to training. We completed a nine-hour test in "P" and landed at 0315 hours under a large, luminous moon. Before coming in for a landing I sometimes put down our landing light on the wing. Here at Skitten it was not an uncommon sight to see rabbits jumping across the runway as we landed, some of them occasionally getting in our path and dying an "honourable military death". A dramatic change in this situation came about ten years later when the disease myxomatosis was introduced. It spread quickly through the rabbit population of the United Kingdom. Very few rabbits were left, although enough survived the epidemic that thirty years later, when I visited Wick aerodrome and Skitten again, I found the rabbits as numerous as ever.

After ops I slept all the next morning. The afternoon was taken up with a lecture on anti-aircraft guns. I was also given the additional job of organizing flying rations; there had been some complaints. Usually if the flight was to take four hours, one set of rations was handed out; if the flying time was to be eight hours, there were double rations, even the odd orange. In Bomber Command, where the flights were shorter, around six hours, normal rations would always be issued, again sometimes with oranges. Then if we did not take off, or even if we were recalled after an hour or so, the Messing Officer would come tearing around trying to repossess his rations, particularly the oranges. Needless to say, he eventually gave it up as a bad job, as the crews would either devour their oranges directly or hide them away in their battledress pockets. I always managed to save enough that whenever I went on leave I could take a half-dozen or so to my cousins and my Aunt Mary in Stafford. They had seen no other oranges since the beginning of the war.

Another new machine, "E for Egypt", was assigned to my crew. It was coated with some sort of thick, sticky substance from its time in storage. With groundcrew at a premium, and with my whole crew impatient to get some ops in, we were soon out with pails of warm water and scrubbing brushes. It took some time for us to get all the paste off the wings and control surfaces. Ronnie Riding was off on ops that night, and Martin had nicked a sub the night before—things were looking up.

We took up "P" on Friday to patrol the Faeroe Islands, between Scotland and Iceland. Somebody glimpsed the wake of a U-boat off the starboard wing. I called action stations immediately: Len was quickly up in the front handling the searchlight controls; Smitty sent the signal 472—"sighted sub, attacking"; Ron dropped the searchlight. Everyone was keyed up, as we'd had little action for some time. I opened the bomb doors, determined to make an attack if at all possible. I made sure the engine fuel mixture was in rich, increased the revs of the propeller, cut back the boost a bit, and we dived toward the wake of the disappearing sub. I dropped the stick of depth charges and the light was switched off. Red, the rear gunner, reported the explosion of the depth charges when he saw the plumes of water spray high into the air. As I swung around on a reciprocal course, Len switched the light on again. He swept it back and forth, but all that remained was a layer of foam on the water temporarily marking our place of attack. No debris could be seen. Well, at least we must have given him a nasty fright.

We started a creeping line-ahead search, sending signals back to base indicating our method. Nothing more was seen, so we eventually returned to base.

As usual, I slept all morning after our debriefing. When I finally woke up, my crew and I walked over to have a more intensive interview with the Winco. There was a party in the mess that evening; with Martin's obvious success two nights earlier and my crew's attack, we were all feeling better.

We worked hard getting "E" ready at Wick in the morning. Ronnie Davies, my navigator, had an interview with the Group Captain Station Commander for a commission; he deserved it, for he had worked hard.

On Monday it was pouring rain, so I cancelled the proposed aircraft swing to correct the magnetic compass errors. We had a lecture and pictures from Wing Commander Combe that afternoon. Southall was off on ops, but was only up fifteen minutes before he found his kite unserviceable and returned to base.

The next day my crew was off on ops in "O", to return after an hour when our generator went unserviceable. Bad weather limited us to training for the next couple of days, but the generator still wasn't working when tested two days later. "E" appeared to be in good shape for us, as it was finally possible to swing the compass, but one day I went out to work on it and found the dinghy poking out of the nacelle storage. I was furious, thinking somebody had been messing around with my aircraft, until I discovered that the problem was due to a faulty release mechanism. It had released itself, and the dinghy immediately did its job and automatically inflated with the carbon dioxide bottle.

Later that week I discussed my application for transfer to an RCAF squadron with the Adjutant, who had first brought the formation of Canadian squadrons to my attention. I also received two presents, chocolates and socks from Mrs. Sifton. The gifts were accompanied by a letter which, among other things, informed me that Bob Dale from Toronto, who had served with me on 150 Squadron in Snaith, was back in Canada.

"E" finally went up on its first air test on October 31. We carried out a recce over Brora on the east coast of Scotland, then tried some blind flying approaches with the ASV. We had the afternoon off, so I visited Thurso. I had chosen a poor time, for all the shops were closed while the town carried out anti-invasion exercises.

The mechanics told us that "E" was still not ready for ops, so I air tested "O" for ops on Sunday night. There was some icing, but we returned safely after nine hours, eleven minutes. A letter from George and one from Dr. Chesters of the University of Birmingham arrived the next day. Dr. Chesters also sent me special test tubes for sampling spores and airborne micro-organisms. The test tubes had agar culture medium in them, so that any living spores could germinate. I also received three hundred cigarettes from Mrs. Medhurst in Toronto, which I passed along to my groundcrew.

On Tuesday we took "E" up on blind flying exercises, and then started out to the Faeroe Islands with a full bomb load for an oil consumption test. Halfway to the Faeroes my navigator informed me that, as he had been looking out the astrodome, he had discovered that the aerial on top of the fuselage had come loose and was flapping around the tail fin and one of the elevator controls. It wasn't very difficult to picture us ploughing into the ocean, should these become entangled with the wire, so I swung the kite around very carefully with aileron control and the uneven use of engine power. We returned on a reciprocal course. On our return the Orkney Islands and the naval base at Scapa Flow passed by under our port wing, but the Navy was not at its anchorage. We could see it out in magnificent full array just west of the Orkneys. In the midst of the ships were two big, apparently new, battleships on shakedown cruises. We did not recognize them, but on landing we checked and found that they were the *Anson* and the *Howe.* Our Intelligence Officer should have let us know that the Navy was at sea on our flight path. Had we flown over the battleships at night, it might have been fatal. Experience had proven that the Navy tended to shoot first and ask questions later.

The next night we took off for our first operation in "E". Excitement was high, for unserviceable planes and lousy weather had been holding us back all too frequently. All seemed to be going well, when suddenly, hell, we received a recall signal BBA. The weather was fine, and everything about "E", including the engines, was running smoothly. The problem? The idiots had given us the wrong patrol area!

Ronnie Davies and I rode our bicycles on Thursday to visit John O'Groats on the most northeasterly tip of Scotland. It was a long, relaxing ride on a beautiful day, and our destination was a lovely place. For a few brief hours we almost forgot the war.

The next day I was Duty Officer, and the wind was fifty miles per hour, causing a shipwreck on the beach near Wick. The high winds were typical of the weather from Wick and off to the north. They had a great influence on the time we spent on our patrol areas: if there was a strong headwind of, say, fifty miles per hour when we were returning, and we were flying with an air speed of 135 miles per hour, it meant that our ground speed was only 85 miles per hour. Thus, if the distance to our patrol area was three hundred miles, it could take over four hours just to get there.

November 8 was again very windy. Nevertheless, we took off on an operation in "E" at 1700 hours. The plane was fully loaded with depth charges and petrol, including the fuel overload on which we were running. I climbed up until just below the snow-spitting clouds, and we continued flying at an altitude of 1000 feet, our patrol height. We passed to the east of the Orkneys, then west of Fair Isle, and on between Foula Island and the west side of the Shetlands. It was a dark, forbidding night with strong winds from the northwest. Suddenly the starboard engine belched sparks and began to lose power. Automatically, I opened the throttle on the port engine and increased the revs, applying opposite rudder to prevent a swing to the right. We had already dropped to about eight hundred feet. Checking the petrol switches I changed to the wing tanks with the crossover feed open. The waves below were clearly visible, and growing closer every moment. I jettisoned the depth charges. We were still sinking so I desperately pulled the fuel jettison lever and shouted, "Dinghy, dinghy!" to the crew, an order to prepare to man the dinghy stations in case we had to ditch. Smitty had started to send out an SOS as soon as the power died, and Ron Davies was preparing a course for base, meanwhile shouting that Sumburgh Aerodrome on the southern tip of the Shetland Islands might be better to try to reach than Wick, which was over a hundred miles away. I gradually eased the plane around to the right, both to get closer to the Shetland Islands and to bring us onto a reciprocal course for base. By this time we were below 500 feet. I gave the crew immediate orders for dinghy stations. Ron grabbed the Verey pistol and some cartridges and scrambled back behind the main spar. He dropped the plastic cover of the astrodome to prepare an exit for himself and Hutch, the ASV operator, Smitty, our wireless operator, and Len, the second pilot. Red, the rear gunner, pivoted his turret to one side and jettisoned the doors, so that he could get directly out of the plane. Len helped to jettison the escape hatch above my head before moving back in the fuselage to prepare for escape out the astrodome. I eased the plane toward the coast, but it was only a few seconds until we were just one hundred feet above sea level. It would only have been a few minutes before we crashed, so I decided it would be better to ditch while the plane was still under control. The port engine was roaring, the starboard engine had been continuously spitting out sparks, but doing little else, and its propeller was just turning over slowly with the force of the slipstream wind—no joy from the throttle control. I had opened the bypass gas valve earlier, but no response, even with both engines drawing petrol from the main wing tanks. The water drew closer and closer; just before we went in I held the nose up and cut the port engine. The whole plastic nose caved in immediately upon impact, and suddenly green water was gushing around me. I was thrown upward and forward out my escape hatch, and the next moment was swallowing a mouthful of brine as I cannon-balled deeply into the water. When I came, gasping and choking, to the surface, I peered around in the blackness of the night. Only the tall, shark-like tail fin of the *Wimpy* was still visible above the rough surface of the water. To its right I finally spied the dinghy, open but lying on its edge partly submerged. It must have come out automatically, but was still held to the sinking plane as if by an umbilical cord. I swam toward it, kicking off my flying boots as I went. My Mae West stood me in good stead. Two other figures, then three, suddenly appeared to my right. I made it to the dinghy about the same time as Len and Hutch. Luckily, the cord broke as the plane sank deeper. The dinghy was left right side up. I helped to push Hutch into the dinghy, then Hutch pulled Len while I pushed. To our frightened eyes the waves appeared to be fifteen or twenty feet high, and it was snowing, or was it sleet, or rain? I climbed aboard and looked around for Ron Davies, who had been swimming right behind me. As he reached the side of the dinghy I leaned over and grabbed his collar. A portly individual, he must have been well over 200 pounds. Ron tried to climb in, but couldn't make it alone. We were all struggling to get him aboard when a big wave splashed over us, knocking us down. Ron disappeared over the side as we lost our grip on him, so I slid back over the side of the dinghy to try to find him, when he came up again. He looked like a big walrus coming out of the sea. Hutch almost fell over laughing, and even Len shook a bit. I felt the contagion of the almost hysterical, tension-relieving laughter; it really would have been funny had it not been so serious. With Hutch and Len pulling and me pushing, we managed to get Ron aboard at last, and I scrambled in again. There were only four of us out of a six-man crew. Red and Smitty had not appeared. We tried to raise ourselves up on the dinghy to search the water around us, and almost as soon as we began shouting a voice came out of the darkness—it was Red. "Are you all right?" Hutch and I yelled together, with mingled relief and anxiety.

Red's disembodied voice came weakly back; "Where are you?..

"Here. Can you swim to the dinghy?" Hearing but a faint reply, we unshipped the paddles and began to paddle as hard as possible toward Red's voice. We couldn't see him; the waves were tossing our dinghy high into the air and back down again. It was impossible for us to make any headway. Red found it no easier, and his voice gradually faded away. Desperately, hoping he still had the strength to stay afloat in the rough sea, we shouted, "Red, try to make for the shore if you can." (Land could be seen dimly at odd times in the distance toward the east.) "We'll keep trying to pick you up." Frustrated, helpless, and terrified, we continued paddling for over an hour in the direction we had last heard Red's voice, but to no avail, the wind and waves were against us. I asked Ron to fire a cartridge from the Verey pistol he had brought from the plane. The red flare seemed to rise ever so slowly, and cast an eerie glow through the blackness around us. We saw nothing but water. Ron reloaded the pistol and pointed it into the air, but nothing happened. The cartridge had swollen with the salt water and was jammed in the barrel. There was still no sign of Smitty.

By this time we had unfolded the dinghy's sail and drawn up the emergency rations. For hours we continued to paddle in what we hoped was Red's direction. The waves gradually began to diminish in size and strength. Finally we saw steep cliffs on our left; white breakers shimmered, ghostlike, in the darkness, and a rock appeared in the water ahead of us. We paddled the dinghy around to the other side of the rock, where the water was slightly calmer, and were thrown violently against the rocky shoreline as we attempted to beach the dinghy. Len and Hutch were the first ones on dry land. I balanced the dinghy while Ron clambered onto the slippery rocks, and finally I disembarked, rather clumsily, still clinging unsurely to the dinghy. Len and Hutch had already started to head up the cliffs, but I called them back. We couldn't tell where we were, or whether we could get to the top of the rocks; and with the tide, it would have been foolhardy to abandon the dinghy and the emergency rations. Looking out to sea we saw what appeared to be flames several miles out on the surface. Was it the petrol from our aircraft, ignited by exploding depth charges or by our flares? I wondered where Red was. And Smitty—there had been no sign of him; he must have gone down with the aircraft, probably sticking to his wireless set sending out his SOS to the last. . . .

We pulled the dinghy onto the shore and up over the rocks. The slope up the cliffs was steep, but wasn't as bad as the almost sheer cliffs to the right and left of us. We staggered upward, one man with the ration box, the rest of us carrying the dinghy. I was in my stocking feet, having kicked off my boots while swimming to the dinghy, but I felt no pain despite the sharp rocks, as my feet were numb from the icy sea-water. After climbing eighty feet or so, we came out onto a level plateau above the rocky beach. Here we left the dinghy, placing some rocks on it to prevent it from blowing away. Pausing to catch our breath, and to thank God that we were still alive, we looked back down over the sea with its phosphorescent breakers exploding against the jagged shoreline. Painful thoughts of Red and Smitty . . .

A cold wind was blowing with a drizzly snow. I decided it better to keep the group moving up over the plateau to find shelter after we were rested. As we continued on our weary way, a moving light suddenly appeared in the distance; it looked like someone with a flashlight. If only he had appeared sooner! Our search along the steep, rocky shore for any sign of Red or Smitty had necessarily been limited by our lack of light. As we drew closer, we found that the light was held by a local fisherman/farmer, who had apparently seen something burning out on the ocean and thought that a boat was in some difficulty. He was surprised to learn that a plane had been flying in such rough weather.

Almost our first words to him were of Red and Smitty, and he assured us that he would organize a search for them immediately. Meanwhile, he implored us to go to his home, just up over the hill, to warm up. Cold, wet, and exhausted, we made our way the short distance across the moors to his thatched cottage. It was very early in the morning, probably about 0300 or 0400 hours, although I wasn't sure as my watch had stopped with the salt water. The fisherman's wife was nevertheless waiting up for us, and quickly prepared us each a cup of hot tea. With this and the warmth of the cottage we gradually thawed out. Outwardly, my crew didn't look too bad, but they returned my scrutiny with concern. My right eye was bleeding from a cut, and a large bump was rising on my forehead. My knees were sore as hell—I must have hit them on the control column as the plane nosed into the water. We said little, and I think we all must have been afraid to mention our two missing crewmates; though our minds were full of thoughts of them, willing the impossible to be true, picturing them as we had always known them— hale and hearty and full of life. After three hours or so an ambulance from RAF Station Lerwick bumped across the fields, and we quietly climbed in, no doubt still partly in shock. After what seemed to be an exceedingly long, slow drive we were ushered into the Officers' Mess in Lerwick. There were several officers there in spite of the early hour, having heard of our crash. The Medical Officer took a quick look at each of us and asked about our injuries. The bump on my forehead was the size of an egg, the blood had congealed from the cut across my right eye, and the upper parts of my legs, just above the knees, were turning black and blue. But aside from all the aches and pains we weren't too badly off physically, with no broken bones or major injuries.

The Medical Officer held up a decanter containing a coloured liquid. "Teetotallers or not," he said, "drink this." He poured a big tumbler of rum for each of us and watched as we gulped it down, with a little water to lessen the burning sensation in our throats. After assuring us that a search was underway for our mates, he ordered us to hit the hay. There was nothing more we could do. Numbly, we followed an officer as he led us into rooms with beds and sheets, and in minutes we were asleep.

I woke up late the following afternoon and found my way to the Ops Room. My muscles were so stiff and sore I could hardly move. I looked a mess, too; my recently acquired wounds still looked fresh and ugly, and I had no shoes, although I had managed to borrow a pair of slippers. There was no word as yet of Smitty or Red. I glanced at the ops board on my way through and suddenly paled as the words "BRAMWELL STILL MISSING" caught my eye. It couldn't be! Red, Smitty, and now Bramwell, all in one night. There had to be some mistake! But the ops officer confirmed that it was indeed F/Sgt Ron Bramwell. Bramwell, my roommate of early Chivenor days, was missing with all his crew. The two of us, along with Ronnie Riding, had taken off the night before on "Flora" patrols within a few minutes of each other. Bramwell had been just ahead of me when he picked up a blip on his ASV and homed in on it. When their searchlight illuminated its quarry, it was not a U-boat, but a British armed trawler. It opened fire on Bramwell's machine and hit him. Ops in Lerwick as well as in Wick received his wireless signal, "Shot up by trawler; engine hit, controls damaged, trying to make . . . SOS, SOS . . ." Nothing more. A day or two later a search aircraft found an upturned empty dinghy between the Faeroe and Shetland Islands.

10016 - 114 St -
Edmonton Alta
Feb 1, 43.

P/o Mr Donald Fraser
R.C.A.F. Great Britain.
Dear Mr Fraser:
I acknowledge with greatful appreciation the kind letters of sympathy and pictures You sent me at the time of Jims passing. I need not tell you the shock I got at the dreadful news, Jim as you may have known was my only son and his sisters and I feel his death Very keenly, as I well imagine The boys who were with him do to, he often spoke of the boys to me, he had a very nice disposition and was Very well thought of, as you would know had you been

From a letter written by Mrs. Allan J. MacDonald of Edmonton, Alberta, to P/O Donald Fraser, February 1, 1943.

172

When our SOS was received, the Operations Officer in Wick signalled to Ronnie Riding to cut short his patrol and begin a search for us. Almost immediately after this order came in he received a second signal: "Look for Bramwell." Of the three kites on ops that fateful night, two were down and the other was searching for them. Apparently, after our SOS, a motor launch was detailed to leave Sumburgh RAF Station on the south end of the Shetland Islands. She raced up the west side of the Islands to look for us, but was soon forced to abandon the search and return after she had to retrieve one of her own crew members who had been washed overboard by the violent seas.

From the operations room in Lerwick we were given transport to Sumburgh aerodrome, where we were kitted up from stores. The Red Cross brought in a great big bag of chocolate, all broken pieces, but solid and good. I hadn't seen so much chocolate since I left Canada almost two years before. Later in the week our new Flight Commander from Wick flew up to get us in "S" for Sugar. The Medical Officer at Wick examined us shortly after we arrived. He gave me some pills for the splitting headache that had been bothering me, and let us know we would be getting some leave. By this time the search party had found Red's body washed ashore in the Shetland Islands. His funeral was scheduled for Saturday.

On Friday our crew met with the Winco to go over the details of the ditching. Everything around the station had changed since the night we left. There were few kites around; 179 Squadron had been posted to Gibraltar. The Winco said that I was to stay with 612 Squadron as an instructor for a while. They were flying *Whitley* twin engine bombers and would eventually get other machines, perhaps Leigh Light *Wimpys*, who could tell?

When I had first returned to Wick, or rather Skitten, from the Shetlands, my room was locked up. A new batman was there, and when I asked him to let me in he said: "Oh, no, that's Pilot Officer Fraser's room. Poor guy went for a burton last week." It was the custom to immediately lock up the room and belongings of anyone who went missing or was killed, so that others could not scrounge all his belongings, particularly his flying equipment. I had a hard time trying to convince the batman that *I* was the late Pilot Officer Fraser.

On Saturday, November 14, I turned out with the firing party and all that was left of my crew for Red McGrath's funeral. We fell in outside one of the huts near the hangar, where a truck with a flag was waiting to take Red's body to the cemetery. But there was no body. It was being flown over from the Shetlands, and the *Hudson* carrying it had had engine trouble and was delayed taking off. As we solemnly waited for the *Hudson,* one airman tried to lighten the somber mood as he reminded us, with a mixture of humour and sorrow, "Well, we always said that Red would be late for his own funeral.''

Forty minutes passed. Finally a *Hudson* circled the aerodrome and landed. Red's casket was taken out while the padre said a few words, and loaded onto the truck. The Winco offered us transport to the cemetery, which was about two miles away, but I thought it better that we pay our respects to Red by marching behind the truck that was carrying his body. On foot, we followed Red's flag-draped casket out of the aerodrome gates, through the town of Wick, down past the Bank of Scotland, over the bridge, up the hill, and into a bit of open country. As we entered through the cemetery gates we broke into a slow march, while six of Red's fellow sergeants carried the casket to the grave. The service on that bleak and windy afternoon was given by the RAF padre. A station photographer took pictures to send to Red's mother in Edmonton. When the padre had completed the service, the firing party fired three volleys, and pieces of soil were scattered on the casket as it was lowered into the ground.

Red was buried by the south wall of the cemetery, next to many other servicemen. He lay beside those Navy men whose bodies had been washed up from shipwrecks, and fellow airmen who had been killed in crashes or in *Luftwaffe* bombing raids during the past two years.

Wellingtons of the RAAF in the shadow of the Rock.
(Imperial War Museum)

Six years later, when I accepted a position on the Faculty of the Department of Botany at the University of Alberta, in Edmonton, I visited Red's family. His mother had died on New Year's Day 1945, but I met with his sisters, some of whom were by then married. They had appreciated the letters and the pictures of the funeral that I had sent to them, and for a half-hour or so together we remembered Red. I think it brought us all a measure of peace.

After Red's funeral the Winco drove me back from the cemetery in his car and we had a quiet, philosophical discussion. I appreciated the leadership of Wing Commander Combe. He was a permanent RAF type who had flown the Vickers *Wellesley* single engine bomber, the geodetic predecessor of the *Wimpy,* on long-distance prewar flights from England to Australia. He was also something of an athlete, often seen out in track gear running around the perimeter of the aerodrome at Skitten. I tried to locate W/C Combe in 1980 and was sorry to learn from the RAF Records Office that he had died two years earlier.

Everybody on the squadron was preparing for Gibraltar, getting innoculations and leave passes before going overseas. On the 15th of November I was paid seven pounds, then collected leave passes for the survivors of my crew, packed, and went to the Station Hotel in Wick with Ronnie, Len, and Hutch. We spent a quiet evening playing bridge, and the next morning caught the 0825 train for London. We ate my mother's fruitcake on the way down, for there was no dining car, and we nipped out at various stations to the NAAFI to get tea or coffee and sandwiches to go with the cake.

We arrived in London at 1150 hours on the following day, and I went to the Officers' Club at 46 Grosvenor Street for the night. I had tried contacting George's unit, but he was out. Before turning in for the night, I met Hutch and we went to a show together, *Yankee Doodle Dandy.* The next day I visited the RCAF Headquarters to meet with Squadron Leaders Birch and T.C. Shore at Adastral House, Air Ministry. I was still trying to transfer to an RCAF squadron, but these officers made me no promises, although they confirmed that more Canadian squadrons were being organized. I also asked if any instructors' courses were available, because I still planned to go into teaching after the war and I thought that the training provided by an instructor's course would come in handy. Again they were unable to tell me much. It would be another one and one-half years before such a course would materialize, at the Flying Instructors' School at Trenton, Ontario. Not that I wouldn't do a lot of instructing before then, but it was always to be at Operational Training Units. It was often considered more advantageous for OTU staff to have a tour-screened pilot with an interest in teaching rather than someone who had taken an Instructors' Course but had no operational experience.

"Red's" Funeral. The funeral cortege of "Red", J.P. McGrath, crosses the bridge in Wick, November 17, 1942. The author is on the right, directly behind the casket.

(RAF Station, Wick)

The author (centre) with Ronnie Davies, his navigator (left) and "Hutch" Hutchinson, his ASV operator, out on a rabbit-grouse hunt on the moors of Wick.

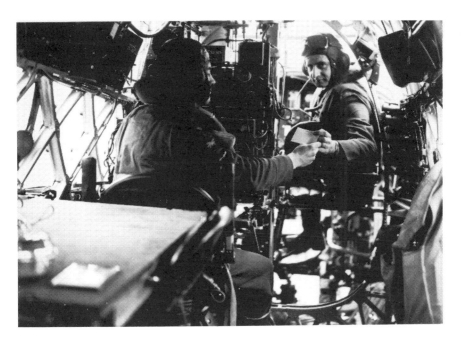

The wireless operator passing a message to the 2nd pilot in a *Wellington*.
(Imperial War Museum)

A Mark XIV *Wellington* fitted with 10 cm radar ASV and the retracted
Leigh Light.

(Imperial War Museum)

By Thursday the 19th I had finally contacted George, and we arranged to meet that evening in Guilford for dinner. He had heard nothing of my forced landing, and when he saw my bruised face with the partially healed cut over one eye, his welcoming grin faded quickly. As we sat over our drinks I sketchily outlined the story for him, bringing the events back all too vividly to my own mind. Over dinner we both tried, not entirely successfully, to avoid the topic—I was torn between a desire to tell George all I had felt that night, to be able to talk over the whole thing with someone close to me, and my need to temporarily block the night from my memory, to forget it for a while until I could face it with less pain.

Before I could entirely submit to the healing passage of time, there was one last task to face. On Friday I took the train to Cambridge, then the bus to Bury St. Edmunds, and finally walked a few miles to Badwell Ash, Smitty's home. Smitty's mother had died earlier that year and his father had passed away when Smitty was young, but his sister and brother were still living in the area. I visited the sister and her husband for a short time, and they seemed glad to be able to talk with me about Smitty, but I felt there was little I could say. After expressing my sympathy and my own feeling of loss, I described how Smitty had stuck to his set, sending out SOS signals until the end. He must have gone down with the plane, for his body was never found. The sister then suggested that I visit a neighbour, whose daughter had been going steady with Smitty. Smitty had talked about her often, and I had gathered that once the war was over he wanted to marry her. She was at work when I appeared on the neighbour's doorstep, and I was having tea with her parents when she returned home. I stood as I heard her footsteps coming toward the room, and I could see her mother and father glance apprehensively toward one another. She stopped at the doorway when she saw me standing there in my uniform, then burst into tears and ran from the room. I left shortly afterward, and Smitty's brother drove me back to Bury St. Edmonds in his truck. The grey, overcast sky and a cold drizzle matched the day's mood.

The next day I drew ten pounds from the bank and visited the sister of my family's minister, the Rev. Dr. McCree of Glebe Presbyterian Church in North Toronto. I happened to see a casualty list that day. It recorded, as killed in action, one of my old Regina/Prince Albert/Camp Borden/*Rajputana*/Benson pals, Charlie Tourville from Victoriaville, Quebec. He had been posted to 99 Squadron on *Stirlings* when I went to 150 Squadron on *Wimpys*. George dropped over that evening to let me know that he would not be able to get leave until the next Sunday, and, I think, to make sure my trip the day before hadn't done me in. I decided to visit Chivenor while I was waiting for George to join me. It may have been a mistake, for I was overwhelmed by the feelings of alienation I experienced at the aerodrome site. All familiarity had been reduced to a purely physical, external nature—the officers and aircrew were all new. I only stayed at the station for a short while before going to find the Scoynes. Thankfully, they were the same, and they welcomed me warmly, asking me to stay with them for the night. That day with the Scoynes must have speeded my convalescence immeasurably.

Besides offering relaxation, cheerful non-war gossip, and the opportunity to play a few tunes on his piano, Mr. Scoyne and his brother-in-law took me ferreting for rabbits. Mr. Scoyne borrowed two ferrets from a friend and we drove up on the sand dunes, part of an old pasture. The idea was to scare the rabbits from their holes into one of the nets which were placed around all the exits of their burrows except one. It was through this opening that the ferret made his entrance. The rabbits were deathly afraid of these weasel-like rodents, and would come hurtling out of one of the exits and get caught in the net. Mr. Scoyne would then grab them and give each a "rabbit punch" behind the neck to kill it. Toward the end of the afternoon we had twenty rabbits, enough meat for many a meal.

Rabbit dinner was a welcome change in wartime England, where meat was in short supply, but in our enthusiasm for a good meal we made one run too many. The ferret caught up with one of the remaining rabbits, seized it by the neck, and then settled down about ten feet underground in the burrow to have his supper. Ferrets were valuable animals in these parts, and indeed this one was borrowed from a friend. What now? Nothing for it but to dig! Mr. Scoyne, his brother-in-law, and myself spent hours digging, digging, and digging. Finally, after darkness had settled in, we came to the burrow with the ferret and its prey. With no complaints the well-fed ferret went back into its cage, and we returned home.

Another delicacy I sampled at the Scoyne's was Devon cream. It was forbidden to make this delicious treat during the war years of rationing, but of course all the farmers made a little. It reminded me of the tales of Kentucky moonshiners who made whiskey or applejack, then went to great pains to avoid the "revenuers". Devon cream has the consistency and colour of light butter, but it melts in the mouth like ice cream, and tastes better than either.

The next morning I bade farewell to my friends and left for Stafford to visit my Aunt Mary and Uncle Horace Binks. I had to go through my story once again, but it was somehow less painful to tell. That evening Horace and I took yet another long walk in the rain and the blackout.

The next day I decided to go into Birmingham to visit the University and Drs. Gunn and Chesters. I also hoped to see my cousin John, who was a second year student of medicine at the University. Uncle Horace drove me to the railroad station, and when I bought my ticket the stationmaster warned me that the train for Birmingham was about to leave. I dashed up the overhead stairs and saw the train just pulling out, but with a burst of energy I made it, hauling myself onto one of the last carriages. Finding an empty compartment I settled back, for I knew that it would take about an hour to get to Birmingham. The train rode surprisingly well, and steamed along without stopping anywhere. "Must be a special express," I thought. Unfortunately, I was absolutely correct. After an hour had come and gone, and I couldn't see any sign of the train slowing down, I got up and wandered along the compartment corridor. Seeing a uniformed trainman, I stopped him. "When do we get to Birmingham?"

"Birmingham?" he repeated with a puzzled look. "You're on the wrong train, son. We're going to London. The Birmingham train was right behind us at the station. We were late in leaving Stafford."

My heart sank. "Now what will I do?"

Seeing my concern, the man thought for a moment, and replied, "Well, you can still get to Birmingham, but it's going to take you all day. Get out at Wolverhampton, then take the train to Coventry and change there for Birmingham."

He was right. It was late afternoon, after a six or seven hour ride, when I finally arrived in Birmingham. I hotfooted it to the University and managed to catch Dr. Chesters still in. He was quite agreeable about identifying any spores that I might send him, so after thanking him I walked over to the Medical Department to see if my cousin John might be there. A secretary informed me that he was dissecting in the anatomy room, and would be there until after 1800. After taking several wrong corridors I finally found the door labelled Anatomy. Peeking in, I saw John across the room, his back partly toward me, bending over a cadaver, with three colleagues similarly engaged. The room had about thirty such tables with cadavers on them and four students at work per table—a gruesome scene. Summoning up my courage I tip-toed across the room till I was right behind John, who remained absorbed in his task and didn't notice me. They were dissecting the liver. During my university days I had cut apart just about everything, skate, frog, rabbit, alligator, chicken—everything, that is, except the human body. Yet the names of tissues, organs, and many of the muscles are the same. Knife in hand, John had hesitated as though wondering where to make the next cut, so I leaned over his shoulder and whispered, "The falciform ligament—the one holding the liver in place in front of the diaphragm."

Startled, he jumped slightly and spun around. "Don! What on earth are you doing here?" he laughed. After a brief chat he went back to work, and, fascinated, I stayed to watch. We spent the next hour tracing out the different parts of the gut. With my biology training, I had much in common with him and his fellow medical students. The demonstrator came around occasionally, but he did not disturb me as I stood there in my uniform beside John. By 1800 hours the lab showed no sign of completion, but I had to catch the last train back to Stafford, so I left John to finish his dissection and made my way back to the railway station.

Aunt Mary apparently decided that I needed some pampering, and gave me breakfast in bed the next day. The weather was raw, wet, and windy, so after a long, lazy morning of reading and chatting, I took my cousin Roy to a show, *The Foreman Went to France.*

Over the next three or four days I took life slowly, seeing another movie—*Captains of the Clouds*—going out for walks with my uncle and cousin, touring a local factory where I saw motors being made, accompanying my aunt to church, and sending letters to my family back in Toronto. George joined me at Aunt Mary's on Sunday afternoon, making those few peaceful days all the more pleasant. But George was firmly convinced that for a full recovery I would need a bit more excitement than that, so the next morning I said goodbye to breakfast in bed and we caught a train for London. It was still wet and foggy, but for the types of activity George had in mind it didn't really matter. In the next two days we saw two plays, ate an enormous amount of delicious food, and sampled a number of local nightspots—we had to concentrate our pleasures when we could. George and I parted on Thursday, and I caught the 1920 train to Wick, where I joined two of my crew for the bus trip back to Skitten. My convalesence, officially at least, was over.

Thirty letters and three parcels, including a Christmas parcel from my mother, were waiting for me on my return on Saturday, December 5. I was interviewed on my return my Wing Commander Longmore of 612 Squadron, and he let me know that I was in line for an instructor's course. My crew had been split up—Hutch was to go to a Coastal Command squadron, probably on *Catalinas,* and Len would leave for a Captain's course to learn to fly *Wimpys.*

On the 8th I supervised dinghy drill at the flights before heading over to Wick to visit the Photographic Section. The latest bit of news going around was about a *Hurricane* fighter that had gotten lost the previous night. Apparently the radio-telephone operator in the Control Tower was talking to the frightened pilot, trying to bring him down onto the aerodrome, when the radio suddenly became silent. The pilot probably passed right over Wick and ditched in the North Sea.

I was kept busy during early December instructing in the flights. I acted as Air Sea Rescue Officer and dinghy drill instructor. I was also very occupied with my studies, both in the operations room and at my Botany, Zoology, and Military Studies work for the University of London. But I still had time for the occasional chess game with Ronnie over eats from my Christmas parcel from home.

On Saturday, December 12 I had to go over to Wick in the morning for clothing cards, and while I was there I drew two .22 rifles and a shotgun so Ronnie, Hutch, and I could go shooting over the moors in the afternoon. It was a lovely day as we tramped over the open country. We saw one grouse and a rabbit, and took some unsuccessful shots, but our hearts just weren't into hitting them. They both escaped easily over the peat bogs. It was a good area for shooting, and we also had an excellent vantage point for viewing the occasional *Whitley* taking off for a test flight from Wick. Apparently the pilots were equally adept at sighting hunters; a few months earlier one of the Australian pilots had been out with his *Wimpy* on an air test and saw a hunting party down on the moors. He dived down to almost zero feet and went skimming over the grass, hedges, and heather. Down went the hunters, faces to the ground. As the *Wimpy* rose again, the hunters jumped up, shaking their fists, and were down again just in time to escape the Aussie, who had come around again in his low-flying *Wimpy*. This continued for some time, until the pilot finally tired of it and flew off, to land back at base. All might have been well, except that when the groundcrew did their daily inspection of the machine, they found the underside of the fuselage peppered with holes from buckshot. The hunters, being quite incensed and, indeed, in some danger, for there was always the possibility that they could get their heads chopped off by the whirling propellers, had taken a few pot shots at the *Wimpy*. Needless to say, there was a minor investigation, and the pilot went up before the Commanding Officer for a reprimand.

A few days later I became acquainted with Flying Officer Norman Roseblade while we went over the bombing gear together one morning. A 612 Squadron pilot, Norman was from Toronto, so we hit it off right away. He, too, had finished his tour on operations and was waiting for a posting. In the meantime, he was, like myself, doing some instructing, checking over equipment, and generally preparing for the new crews who were to be checked out on the *Wellingtons*.

Roseblade had relatives in Aberdeen, and during one of his visits there he went skating at the local ice rink. Noticing a comely girl having trouble skating, he offered his help, and ended up spending a large portion of the remainder of his leave with her. During his next few leaves, Roseblade came to know her well; it was not far, at least by air, from Wick to Aberdeen. The next thing I knew, they were getting married. Later he was posted to a torpedo *Wellington* Operational Training Unit in Limavady in Northern Ireland, near Londonderry, where I was to see him again six months later.

Well, life went on at the RAF Station at Wick and Skitten during the last part of 1942. As time passed I continued my work with my microscope. By that time I had many slides that had been exposed to the air with my spore trap during flights. Their vaselined surfaces had captured hundreds of plant fragments. Most of them remained unidentified, but I was always amazed at the number of types of plant tissue I could catch even at altitudes over 5,000 feet. Unfortunately, I had lost my spore-sampling apparatus when our *Wimpy* ditched. Another pastime was visiting the local flicks or movie houses. I recall some of the titles of the time; *Fleet's In* and *China Seas* with Clark Gable and Jean Harlow were two I particularly liked.

As Christmas approached I remembered Red's grave and inquired about getting a headstone for it, but was informed that the Government would be erecting a serviceman's stone, as indeed they later did. I saw it almost thirty years later, in July 1971, on a day when the weather was slightly warmer, but just as windy, as those well-remembered days. The church sexton was in the cemetery that day, and he mentioned that the father of one of the lads buried there flew over from Canada every year to visit the grave on a specific date, probably the date his son was killed. After flying to Wick and motoring to the cemetery, the father would place a wreath of flowers on his son's grave, then return to London to catch an afternoon flight back to Canada. The special servicemen's section of the cemetery, with its official headstones, had been well kept through the years. Red's grave had a rose growing up in front of the headstone, partially hiding the RCAF crest. It was good to find that it was Warrant Officer James Patrick McGrath on the stone, for Red had received his promotion posthumously.

Christmas day 1942 we had the Sergeants over to our mess in the morning, then went over to their mess in the afternoon to serve their Christmas dinner. It was cold and windy outside, but inside, spirits were warm and the mood was genial.

My Christmas surprise came a day late, on Boxing Day. Squadron Leader Moore told me that my posting was finally coming through, and that I was to see the Winco about it the next day. So, on Sunday, December 27, I learned that I was posted to Silloth, No. 1 Operational Training Unit, where they flew *Hudsons, Ansons,* and *Oxfords.* Ronnie was to go to 210 Squadron on *Sunderland* flying boats, Hutch to 422 Squadron flying *Sunderlands* at Oban, and Len to 6 Operational Training Unit on torpedo *Wimpys.* Thus my crew was finally split up.

Chapter Nine
Operational Training Units
and a Step up the Ladder

ON MONDAY, DECEMBER 28, I packed up everything, cleared from the Station, and took my luggage and bicycle to Wick. After lunching there I left for the last time on the slow train to Inverness, eventually arriving at Silloth on the Solway estuary in Cumberland, at 1400 hours the next day. The Chief Instructor told me that there was an instrument flying course on *Hudsons* at Silloth as well as an *Anson* and *Oxford* flight for checking wireless communication and training wireless operators. I had never flown *Ansons,* nor the twin-engined *Oxfords* before, having gone straight from single-engine *Harvards* to twin-engine *Wellingtons* at Benson almost two years before.

The same day I arrived I took up one of the *Ansons* for the first time, but had little trouble. After checking the aircraft's instruments and general layout, I did one quick ten-minute circuit with the instructor before going solo. A pilot with previous experience always did that one circuit with the new instructor, mostly for formality's sake. Once he knew the instruments of the plane, the petrol, cocks, and the general stalling and flying characteristics, handling most new aircraft was a piece of cake.

Silloth was quite different from Wick, both geographically and in terms of my duties. I flew up to six hours every day, a welcome change from ground duty and standdowns at Wick and Skitten. While checking out the wireless operators it was possible to cruise over a wide area, to continually see new territory, quite interesting to a developing geographer. That first day I flew over Carlisle and Gretna Green, the latter well-known as the spot where so many English couples, having crossed the Scottish border, could get married with a minimum of regulations. Everything on that first trip was satisfactory, except that I was dead tired. Flying immediately after the long, sleepless trip from Wick was exhausting. A day or so later, I slept right through New Year's Eve and missed the celebrations in the Mess.

New Year's Day, January 1, 1943, was not remarkably different from other New Year's Days during the war: a parade scheduled for 0830 in the morning was put off until 0915 hours; it was raining and low clouds blew in on a warm front. There was no flying, so I did 45 minutes instrument practice in the Link Trainer. The following day, Saturday, I flew four hours and saw snow on the hills to the south. That day I got many letters, including ones from Mother, Smitty's sister, and a neighbour, Helen Walden. The pattern repeated itself for the next few days, except that on Sunday evening I also went to the Presbyterian church in Silloth.

Tuesday, January 5 marked the 17th birthday of my youngest brother, Graig. While the family was undoubtedly celebrating the event back home in Toronto, I was finding it increasingly difficult to think about celebrating anything. I had been suffering from a cold, with all the accompanying aches and pains, ever since coming down from Wick, and I was finally forced to report sick with the flu. The Medical Officer handed me a batch of pills and ordered me to bed for a few days. Meals would be sent over from the Mess. Nothing could have sounded better to me right then than the suggestion of bed rest, so by early afternoon I had climbed into my bunk. I had lit a fire in the little stove in the corner of the room, but it hadn't lasted long, and despite the cold I didn't feel up to getting it going again. A little later there was a knock at the door. Croaking "come in" through my red-hot, inflamed throat, I peered out bleary-eyed from underneath the bedclothes. I just might have fallen over had I not already been lying down. Coming through the door with a cup of hot tea was the cutest WAAF I had ever seen. With a cheerful greeting she deposited the tea into my hands, then went directly to the stove and had a fire roaring in moments. Announcing that she was my "batman" for the duration of my illness, she left with a smile. I wondered momentarily if I had just conjured her up from my fevered brain, but the soothing tea and warm fire soon took over, and I slept. I wakened a few hours later when the door opened, and there she was with my supper on a tray. As I was unable to eat much, my "batman" made sure that I was comfortable and then sat down in the corner, unravelled some knitting, and was all set to keep me company for as long as I wanted. At any other time I would have been only too happy to have her there with me, but as things were, I was in a rather hostile mood and feeling seedy—nose running, eyes inflamed, and all aches and pains. I tried to be polite, but assured her that all I wanted was to sleep, in spite of her hospitality. Understandingly, she bade me a gracious good night. Just my luck to have the most gorgeous thing I'd seen since I arrived in the UK meet me when I was looking and feeling my absolute worst. But a big dollop of rum added to my tea helped me to forget my troubles, and soon the rum and my pills began to take effect, and I drifted peacefully off to the land of dreams.

With the help of my WAAF I recovered quickly. The Medical Officer must have considered me healthy, anyway, for I was given additional duties in the operations room when declared fit for service again.

By this time I had a balance of 174 pounds in Lloyds Bank in London. More good news arrived with a letter from George, whose jubilant note announced his engagement to Jean Cowe of Donalda Farms near Toronto. Jean was a nurse in the Toronto General Hospital. She had been introduced to George by another 48th Highlander, Lieutenant Bill "Dusty" Miller, who was engaged to Jean's twin sister, Flo. After George and Bill went overseas in December 1939, I used to take Jean out to University dances and shows until I myself was posted out.

One night I went to see a show in Silloth, *The Maltese Falcon.* How the late night television shows of today bring back memories! I find this movie just as fascinating now as I did then. But I didn't spend all my time at Silloth at the movies. Planning the training sessions kept me busy in the ops room, and I also worked in the navigation section, as well as studying Botany in my free time. I was continuing to receive many cigarettes as gifts, though I still hadn't succumbed to the habit, but George and my buddies on the base benefitted. I used to give the cigarettes to my grateful groundcrew when I was on operational duties, which helped to strengthen our good relationship. For example, old "N for Nuts" had an excellently maintained automatic pilot, because the instrument lad in charge would come up with me in the air for hours on end just to adjust it, something he was by no means required to do.

One day while I was at Silloth I saw a *Hudson* go down in the Solway estuary. Another *Hudson* crashed there a few days later. This area had had many *Hudsons* crash into it, and so many wrecks could be seen on the sands at low tide, it was called "Hudsons Bay" by the Canadians.

Relatives, neighbours, and friends at home really seemed to think a lot of types like me overseas. At one point I received 25 letters within two days. Letters and gifts from home always gave a tremendous lift to spirits and morale.

On January 18 I visited the station dentist to see what he could do about yet another painful toothache. Almost before I knew it he had pulled my upper right wisdom tooth. The tooth was decayed and was better out, said the dentist, and no doubt he was right, but the resulting pain from the extraction seemed little better than the original toothache.

An interesting lecture on Russia was given a few days later by a Flight Lieutenant Griffith. He had been with a *Hurricane* detachment the previous summer at Murmansk where they had checked out the Soviet pilots on the *Hurricanes* being turned over to the Red Air Force. The RAF pilots even flew some escort missions for Russian bombers on ops against the *Luftwaffe* and the German army in Northern Finland, particularly around the nickel mines of Petsamo. A second lecture on Russia was given the following day.

Saturday, January 23, 1943—I was 25 years old. It scarcely seemed possible. To mark the event I went to Carlisle that evening for dinner and a dance. The next day I had a medical examination which went smoothly except that I had been having some trouble focussing my right eye. I was told that I might need to get correctional glasses for flying. After the exam I played a bit of chess to kill some time and saw the film *The Man Who Wouldn't Die*—perhaps, I thought, this should be my objective. Coming back on the train from my medical I met an elderly gentleman, Captain Alexander of the Royal Navy. We were travelling in the same compartment, and chatted comfortably until arriving late in Newcastle. We had both decided to stay the night, and after running into each other several times at hotels that were filled, we ended up sharing a double room, the only one available, in the last hotel. He reminisced far into the night, first at the bar, then in our room. His description of one of his experiences during the First World War made a strong impression on me. He had been commanding a destroyer and was ordered to take it up a certain river, something not normally attempted because of the river's shallow depth. Orders were orders, so, after lightening the ship by unloading ballast and fuel, he waited for high tide, then steamed up to his destination. Needless to say, when the tide went out the destroyer was high and dry on the mud flats. Captain Alexander was later called up on the carpet for stranding his ship. The order for him to go up the river had been a mistake, as Alexander had suspected, but as Tennyson's "Charge of the Light Brigade" so definitively puts it:

> *Theirs is not to make reply,*
> *Theirs is not to reason why,*
> *Theirs is but to do or die.*

Captain Alexander was returning from a meeting with Soviet naval representatives. They had been very suspicious when he displayed several different types of radar and explained that Marks III and IV were experimental only, and that only five sets had been made. The Soviets insisted that they should have 100 sets of each model. For hours Alexander had argued, but he was unable to convince them that only five sets were made of some types because they hadn't worked as well as planned. In the end other Marks may have had their numbers changed to III and IV, to satisfy the Soviets that they were getting 100 sets of each.

When I arrived back at Silloth I found a parcel waiting from Mother. It had been mailed December 17 and contained a watch to replace the one that had been irreparably damaged with salt water when I ditched. As an officer of the RAF I had received three pounds for its replacement, but my crew, whose watches were also ruined, received nothing, because they were "only" Sergeants.

I was now working hard on ship recognition and also flying a great deal and drawing up lighthouse charts. One of the Canadians at Silloth, Murray Goldberg, who had helped me with swinging compasses on the *Hudsons,* told me that he was leaving the next day for a posting back to Canada. Ah, for the luck of some people! The next day I was detailed to assist with funeral preparations for five chaps who had been killed in an *Anson* crash two months earlier and had only just been found. It was not very pleasant, but it had to be done—one was constantly reminded that he could easily be next.

There were a few *Oxford* twin-engine trainers at Silloth, so I had a chance to check this type out as well. They were faster and more manoeuvrable than the old *Ansons*—a much more pleasing kite to fly. They stalled more smoothly and dipped a wing, whereas the *Anson* usually just bashed straight down when it lost flying speed. On the other hand, the engines of the *Oxfords* stalled when throttled back to idling speed, thus you had to land too fast and wheel the plane along the runway on two wheels rather than making a three-point landing. You then could try to cut back the engines, catching them before they stopped, and taxi off to the dispersal, hoping not to run into something, or else stall our engines somewhere out near the end of the runway. If that happened there was a wait for what seemed like hours before a tractor chugged its way out to tow you in, or you could try to start the stalled engines and taxi in with them over-revving. Needless to say, the *Oxfords* were unpopular with us for training flights. I still made some interesting flights: often officers from other stations came to Silloth when leave-bound for Ireland and we would arrange a training flight to take them to Long Kesh near Belfast. At other times I took the students out to circle the Isle of Man before returning to Silloth. On another trip we flew south along the coast to an aerodrome near Blackpool. Caution was always necessary: one day I was flying along the coast and found that the anti-aircraft ranges were busy, and were shooting just beyond my starboard wing, far too close for comfort.

On February 10 I received word that permanent staff, like myself, were to move off the station to be quartered in the Skinburness Hotel, about three miles away through the main station entrance. There I had a hotel room to myself, and all meals, except for lunch, were at the hotel. Some of the RAF types quartered there complained to the woman in charge that they were not getting enough food in their ration allotment. As far as I was concerned, the change in diet more than made up for any deficiency in amount, but then, I always had my parcels from home. One of these included a large can of corn on the cob. When that parcel arrived I had the cook boil up the cobs so I could share them with my mates. The RAF types tried to eat them with a knife and fork, much to the amusement of the Canadians. The corn tasted so good that I asked some of the Land Girls to plant some corn the next time I was down at Chivenor. I never did get back to see if it had ripened.

Thursday, February 11—given some leave, I decided to head north for Aberdeen, visiting the University of Edinburgh on the way there. I looked up Dr. Angus Graham, a Canadian post-doctorate fellow I had met on my last trip. He decided my visit was reason enough to celebrate, so we bought some sausages (which turned out to be mostly meal and fat), dug up some potatoes in the University Victory Gardens, and returned to the lab to cook them up. Gus introduced me to Dr. Bill Ramsey of the Dick Vet School, and he invited me to stay with him and his wife on my way back from Aberdeen. I also ran into Sergeant Cyril Kendrew, of the 48th Highlanders of Toronto, my brother's regiment. Bill and Gus had other plans that night, but Cyril and I went together to the circus at the Empire Theatre in the late afternoon. I met Gus's girlfriend Claire, and afterward we all went to a dance, a swell evening. Gus saw me off on the train for Aberdeen the following afternoon, while Cyril headed back to London. The high point of my stay in Aberdeen was a Scots dance, just like those of the Cairngorm Club in Toronto, with Eightsome Reels and Reels O'Tulloch. After visiting with Auntie Jeanie and Great Aunt Kate and other relatives for a few days, I went back to Edinburgh where I stayed with Dr. Ramsey and his wife at their apartment. My brief stay there was quite busy. I took the Ramseys to the show *Bambi* the afternoon I arrived, and the next day I visited Gus's lab again and then went to see the Botanic Gardens. Later we climbed the hill near Edinburgh known as Arthur's Seat. That evening the Ramseys invited Gus, Claire, and myself over for dinner, and then it was back to Silloth for me.

When I arrived back at the base I found a letter from my mother, who wrote that Mrs. Sifton, my old Professor's wife, had cancer. Mrs. Sifton had always been exceptionally kind to me, and, indeed, it was because of her friendship and encouragement that I chose to go on for my PhD studies after the war with her husband, Dr. Sifton, in the Department of Botany at the U of T. At that time, although her health was failing, Mrs. Sifton held weekly receptions for her husband's graduate students while they were preparing for their PhD preliminary orals. Her kindness and warmth helped a great many of us through those days of mental toil.

I was enjoying my billet in the Skinburness Hotel at Silloth. Besides tastier meals and comfortable quarters, it provided me the opportunity of seeing more of the countryside. I often cycled on the back roads to No. 3 Squadron—a distance of only one mile, rather than the three miles over the main road to the front gate. Almost thirty years later I was to retrace this path in a rented car when I revisited Silloth. The huge hangars were by then filled with a half million squawking chickens —no sound of roaring airplane engines. The runway was deserted, but there was a campground on the far side of the aerodrome and a wood-working factory established in one of the old service and maintenance buildings. I asked the watchman if there were any planes flying. "No," he answered, with a slow shake of his head, "nothing at all." We drove the car through the opening in the barbed wire fence, past the old 3 Squadron flight offices, deserted now, the back guardhouse, now made into a little office for the local contractor, then across the taxi strips to the main runway. I was driving down the runway from which I had so often lifted the wheels of a plane when, lo and behold, coming toward us was a small van with a flag. A twin-engine plane followed closely behind it on the ground. We quickly drove off the main runway across the aerodrome to the old control tower. The twin-engine plane took off and circled for a practice landing. Although we had been assured that there had been no flying for ages, there was to be a change. The local steel company had acquired this twin-engine plane for communication purposes, and the pilot was just checking it out. He would use Silloth for his base. For some reason, I found this information immeasurably cheering.

On Friday, March 5, 1943, No. 1 (Coastal) Operational Training Unit was posted to Thornaby. It hadn't been decided whether No. 3 Squadron would follow, but I was told that in any case I would be staying at Silloth with the Chief Instructor and Chief Ground Instructor.

In mid-March I was invited to go horseback riding on the sands with an officer who had just returned from Gibraltar. He was a tall, lanky individual who had ridden much in peacetime. My only experience had been riding the "old grey mare" up on the farm, bareback. There were only two horses available that afternoon. My friend assumed that, since I was from Canada, I must be a cowboy. He shoved the big, partly broken stallion at me and hopped on a little mare with his feet almost touching the ground. His horse galloped off, and mine immediately gave chase. I felt precariously high on top of the stallion; the stirrups were too long and, as I had no chance to adjust them, I bumped gracelessly along. This uncomfortable progress continued up and down the sands for well over an hour, and I rode in constant terror of falling off at any minute. At last we returned to the stable, and I quickly confessed that I had had enough. That night, and indeed over the next few days, I literally took my tea off the mantlepiece, having trouble sitting down on my bruises.

On March 23 I flew three hours in a ropey kite and landed at noon to find that I was posted to No. 7 (Coastal) Operational Training Unit at Limavady, Northern Ireland, where they were flying *Wellingtons* fitted up with torpedoes. I was none too happy about this posting, but when I talked with the Squadron Leader the next day he said that he had already tried to get it cancelled. He thought they must be in need of *Wimpy* instructors over in Ireland. And so I once again collected my gear, got clearances, and crossed the Irish Sea to arrive at Limavady at 1530 hours the next day. It was quite close to Londonderry on Loch Foyle. Everything was green and very wet in Ireland. As we landed at Larne from the ferry, I noticed piles of boxes, apparently food, on the wharves. It seemed that there was a strike on and food was not being shipped to England. In Ireland, one could still walk into a restaurant and order steak and chips and get a big steak, something unheard of in England and Scotland. I was told that there was no compulsory military service in Northern Ireland, and was then warned to be careful should I visit Belfast. It was not safe to walk in the Falls Road area, particularly at night. English types were not welcomed, and it was doubtful whether the Canada flash on our shoulders would be seen or heeded.

When I arrived at Limavady on Friday, March 26, I found a lot of operationally tired *Wimpys* waiting for me. I checked out on one of them and it seemed to be alright, but it bounced all over when I came in for a landing. Of course, part of that could have been due to my vision problems. The Medical Officer at Silloth had suggested that I see an opthamologist, and after my *Wimpy* flight I took his advice. The specialist informed me that my right eye had astigmatism—my vision was 20/60 instead of the usual 20/20. He must have wondered how I'd made it so far as a pilot. I had found by experience that if I looked through my right eye at an angle, my vision improved, but of course, while flying one could not always do this. He prescribed a pair of correctional goggles and they helped considerably. Some inflammation had also developed, so I washed both eyes with a zinc-sulphate solution before leaving the hospital.

Several days of drizzling rain put a brief halt to the flying. One afternoon I went into Londonderry where I saw a British submarine, the *N33*, moored up at the wharf in the harbour. After making my way down to it, I met a crew member who invited me aboard; so I climbed down the conning tower hatch to explore the cramped space onboard. The submarine was there for exercises with convoys and anti-U-boat escorts in the area outside Loch Foyle.

The aircraft at Limavady were *Wellington Xs* with *Hercules* engines, with which I was unfamiliar, so I spent a few hours going over the information on these. Being a new arrival on the station I ended up with a fair amount of Duty Pilot responsibility for night flying. One Saturday night a student pilot turned up in the briefing room for his night cross-country flight in his best uniform. The other crews were the usual, somewhat unkempt looking group chatting away, wondering what the weather would be like. I noted that this particular pilot was not paying much attention to the briefing, so I called him up afterward to find out what he was up to. In response to my questions, he replied, "Well, the weather isn't too good, is it? I figure the flying will just be cancelled tonight anyway." Apparently he was all set to hop a bus into town for a dance. I reprimanded him in no uncertain terms and told him to smarten up, for the lives of his fellow crew members depended on him. He seemed to be properly chastened, and all trips that night went smoothly. Yet a few nights later this individual failed to get his *Wimpy* off the ground and pranged with his wheels up. No one was injured, but after several close calls like this the Squadron Leader took him off the course.

Air Chief Marshall "Bomber" Harris in 1942.
(Imperial War Museum)

Air Chief Marshall Sir Arthur and Lady Harris (left) and Professor D.A. Fraser during a meeting at Sir Arthur's residence at Goring-on-Thames, to discuss the merits of the Wellington Bomber, in July 1971.

The author examinig the four bolts that held the
wing of the *Wellington* to its body. Failure of these
bolts in some machines lead to the wing falling off
in flight.

We had a change in students when a group of Free French pilots
arrived with their crews from North Africa. They were the General
Giraud French (former members of the Vichy French Air Force who
had come over to the Allies after the invasion of North Africa), and we
were informed that they were to be considered as separate from the
De Gaulle Free French. We all wondered what was taking place. Were
the higher authorities, including Churchill and Roosevelt, trying to
establish a second Free French group in opposition to De Gaulle, even
after De Gaulle had rallied the Free French to fight with the British in
those dark days of 1940? What were politics coming to? Despite our
doubts most of us were content to leave the politics to the politicians
and carry on with training the new students. Usually only the Captain

of one of these crews knew any English, so it could get a bit dicey when doing takeoffs and landings with them. They naturally began to pour out a stream of French whenever they got a bit rattled; particularly when they came in to land with the wheels up, or too high, in coarse pitch instead of fine, or in lean mixture instead of rich—but they were an interesting lot.

One afternoon I was standing outside the Flight Office watching the *Wimpys* take off and land on their training flights. I noted that one *Wimpy* was coming in slowly, about 500 feet up, on what seemed to be a perfect approach to the runway on the far side of the aerodrome. Suddenly, to my horror, the plane's nose lifted up, the right wing dropped, and the aircraft plunged directly into the ground with a tremendous crash and burst into flames. A cloud of dense, black smoke spiralled upward. It did not take long for the fire truck and ambulance to arrive with sirens blaring, but they found little more than a blackened hole in the ground. Investigation proved that the accident had been caused by something often warned against. The trim tabs for the elevator controls were supposed to be put in neutral before the flaps were lowered for landing, because of an automatic interlocking control. When the initial fifteen degrees of flap were dropped on the trailing edge of the wings, the extra lift caused the nose to rise. An automatic elevator trim tab adjustment was supposed to counteract this by lowering the nose. When it did not work, there was a possibility that the trim tab wire controls could become overstressed and snap. Now, what we had been warned against appeared to have actually happened. It was a shattering experience—death resulting not from enemy action, but from a mechanical failure, something all too common in those years.

Years later, in conversation with Air Chief Marshal Sir Arthur Harris and again with my only Wing Commander to reach the rank of Air Vice Marshal, John Russell, I learned that one of the production series of *Wellingtons* had faulty wing attachments. This caused the wings to collapse during violent flying manoeuvres or in severe air turbulence. Then, in 1971, I had the opportunity to examine sections of the last existing *Wellington,* then being readied for exhibition in the RAF Museum at Hendon, near London. Each wing was attached with a single pin. It must have been a shock, to say the least, to be flying along and suddenly have a wing fall off. After the first flight in a *Wimpy* one's confidence was already a bit shaken. Unlike the strongly rigid wings of a *Hudson* or *Harvard,* the geodetic construction of the wings and fuselage of this plane allowed some flexing. It was quite an experience for a new pilot or other crew member flying for the first time in a *Wellington,* to notice that the wing tips were wobbling rapidly up and down while the rest of the wing was stationary.

The evening of the crash we had a special showing of *You Can't Take*

It With You with Lionel Barrymore to relieve the strain of the day. Hollywood created one of the vital parts of an airman's life during the war, helping to take one's mind off the daily tragedies and tension.

My old friend Norman Roseblade was already at Limavady when I arrived, and occasionally the two of us went to a local dance or on trips to Londonderry between instructional duties. Letters continued to arrive from home with unabated frequency and quantity, especially from the girls. Some were personal, others were from different groups to accompany their parcels. I hope that this account is read by some of the gals that considered it part of their personal "war effort" to write to and dance with us servicemen—we really appreciated it!

DÖNITZ

GROSSADMIRAL A. D.

2055 AUMÜHLE (HOLSTEIN),

PFINGSTHOLZALLEE 4

TELEFON 30 69   3. 8. 1974

Sehr geehrter Herr Professor Dr. Fraser!

Ich danke Ihnen für Ihr Schreiben vom 23. 7.
Sicherlich waren die englischen Flugzeuge mit Scheinwerferlicht, welche in der Atlantikschlacht gegen die deutschen
U-Boote eingesetzt wurden, ein sehr gefährliches, weil erfolg-
reiches, Abwehrmittel gegen ein aufgetauchtes deutsches U-Boot.
Wenn das Flugzeug dieses aufgetauchte deutsche U-Boot vorher
mit Radar geortet hatte und auf das U-Boot zuflog, ohne dass
das U-Boot hiervon irgendetwas ahnte, so war es für das
U-Boot dann ausserordentlich gefährlich, wenn es dann plötzlich
mit Scheinwerferlicht angeleuchtet wurde und mit Bomben
angegriffen wurde.

Ich wünsche Ihnen zu Ihrer Arbeit alles Gute und bin mit den
besten Grüssen

Ihr

Letter written by Grand Admiral Karl Dönitz, former head of the German U-boat fleet, to Professor Donald A. Fraser, August 3, 1974. In this letter, the Grand Admiral confirms that Leigh Light-equipped English bombers were a serious threat to German U-boats in the Battle of the Atlantic.

The two antagonists meet again in Aumühle (Holstein), West Germany, in 1976. Professor Donald A. Fraser (left), formerly a Pilot with the RCAF and a member of 172 Leigh Light *Wellington* Squadron, and Grand Admiral Karl Dönitz, former head of the German U-boat fleet.

On April 23 the Roman Catholic padre from RCAF Headquarters in London visited our station to meet the Canadians based there. I was the only Canadian on permanent staff—most were there to go through the training course. For this reason, I, rather than the RAF Benefits Officer for the station, was appointed the padre's representative. Soon after his visit cigarettes and various papers, such as *Wings Abroad,* began to arrive from RCAF Headquarters for me to hand out to all Canadian trainees.

On the 24th I was off again to Londonderry with Roseblade to see the British submarine *N50.* I had mentioned my recent unofficial visit to the *N33* to some of the instructors at Limavady, and now there was more interest among Coastal Command aircrew to visit the Navy, especially the submarines. I personally thought that the more I knew about subs, the better I would be equipped to understand their behaviour when I went back on ops against the German U-boats. Of course, one never could tell just when or where the next posting would be.

Grand Admiral Karl Dönitz, head of the German U-boat fleet in World War II.

(Imperial War Museum)

Another day I visited in Belfast with the McNally's. Mr. McNally was the brother of one of our neighbours in North Toronto, Mrs. Watson, and his daughter was going through the University of Belfast in Medicine. I was sorry to hear after the war that Mr. McNally had died suddenly of a heart attack.

The weather was improving as summer approached. I bought a new tire for my bicycle for twelve shillings six pence, and thereafter put it often to the test as I spent free mornings or afternoons cycling about the neighbouring countryside.

Wednesday, May 8 I received a 48-hour pass, and was off again to Belfast. This time I stayed with the Camerons, friends of Roseblade, and visited with their friends, the Sloans. I also had the chance to take their daughter, Rita, to a dance. There were times when I just couldn't get enough of the civilian wartime spirit! The next day I rounded out my busy weekend by doing some shopping—I bought several books, including a bible, and also a knife and a screwdriver. I was back at Limavady by 2200 hours.

Back with the squadron I continued lecturing on the petrol and oil systems of the *Wellington,* and issued pilots' instruction booklets to all the new pilots. I also directed a dinghy drill, as I was by this time the Air/Sea Rescue Officer for No. 2 Squadron. At night I was still serving as Duty Instructor. One evening I was kept on the run when a Pilot Officer Bridges and crew went missing on an evening navigation exercise and I had to organize a search for them. I stayed up all night in the control tower and operations room redesigning the usual navigation flight exercises for the next morning into a search pattern for Bridges. By the afternoon I was dead tired and feeling just about ready to keel over, when a signal came through that the corvette HMS *Columbine* had picked up the bodies of two of Bridges's crew in Loch Foyle. This information led us to suspect that he had crashed quite close to the station. The *Columbine* was on its way out to sea to escort a convoy, and had to maintain her course, so the two airmen were buried at sea. There was no word about the others.

Bridges's crash lent emphasis to my duties as Air/Sea Rescue Officer. A few days after the accident I took a group of students into the YMCA pool at Londonderry. There I put the crews through a wet dinghy drill. I had the crew members don their Mae Wests over their battledress, then jump off the diving board and swim or otherwise make their way to the other end of the pool. Those that knew how to swim had to help the nonswimming members of the crew. Returning to the deep end of the pool, they righted the dinghy that I had placed there upside down, climbed in, and paddled back to the shallow end. I timed the whole exercise and gave a prize to the crew that performed it in the shortest period of time. This stimulated competition and pressed the crew members to strive for speed, something which would be essential if they were involved in the real situation. I was to continue this rescue training at the other stations where I was posted—my own experience had shown me how much more we should prepare ourselves for the all too frequent emergencies.

In my role as lecturer I also was teaching the new crews about the *Wellington Mk X.* There was considerably more power in the *Hercules* engines, and with an all-up weight of almost 36,000 pounds it was a much heavier machine than the 29,500-pound *Pegasus*-engined type.

Despite this weight increase it was possible to fly a *Wellington Mk X* on one engine because of the extra power. Also, when one engine cut, it was possible to fully feather the propeller, that is, turn the propeller blades parallel to the slipstream. Thus there was not the 10% loss of power through drag as with the non-feathering propeller on the *Pegasus*.

Although the invasion drill at Limavady didn't come close to the standard set at Chivenor, the Station Commander did have special exercise days for all personnel. On one day most of the station went on a fifteen-mile route march, really more of a hike, up over Bevenah Mountain, which stood off to one side of the aerodrome. I have no aversion to a good hike, but tramping up and down that mountainside was no joy.

I was also directly involved in the organization of baseball games with the Canadian aircrew trainees. To give them more competition, I kept an eye open for the arrival of Canadian naval vessels in the port of Londonderry. When I noted a Canadian destroyer or frigate in the harbour, I sent down an invitation for the crew to organize a baseball team and play against our RCAF team as our guests at Limavady. I would send down a bus for them and arrange a meal at our local NAAFI. It was invariably a hilarious interlude from training, for the Navy types usually arrived to play before they had gotten rid of their sea legs. They were often unable to even walk straight on land, let alone play ball. Besides the hearty food from the NAAFI, liquid refreshments contributed to the joviality. The ball games were never anything worth writing home about, but we sure had a lot of fun.

One afternoon I was organizing flight exercises when a message came through to the flight office that I was to report directly to the station Orderly Room. Wondering what was up this time, I saw that all was in order at the flights before walking over to the Orderly Room on the other side of the aerodrome. The erk on duty came over to the counter and said, "A signal's come in from Air Ministry; you're posted overseas." Well, my heart took a jump, but posting was part of the game. It would probably be India, I thought, or perhaps Rhodesia, where they had a flying training scheme. The Orderly Room clerk continued as he pulled my records out of a folder, "Okay, let's see—here it is. Your posted overseas to No. 34 OTU, RAF Station Pennfield Ridge, New Brunswick. I don't know where that is." I almost keeled over. My overseas posting was to Canada!

Chapter Ten
The Voyage Home

IT WAS HARD TO BELIEVE–a posting back to Canada. Only a few months before I had been called to Station Headquarters to sign a form confirming my acknowledgment of the agreement for overseas posting. Apparently, with Canada approaching the conscription issue, it was found that RCAF aircrew seconded to the Royal Air Force early in the war had not signed the necessary authorization forms. And now in the United Kingdom I was being posted "overseas" by the RAF—to Canada. Oh, the anomaly of it all!

On May 27, 1943, I picked up the clearance chit from Station Headquarters and hurriedly made the necessary rounds—to stores where my record of loans was checked; to hand in my parachute and get my clearance chit signed; then to station sick quarters and the Flight Commander for signatures. That evening I went to a last show with Norman Roseblade. He bought my bicycle for three pounds. It was a good bargain, for I had just had it overhauled the previous week and one of the tires had been replaced. I lost track of Roseblade until mid-1945, when I was in charge of a Forest Soil Survey in Northern Ontario. I had picked up a somewhat dated Toronto newspaper and was surprised to see a picture of him with the caption: "Flight Lieutenant Roseblade, reported missing since May 8. Buried in Oslo, Norway following the recovery of his body found washed ashore late July." It was a sad shock to me, and a tragic loss for his family in Toronto and bride in England.

On the 28th of May I walked down to Limavady village, bought a new pair of shoes, and had a beer in the local railway hotel where the brother of Mary, my London girlfriend, worked. On learning of my posting, he said, "It's on the house." Next I sent cables home to my mother and to Mrs Sifton, my Botany professor's wife. The afternoon train took me to Belfast, where I caught the midnight boat to Stranraer, and went on to London for a few days before reporting to No. 5 Personnel Departure Centre at Blackpool. I had no idea how or when I would be transferred to Canada, only that I was on my way. I wondered what I should do to celebrate the occasion. It was like a dream come true. I made the decision that I needed something permanent to remind me of this posting, and chose to grow a moustache, which I still wear to this day.

I arrived in London at 10:30 a.m. on Saturday the 29th and went to Canadian Military Headquarters to find out where my brother George was located. But I was not to see him for another two years. His regiment was on its way with the Canadian First Division to the Mediterranean and the invasion of Sicily.

Thirty-seven years later I stood in front of the memorial at the Agira cemetery in Sicily, where 490 Canadians are buried. This was not the first war cemetery that my wife and I had visited on our journey into the past, but it was the most difficult to find, as it sits isolated amongst the hills in the centre of the island. It is a completely Canadian cemetery —both the Americans and British who fell in Sicily are buried elsewhere. This was also the only cemetery that we had visited where a full day in a rented car was necessary for the trip—we had been unable to find lodging closer than Catania on the southeastern shore of Sicily. The trip out seemed quite long, because, although we had started on the modern double highway between Catania and Palermo, half of it wound through the mountains and villages that hang on to the cliffs like eagles' nests. Yet all the roads were paved, and some of them were quite new. This even included the unexpectedly well-marked spur from Route 121 to the cemetery itself. The hardtop was a blessing, for it poured rain, and the clay of the surrounding fields became as slippery as ice. Without the paving we would have been unable to reach our destination by car and would have been in sorry shape for the trip back to the city. Although we had been looking forward to the warmth and sun of Sicily in early April, we were soaked by an incessant rain from the low, scudding clouds, that permitted only an occasional glimpse of the surrounding peaks.

At the cemetery, the Cross of Remembrance dominated the site. We were impressed by the number of local inhabitants who had signed the visitors' register within the last eighteen months. There was only one North American entry, from the United States, before we added ours in fond remembrance of the late Lieutenant Bill "Dusty" Miller, whom I had last seen in Littlehampton in 1942.

Sunday, May 30, 1942—I slept in that morning, then picked up Mary at her residence near Westminster Abbey. We spent the afternoon in the sunshine at Kew Gardens. We parted warmly as friends, and by the evening I was back at the Dominion Officers' Club writing letters.

I was visiting RCAF Headquarters the next day when, lo and behold,

I ran into F/O Gordon Tinker, who had attended Eglinton Public School with me. Gordon was an administrative officer at Headquarters, and he informed me that my promotion to the rank of Flying Officer was coming through. I also found out that I had an additional $210.20 in my account in Ottawa as deferred pay. This was the difference between the RAF pay and the RCAF pay.

On the first day of June I caught the 0830 train from Euston Station and arrived in Blackpool at 1430 hours. At No. 5 PDC, where I was billeted in the Vancouver Hotel, I met two other officers, Pilot Officer John Henderson, and Flying Officer Williams, who were also going to Canada. The beach of the Irish Sea in front of the hotel was black with oil sludge from sunken tankers; not very good for swimming, to say the least. It graphically reminded me that U-boats were still a menace, and I wondered about the impending return trip across the Atlantic. The next day I handed in my gas equipment, webbing, and revolver holster, and had another clearance chit signed. Then, after making a list of friends and family back home, I went souvenir shopping. That night we saw a good show with Bing Crosby, *Silver Fleet.*

During the next two days I picked up my baggage from Limavady, took a brief trip to the nearby town of Fleetwood to visit a friend of the family, and toured around the famous Blackpool Tower and Aquarium. When I learned that I was to leave on the 5th at 1100 hours, I did some final shopping and picked up a sweater, boots, and gloves.

Early on Saturday the 5th, my baggage was collected. It was to be shipped to Canada separately, and I would not see it again for a fortnight, till I picked it up on the railway station platform in Moncton, New Brunswick. The RAF collected three pounds to insure it against damage or transit loss—in other words, if the ship it was on was hit by enemy subs. After a final visit to the Blackpool fair I met with the other officers posted to Canada for a trip to the railway station, where we entrained with other military personnel. At Gourock Station, Scotland, we boarded the ferry that took us out to the *Queen Elizabeth.* It was something of a surprise to be leaving from the very same dock where I had first landed some two and a half years before; oddly enough, it was still raining. Our first meal on board was splendid—there was even white bread!

Our ship left port early on the morning of June 7. She steamed along at 25 to 30 knots in a defensive zig-zag pattern. There were no surface escorts for the *Queen Elizabeth,* but an air escort was with us for the entire crossing. In mid-Atlantic our air cover included a US *Liberator*— a welcome sight that made North America seem closer to us. During the voyage we handed in our English money, to be replaced later with dollars. Life on the ship was very pleasant. Our two meals a day were excellent—I could hardly believe that I was still in the Air Force! Something else that tasted incredibly good was a tall, cold drink I had in the ship's lounge—a *Coca Cola*, something I had not had for over two years.

On the second day we heard that Pantelleria, the Italian island near Malta, had capitulated. The news encouraged us all, and the general consensus was that the war would end soon. How wrong we were!

After a lovely, calm voyage, the *Queen Elizabeth* docked in New York on Saturday, June 12. Anxious though we all were to stand on North American soil, one thing prevented it—we still hadn't been given any money! Some of the pilots couldn't wait, and hurried down the gangplank into town. Noticing an ice cream shop, they were overcome by the temptation of a treat they hadn't seen in years. Having acquired a precious ice cream cone each, they walked out of the shop, telling the owner that the RAF would take care of payment later. Fortunately, the owner was lenient and good humoured, and merely waved them on their way.

I had walked off the ship too, but, because I didn't wish to miss the train to Canada, I just wandered around the wharves and watched the ships. That evening we caught a troop train for Moncton, on which we travelled for the next day and a half until our arrival at 0700 on June 14. Our first step was toward the drill hall for a breakfast with two eggs, something else I had not tasted for many a month.

H.M.T. *Queen Elizabeth*, the ship the author returned in from England.
(Imperial War Museum)

Right after breakfast I phoned Mother in Toronto—apparently everyone at home was very excited to know that I was back in Canada! Mother said that I had picked up an English accent. Next on the day's agenda was a medical, and then we were told that our heavy luggage could be picked up at the railway station. A truck was available, so the four of us who had been together at the Vancouver Hotel in Blackpool grabbed a ride to the station. We found everything in order. I had been prepared to give the luggage up for lost.

Most of the pilots who had voyaged with me were British RAF types being posted to relieve the instructors who had been in Canada for about two years. The groups were split up and issued train warrants to travel to various RAF aerodromes in Canada. Four of us were Canadian, and, eager to see family and friends, we contacted the posting officer to ask about getting some leave. His reply was abrupt: "You RAF types! You all had your leave before you left England!" We assured him that we were Canadians of the RCAF, and, after a great deal of argument, he finally agreed to look into the matter. Meanwhile, one of our Canadian group, a Flight Lieutenant who had been awarded a DFC and Bar for operations from Malta, got on the phone to an RCAF friend in Ottawa. Altogether, results were fast—the next day we were recognized as Canadians, posted to Rockcliffe in Ottawa, and given thirty days leave.

We had a few days before having to report to Rockcliffe, so on the 15th I headed into Moncton with F/L Ivor Beckwith. He hailed from an English community in the Argentine and had come north a few years earlier to join the RCAF. He, too, had flown *Wellingtons* with RAF Bomber Command. Ivor's favourite treat was a banana split, something practically unheard of in wartime England, and we went from one ice cream parlor to the next. My weight was 155 when I arrived back in Canada, down from the 165 it had been when I went overseas. It wasn't long before it went up again to the original 165, then another ten, then twenty pounds, until my liking for banana splits wore off, perhaps because my uniform was getting more than a bit tight. I have had to watch my weight ever since—not always with success.

On the 16th I was at last given my $17.72, the equivalent of the English pounds I had surrendered on the *Queen Elizabeth.* To celebrate, we four Canadian pilots went to a show—Laurel and Hardy in *A Hunting We Will Go*—and we had some more milkshakes. The next day Ivor and I took a long walk through the town and had yet another banana split. Our conversation centred on the imminence of our leaves. It was rumoured that we might be going to Ottawa on the 18th—perhaps I could be in Toronto by Monday! On the strength of the rumours, I bought slippers, a watch strap, blue pants, and a dressing gown. At least I would have some civilian clothes when I got home.

The rumours proved to be wrong, as they so often were, but by 1500 hours on Saturday, June 19, I was packed and on the train to Toronto, for one day at home before reporting at Ottawa. My mother and two younger brothers, Douglas and Graig, were all waiting to meet me as I arrived. Everyone looked fine. My youngest brother, Graig, had grown tall. He was fourteen years old when I joined the Air Force in 1940; now, three years later, he was seventeen, a young man. The four of us went to church together the next morning and we all sat in the back pew, where Mother and many of her friends held "permanent" places. I was recognized by many of the congregation members, and the friendly greetings from these familiar faces warmed and welcomed me. Several had sons serving overseas, like Mr. Adams, whose son Clark had been in my class when I taught Sunday School in 1938, and Mrs. Grant, the mother of Hughie who had been killed on *Spitfires* earlier in the year. Mrs. Fleming's son Jack, also on *Spitfires,* had been shot down over France and was now a prisoner of war. Their sad smiles reminded me again how lucky I had been so far. Mother, as usual, was wearing her black beret. On it were three badges: the 48th Highlanders, the Royal Canadian Air Force, and the Royal Canadian Navy, for Douglas had just signed up with the Navy. He was to train at HMCS *Cornwallis* near Digby, Nova Scotia.

My brief stay at home was over all too quickly, and that evening I caught the night train for Ottawa. But my posting to RCAF Station Rockcliffe was to be quite short, for very shortly after my arrival on the 21st I was given my promised thirty days leave. I was also informed that I had been promoted to Flying Officer, backdated to January 1, and I received my back pay. All in all, Rockcliffe was looking like a very pleasant station, but I wasn't sorry to leave it the next day to catch the 1600 hours train to Toronto. It made me very happy to sleep in my own bed at home.

Much of my leave was spent shopping and visiting with family and friends. On my second day home I lunched with Graig, bought a summer uniform, kit bag, and casting line at Eaton's, and then went on to visit my old high school, North Toronto Collegiate. I was welcomed with open arms and a flurry of questions about my experiences. The principal, Colonel Wood, asked me if I had run into other students from NTCI, and I told them about Jackie Nicholson, who had shared a cabin with me on the ill-fated *Rajputana.* I had heard that Jackie was flying *Blenheims,* and that he had dropped a spare set of wooden legs to the famous RAF fighter pilot Douglas Bader when the latter was shot down over France. Jackie was later listed as "missing".

I also visited the Biology Department at the University of Toronto, and mentioned my interest in collecting airborne micro-organisms. My professors were glad to see me back, but I'm sorry to say, they did not show too much interest in my airborne micro-organism research. Slightly disappointed by their reaction, I crossed College Street and went into the Stewart building, the location of Police Headquarters. There I was warmly greeted by the Chief of Police, General Draper, who had given me a character reference three years before, Albert Corbett, the Chief's secretary, who had been with my father when he died of a heart attack on the job, December 3, 1937, Constable Garrioch, and many others. I mentioned that I had lost my personal Webley .45 revolver when my *Wellington* crashed into the sea the previous winter. Albert Corbett said, "We shall fix that," and promptly arranged for me to obtain a 1917-model Luger. It was a lovely weapon in spite of its age. My father had started the Police Registration Policy for small firearms in 1934 at Police Headquarters, where he also served as receptionist for the Chief. Father had had an extensive collection of revolvers and automatic pistols, and had once traded a Luger for a Chinese jewel box with Albert Corbett. Perhaps it was this same Luger that I had now been given. Years later, after I married, Mother presented my bride with a lovely Stevens single-shot .22 pistol. My mother told her at the time, in jest I hope, "You can shoot Don if he doesn't behave . . . but only in the leg!"

Constable Garrioch invited me to visit him and his wife at their home, so a day or two later I took Mother with me out to their house at Woodbridge on the flood plain of the Humber River. It was a lovely home, with many colourful flowers and vegetables in the garden. The Garrioch's house, and others near it, no longer exist—in October 1954 Hurricane Hazel swept these homes away. Afterward the land was classified as a green belt, and all further building there was prohibited.

Deciding that I should attempt to accomplish something useful on my leave, I polished and inspected our old 1929 Lockwood-Ash six-hp outboard motor. Unfortunately, I somehow managed to break the venturi of the carburetor when I tried to fix it. The motor had not been run since before the war, and the parts had stuck together. The next day I shopped in vain for a spare part, and finally succumbed to the much greater pleasure of looking up old friends. As mentioned earlier, I had received many parcels of food, cigarettes, candy, and gum from a number of organizations, friends, and relatives. One faithful group was Form 4E of the North Toronto Collegiate. The woman who had always signed the letters with the food parcel was a Joyce McLean. I was anxious to meet her, so I called her on the phone and arranged to visit and take her out to a show. It turned out that she was a beautiful, fashionably dressed redhead, and we had a wizard evening. When I later saw her to her home, she rather wistfully told me that she had a boyfriend—if not a fiance. Oh well, one can't win all the time.

A couple of days later I finally found someone who would repair an outboard motor, "Doc" Marshall of Eastern Toronto. He made a new venturi for it, but then the coil blew when the motor was tested, reminding me of the *Pegasus* engines in our old *Wellingtons.*

Douglas was to report to the Navy in less than a week, but before he did he wanted one last visit with his girlfriend, Lily Wilson of Muskoka. So on Saturday, July 3, Douglas and I set out northward in our 1934 Ford. Bob Sedgewick, who was to marry Lily's sister Margaret, was with us. After driving through some severe thundershowers, we arrived at the Wilson's cottage early that evening.

We were up by 0700 hours the next day, swimming and fishing for the greater part of that Sunday despite an incessant rain. That night, having said our goodbyes (Doug's understandably somewhat prolonged), we piled back into the Ford for the trip home. But, no doubt because of the rain, the car refused to start, so we all climbed back out and accepted the Wilson's invitation to stay another night.

The gang at Sparrow Lake, 1943. Note the predominance of women and older or young males.

Monday morning the car still wouldn't start, so Doug caught the train to Toronto so he wouldn't be late for his posting. Left with an unservice-able car, I phoned Bracebridge garage, some 25 miles away, and the tow truck came out. After a push, we managed to get a few grunts and groans from the engine. It fired spasmodically, but then gave up and blew out dense clouds of smoke. The mechanic and I disconnected the distributor, which was located low on the engine in front of the drive-shaft. The casing was full of water—the protective shield covering the intake high tension wires had cracked and allowed rain water to seep in. The casing was dried out, the points cleaned, tape wound round to protect it, and I was on my way home—alone.

I arrived in Toronto at 2200 hours. Imagine my brother's surprise when he trudged up the street at about midnight and found me sitting with Mother on the verandah. I had already been home for about two hours—he had just completed a hot, tiring journey down by train and then on the street car.

Eleanor, Mary Lou and Joyce, fishing partners at Sparrow Lake, Muskoka, when I was on my leave after returning from England, 1943.

Mother had already made earlier reservations for her holidays at Stanton House on Sparrow Lake in Muskoka. I phoned Mrs. Stanton to say that I would be coming along later, then checked with Doc Marshall to see how the repairs on the outboard were coming along. I was able to pick it up on Friday, July 9.

Saturday morning, Doug arranged a 48-hour pass from the Navy while I packed the car, and we managed to leave by 1330 hours. Doug only went with me as far as Bracebridge, from where he went on to Lily's cottage. I went on to meet Mother and Graig at Stanton House, where our family had enjoyed their annual holidays since 1925.

I had a wonderful time. The holiday resort was packed with older people, like my mother, as well as many girls and teenage boys. On one occasion I had three girls as fishing partners in my boat, now powered with the smoothly-running overhauled outboard motor. Oh, it was a hard life! The father of one of the girls and his friend were my next fishing companions. Then, too, there was dancing at Wildwood Inn across the lake, and swimming several times a day after a game of tennis.

On the 12th Graig received a phone call from Mrs. Horniblow in Toronto. Her only son, Douglas, who had recently gone into the Royal Canadian Army Service Corps as a clerk stationed in Halifax, had suddenly died of a ruptured appendix. Apparently he had complained a few days earlier of a sore stomach and had reported sick. The Medical Officer had given him castor oil and sent him back to his barracks. Obviously, clerks did not get the careful and considerate medical treatment that the aircrew were accustomed to. When on Sunday his symptoms changed for the worse, he was rushed to the hospital, only to die of a ruptured appendix.

Doug Horniblow had been in my classes at North Toronto Collegiate and had planned to go on to the Guelph Agricultural College. I recalled one Saturday, before the war, when we had walked ten miles to Donalda Farms, past Bayview, to see hogs that were being innoculated and to discuss a farming career. Alas, he was an only son, and there was some opposition to his leaving Toronto. As a result he took a Shaw's business course instead. When war was declared in 1939 and I told Douglas that I was going to apply for pilot training in the RCAF, he indicated that he would like to join me, but hesitated to do so because of his mother's attitude and the fact that he was an only son. It brought home to me the lucky fact that I was one of four brothers. Not that my widowed mother cared for any one of us less, but she did not stand in our way when we wanted to join up. My thoughts went back to the pre-embarkation days of early 1941. My mother was at the local church's women's tea party held at a friend's home. As often happened, there was a woman there who read tea leaves. I had taken the car over to pick up Mother, and the ladies insisted that I have a cup of tea with them. Then one of the women said that the lady *must* read my future, and could I pass over my cup when I had finished drinking. Worried at the prospect of a grim future, I stared nervously into my teacup. Thinking fast, I boldly swirled the last of my tea around in the bottom of my cup and quickly drank the leaves down. I handed my empty cup over to the clairvoyant, and the church ladies listened expectantly to hear what my future might be. The clairvoyant studied the cup for a moment or two, and then spoke slowly. "Donald does not have to worry about his future; it is in his own hands." Despite her assurances, I thought immediately of the saying, "There's a divinity that shapes our ends, Rough-hew them how we will.''

Graig had to go back to Toronto to work, so he was to attend Horniblow's funeral. My leave was growing short, and I felt that I should spend it at Stanton House with my mother, and all the other friendly people, in the enjoyable pursuits of fishing, tennis, dancing, and hiking. Since then, I have often visited Horniblow's grave in the Mount Pleasant cemetery in Toronto.

Wednesday, July 14—out fishing, I caught a turtle and a snake and let them go, but four pike were not so lucky. After cleaning them I asked the cook at Stanton House to serve them at our table. I must have started something, for the next day I was elected to find wieners for the night's wiener roast. My mother and I drove with a retired couple in their Pontiac to Gravenhurst, some 25 miles away, only to find the stores closed because this was the day chosen by the local merchants for their half-day holiday. I then turned around and drove directly to Orillia, 25 miles to the south, where I bought the wieners for the great party that we had that evening. It was, I thought, fortunate that I had not been driving our own car and using our precious gas coupons for this extravagant jaunt. The old couple had very limited use for their car and had not the same problem with the gas supply as our active family.

Friday, July 16—in another typical day, I played tennis and then went out fishing again, this time with Judge McKay from Hamilton. His daughter Marion was also at Stanton House. We caught two pike and one bass. That evening there was another splendid dance at Delmonte Hotel on the other side of Sparrow Lake.

My leave was nearing its end, but I had enjoyed a near Utopia. On Sunday, my last day at the lake, I had a nice breakfast, went to church, played shuffleboard all day with Graig and others, and took the motor-boat out for a spin.

The following afternoon Graig and I departed for Toronto. Mother came with us as far as the locks on the Severn River below Sparrow Lake, then walked back the mile to Stanton House. It had been a marvelous, relaxing holiday, and the sunny, peaceful area around the lake was a fit place to say goodbye.

Back in Toronto I decided to prolong leave as much as possible, and made reservations to catch the 2325 hours train on Tuesday, July 20. In the meantime I visited the Horniblows and the Dales, and saw a couple of shows with Graig. On Tuesday, the Horniblows came down to Union Station in Toronto to see me off, pressing a box of chocolates into my hand before I boarded the train.

I arrived in Ottawa the next day and went straight out to Rockcliffe Air Station, where I collected clearances and $247 in pay. I also had $213 of deferred pay coming to me. At 1600 hours I left for Montreal, where I caught the sleeper for Saint John, New Brunswick, to go on by bus to No. 34 OTU, RAF Station Pennfield Ridge.

Chapter Eleven
Adventures and Misadventures
at Pennfield Ridge

NO 34 OTU, PENNFIELD RIDGE was flying *Ventura* aircraft when I arrived, but the rumour was that they would convert to *Baltimores* in a few days. The *Ventura* was a Lockheed twin-engine light bomber, a larger version of the earlier *Hudson,* with more powerful 2200-hp engines and a gun position in the lower rear fuselage. On my first day at No. 34 I visited the maintenance and signals sections and started to learn the cockpit drill. Later in the mess I met F/L Derret and F/O "Ace" Kay, both of whom had served in my old 150 Bomber Command Squadron at Snaith.

It wasn't long before I experienced typical Pennfield Ridge weather. We were only three miles from the cold waters of the Bay of Fundy, where a thick bank of fog, about 300 feet high, usually sits over the water. It took only a slightly stiff wind to bring it over the aerodrome. Pilots always had to be on the alert for this sudden appearance of fog, which could quickly reduce visibility to nil. As a side effect of the weather pattern, as much flying as possible was done whenever the skies were clear. I went on a bombing exercise with students on my second day at Pennfield, although I had not yet soloed the *Ventura.* Even during the sunny periods at Pennfield Ridge, I found that few *Venturas* were ever serviceable and ready for flying.

For most of my first week at No. 34 OTU, the weather consisted of alternating rain and fog. To keep myself busy I wrote a lot of letters, lifted weights in the gym, played chess and badminton, and took long, exploring walks, usually down the country road toward the seashore, three miles away. On one day Flight Lieutenant Derret and I caught an early bus to Saint John, where I deposited $200 in the Bank of Commerce after touring the town. I then bought a pair of skates, even though it was mid-summer. One night there was a dance in the mess to keep me occupied, and in the evenings there would be movies such as *The Battle of the North Atlantic* and *Five Graves to Cairo.*

One afternoon when the fog and clouds had broken up a bit we heard the roar of a multi-engined aircraft overhead. A large, four-engine plane appeared through the clouds, circled the aerodrome, and landed. It was an American Air Force *DC-4,* just in from England. After this excitement had passed, it was back to writing letters as usual.

With the weather continuing to be so-so and aircraft serviceability the same, I found Pennfield Ridge to be not much different from Wick, except that at Wick the flying was not just for training. The *Venturas* had some special quirks. For one thing, the hydraulic systems to open the bomb doors and to operate the brakes were interconnected. This was almost never a problem, because the brakes were operated on the ground and the bomb doors were opened just prior to dropping the bombs while the plane was in flight. But, of course, the bomb doors had to be open when the groundcrew was bombing up. If, perchance, the pilot should taxi the *Ventura* out to takeoff position on the runway and then surge forward to take off while the bomb doors remained open, the chances that he would get safely off were marginal, because of the extra drag created by the open doors. If he realized that the bomb doors were open while he was taxiing, he had to stop the machine by putting on the brakes, and then shut the bomb doors. On the other hand, if he continued moving and operated the closure lever for the bomb door, he would have no hydraulic pressure when he had to apply the brakes to stop.

One afternoon I was walking from the Control Tower down the tarmac to the Flight Office when I saw a student taxiing quickly toward me. I walked to one side, and noticed that he was nearing takeoff position with his bomb doors still open. Giving him the usual signal to indicate that his bomb doors were open, I curved my arms inward and moved them out and in. The student pilot saw my signal, realized his error, and, to my horror, bent his head in the cockpit and moved the bomb door lever to "close". The plane surged to the left toward a row of *Venturas*—the pilot braked—no dice—and his props chewed up the wing of one of the parked kites. A hundred thousand dollars damage done, but at least no one was hurt.

I was sharing a room with Flying Officer John "Mordie" Morden, and we were also often detailed for the same duties, so it was fortunate that the two of us hit it off right from the start. Mordie had been at Pennfield Ridge for some time, and was engaged to a local girl. He often took me into town to go out with the two of them, and sometimes the fiancee's sister, to dances or the show. I also met his fiancee's family, the Ellis's, and they always welcomed us whenever we stopped by.

The weather had begun to improve slightly by this time, early August, but despite the clearer skies, flying was still rare, as there seemed to be a continual shortage of serviceable aircraft. And, of course, there were the usual training school accidents, such as an occasional aircraft going down in the drink off Grand Manan Island in the Bay of Fundy. Our shortage of aircraft was often made even worse on those occasions when several aircraft would be up and flying and fog would close in. The planes would then be diverted to Moncton, and we would have to wait for them to fly back when the weather improved.

One night I went for a walk with Jack Rush, the Met Officer, who had taught Latin in Vancouver High School before the war. He was one of the few teachers I'd ever met who really enjoyed his profession. Even at No. 34 OTU he continued teaching, giving German lessons two evenings a week. I was one of his students, and in my estimation he was quite a teacher, for he soon had us ploughing through *The Sinking of the Bismarck* in German.

On Friday, August 20, although I still had not been officially checked out on *Venturas,* I was slated to take a Sgt Fraser and his crew off on low-level and air-to-sea firing. Our bombing runs were excellent, and it was obvious that the Sergeant had the makings of a good operational pilot. Our air-to-sea firing was next and we began a dive toward the target. The two fixed .50 machine-guns in the nose of the *Ventura* rattled away as my student opened fire. Fumes from the guns swirled through the aircraft. Suddenly, there was a terrific bang and air began rushing through the fuselage. This was one of the *Ventura's* weaknesses of which nobody had seen fit to inform me. The machine-guns had caused considerable vibration, and the whole front perspex nose of the aircraft had cracked. Parts flew off, and the slipstream of the aircraft almost knocked me over. Somehow, we returned safely to base. Three days later a similar accident occurred, only this time the escape hatch over the pilot came loose due to the inrush of air and flew off. There was an investigation, because the hatch was worth over $250, to say nothing of the danger to anyone below. A groundcrew man made several searches for the missing hatch, but it was never recovered.

I was on as Orderly Officer for the weekend of 21/22 August, but, having organized the flying early on both days, there was little to do. A tour of the station showed everything in order, and except for a minor prang on Sunday, my duties were minimal. I had a lot of spare time for a dance in the mess on Saturday night.

After finishing off my Orderly duties early Monday morning by raising the flag, I took a few solo practice flights in a *Ventura.* I was much more comfortable with the aircraft by this time, having learned a few of its quirks. Mother had faithfully sent me another batch of letters, and after reading these I played some baseball with the Officer's team, winning 13 to 0. Baseball was a favourite pastime at Pennfield Ridge, and I usually played several games a week. I was later to discover that, despite the exercise, baseball wasn't always a healthy activity.

Later that week I received two very pleasant surprises. When I returned from giving dinghy drill instruction one afternoon, I was told there was a parcel in the mess for me. It turned out to be my microscope and a pile of books from home. A day later, I was informed that I had a 48-hour pass beginning August 26. That night, another foggy one, I studied the homework exercises for my German class until about 2200 hours, then wandered over to the mess for a late cup of tea or hot chocolate. I was usually able to find one of the Dutch students to play chess with, and the game would often go on until well after midnight, but none of them were in the mess this evening. My search for company must have been a bit obvious, for two padres sitting with a Flight Lieutenant in one corner called me over: "Do you play bridge, Don?" I replied that I had in the past. "Do you want a game? We're looking for a fourth." As I would be going on leave the next day, I didn't mind staying up a bit later than usual. We retired to a corner room. The two padres were partners and I was opposite the Flight Lieutenant. Springing two new packs of cards, they began to shuffle them like card sharks. Oh well, I thought, my opponents were men of the cloth; could I have been in better hands?

The evening whizzed by, and early morning crept upon us. I seemed to be living under a lucky star that night, and could do no wrong. My opponents were mystified as they kept going down on their bids. It was not that I was always on the winning rubber, but that the padres always overbid, or so I thought, and the tally of points verified.

Finally, at 0200 hours, the group decided to call it quits. Worn out, I was all too happy to agree. I almost fell over when the padre said, "Well, Don, it's your lucky night. We owe you $35; you can check it— it's so much a point."

Startled, I asked, "But we weren't playing for money, were we?"

"Oh, yes," replied the padre. We don't consider it a game of chance, but one of skill. We'll credit it to your mess account."

"Please don't; put it in your collection plates at church." With that I retired to my room and bed and even sent up a special prayer of thankfulness. It was an episode I would never forget. "Security is mortal's chiefest enemy." There I was thinking myself secure in the bridge game, never dreaming that the padres and I were playing for money. It was my first and last game with them.

The next few days passed in the usual pattern, with a few minor exceptions. I was kept busy with a few bombing trips, some baseball, and a game or two of volleyball. Mordie, my roommate, went into the hospital to have his tonsils out, so I had some extra work at the flights.

A loose filling that had to be replaced took up a bit more of my time, and before I knew it another week had gone by.

On Saturday, 3 September, I finished flying at 1400 hours, then turned up for the final baseball game of the "series"—the Officers against the Works and Bricks team. The game was held on the far side of the aerodrome; a fairly level diamond, but the outfield was covered with clusters of blueberry bushes. There was a fair-sized crowd from the station that Saturday afternoon to watch the game. I was playing centre field, Mordie's position before he went into the hospital.

It was a tight game; the teams were evenly matched. At the seventh inning it was a tie score. Our pitcher fanned one out—the next batter was walked. Then a hit went past the shortstop and there were two on base. A bunt, and the bases were loaded. The tension mounted.

One out, three on base. The next batter connected with the ball, and it flew high over second base. I sprinted in and just managed to catch it. No runner moved from his base, so I tossed the ball to the pitcher.

Another strike, then two balls, a second strike, and then—the crack of bat meeting ball. I came charging in, reached low, and intercepted the ball, simultaneously ensnaring my foot in a blueberry bush. I unavoidably lost my balance and tumbled forward, still clutching the ball firmly in my hands. The crowd cheered; "Three out!" shouted the umpire. I hit the ground with a thud, and felt a sharp pain shoot through my left shoulder. I slowly set the ball down on the ground, and hesitantly brought my right hand up to check my injury. My mouth suddenly went dry and my face paled as I felt the sharp edge of a bone protruding from my shoulder. My collarbone was sticking up through the skin. By now my team had run in to bat, and I was left sitting on the field. Everyone was shouting at me, "Fraser, get up, we want to finish the game!" Dazed and weak, I could neither move nor yell back, and finally one of the crowd came out onto the field. Seeing the broken bone he cried, "Don't move," and called for help. Moving was the furthest thing from my mind, and I was perfectly content to sit tight until an ambulance wove its way through the crowd to where I lay.

The Medical Officer fixed a splint and told me to hold my left arm steady with my right hand. As I was helped toward the ambulance, I heard somebody shout, "Is there an officer in the crowd to take Fraser's place?"

A reluctant volunteer walked up—"but I don't have any running shoes."

"What size?"

"Eight and a half." Off came my shoes. "And I have my good pants on," he continued. My sports trousers were dragged off me as the medical types bundled me into the ambulance. It was a long, bumpy, and, in my semi-naked state, chilly trip across the aerodrome to the hospital. But the game went on!

At the hospital I was wheeled down the hall into a private room where I was told to lie flat on my back. A beautiful nurse soon walked in. "Are you hungry?"

"No."

"How about a cool drink?"

I acquiesced. A little later the Squadron Leader Medical Officer, Dr. Christie, strode in with the nurse in tow. They cut off most of my remaining clothes, my shirt and undershirt, and the doctor examined the break. Hemming and hawing the whole time, he finally said he would arrange to have a weight put on it until Monday, when he would examine it for a possible "reduction". An orderly brought in a sand bag, and it was arranged over my left shoulder. Then I was left alone once more. What luck! There was to be a big party in the mess that night. The nurse informed me that the Officers' team had won the ball game and championship.

Later that night the Group Captain paid me a visit. "Now I see why you're not at the party," he said. After a brief chat he stood up to go, warning me, "Stick to flying; baseball is too dangerous!" He winked as he left to return to the festivities.

After a restless and uncomfortable night, I woke to find my shoulder even more painful than it had been the previous day. By Sunday evening I was absolutely despairing of getting any sleep whatsoever. As a consolation, the two night nurses came alternately to pay me a visit. They were good company, even to the point of seeming interested in my airborne micro-organism research. With their kind companionship the night passed more easily.

The Doctor made his rounds on Monday morning and came in to see me. "A nice, clean break," he assured me. "Now if you were a WAAF, the RCAF would pay for an operation to reduce the break, and I'd put in a nice silver pin. But since you won't be wearing any evening dresses, I'll just fix you up with a splint to hold the bone in place. Collarbones usually heal themselves quite well. The ends of the bones will overlap so there will always be a bump, and your left shoulder will be slightly lower than the right one, but it should be as strong as ever. We normally use a light aluminum Stadler splint for such accidents, but there are none available here. I'll have the carpenter make something up."

Later that afternoon both doctor and carpenter appeared at my door. The carpenter had taken a piece of wood—it looked like a 2 x 4, but probably wasn't that heavy—and nailed on a cross piece. Two leather straps at each end and one at the bottom of the main piece of wood completed the splint. They fixed it on my back, strapped the lower piece of wood around my middle, and attached each shoulder to one of the cross-piece ends. My left arm was then placed in a sling. I felt much better, and could even get up and walk around, but I was certainly rather clumsy and must have been a shocking sight.

With my new-found freedom I wandered into the next room, where a Flight Lieutenant Cripps was laid up with an infection. We hit it off well, so I stayed to chat for several hours. Cripps's wife was in a local civilian hospital expecting to give birth shortly. At two in the morning Cripps and I were playing cards when a beaming nurse rushed in. "Cripps, you're a father!" After some celebration I went back to my room and soon was fast asleep, for the first time in three nights.

The rest of the week passed slowly. Cripps and I played cards and Monopoly, the nurses came in for the occasional chat, and my shoulder was X-rayed to see how it was healing. I was reading my Botany texts to pass the hours and was soon feeling much better. On Sunday I almost went to church, but stayed for Dr. Christie's inspection.

Just before my discharge from the hospital I was called in to see the Wing Commander. "Fraser," he said, "you won't be flying for some time; in fact, your appearance doesn't have a very good effect on our incoming flying crews. They usually jump to the conclusion that you've pranged a *Ventura*. So I'm sending you on two weeks' leave." This was confirmed by Dr. Christie, so I went over to my room to pack as soon as I was discharged from the hospital. But what to wear? I did not have any civilian clothes on the station, and I couldn't fit my uniform jacket over my splint. My problem was solved by a visit to Station Headquarters, where the Group Captain provided me with the necessary release to wear my loose-fitting battledress jacket. (While on flying duties, battledress jackets and trousers, similar to those of the Army, but blue in colour, were worn by the crew, but it was normally against regulations to wear them off the station.)

So the next morning there I was boarding the 0700 bus for Saint John. I deposited $100 in the bank there, for I had had no opportunity to spend money while in the hospital, and then I was on the 1300 hours sleeper for Toronto. The next afternoon I finally arrived home, and was met at the station by Graig and Mother. It was great to see them again, especially so much sooner than we had expected.

I took things easy at home, and received generous helpings of sympathy from my neighbours, friends, and family. I did manage to stir myself once in a while, and all in all I made good use of my leave time. Some of my old professors at the University of Toronto lent me biology books so I could continue my part-time studies. Not wishing to spend all my time hitting the books, I went down one day to Eaton's to buy a set of skis and ski boots. The man who assisted me there, a Mr. Gill, mentioned that he had an old three-speed Sturmer Archer back-wheel axle that he could overhaul and fit to a new bicycle, if I wanted it. I gladly accepted his offer, and chose a new Planet English bicycle. I had always wanted a three-speed, and at last I was to own one. The bicycle, skis, and baseball I was indulging in might lead one to think I was quite the athlete. This wasn't really the case, but I have always been keenly interested in sports—perhaps my enthusiasm outreached my athletic ability and led to my sporting accidents. . . .

One Saturday afternoon I took Eleanor, a girl I had met at Sparrow Lake, to a University of Toronto rugby game. I don't recall who the opposing team was, but U of T won 31:0. Despite the game and pleasant company, I often found my attention wandering. It was an unusually hot day for September, and I was extremely uncomfortable. My back splint and arm sling made me conspicuous wherever I went, so I had borrowed my brother's large, white wool sweater to partially hide the contraption. It served the purpose, but I sweltered all afternoon.

One of the nurses who had attended me while I was in the hospital was a Mrs. Pink, who had been employed by Canada Life Insurance before the war. She had convinced me of the benefits of life insurance, so on Tuesday the 21st I wandered down to the Canada Life building on University Avenue. I thought I must be quite the sight with my back splint and arm sling when I went up to their desk and asked for life insurance. But the girl behind the desk scarcely even took a second look —she just asked, "How much?" Apparently Mrs. Pink had written to them to expect me, so they welcomed me with open arms. I was ushered into the manager's office and right away I mentioned my baseball accident, not wanting them to consider me a bad risk and charge me extra premiums. But he brushed all explanations aside and began explaining the premium deduction policy. I signed the necessary slip and went on my way. I was using the car for this trip, and when I drove up the Avenue hill I ran into some difficulty changing the gears and steering because of my collarbone. Feeling a sharp pain in my left shoulder, I thought, "Ye Gods—have I caused the bones to separate?" My arm was sore again that night.

Generally, the reaction to my injury was rather embarrassing. People along Mount Pleasant Road near my home, who had not seen me since before the war, were stopping to ask about my experiences. They would look at me carefully and, with voices full of sympathy, ask, "Was it fighters?"

"No," I would reply, "it was baseball."

"Don't be so modest," they would continue. "Was it flak?"

I would reiterate, "It was baseball," but, unfortunately, it took some time before they would believe me. Having heard that I had been on ops in Europe flying bombers, they seemed to expect me to return all shot up. I believe that to this day most of them, from Mr. Foster in his butcher shop to Mr. Ball in his drugstore, still don't believe that I was givng them a truthful answer. And then there was the dear little old lady who insisted on giving up her seat for me on the streetcar—to the "war-injured defender of the country"! How could I have ever explained to them that even we "defenders" got some time to relax—and collect related injuries.

While I was visiting a Professor at the University I learned that Jocelyn Rogers, a contemporary of mine who had gone through Biology and Medicine, was now a Medical Officer with the RCAF at the Eglinton Hunt Club Station. We had served together during our University days in the Canadian Officers Training Corps. I phoned him about my shoulder and he told me to come up for an examination and X-rays the next day, 24 September. His diagnosis was that the broken collarbone was healing very slowly, and, accordingly, he sent a telegram to Pennfield Ridge asking that my leave be extended until October 8th. Three days later a telegram arrived granting an extension of my leave. My only reaction, recorded in my diary, was "Whoopee!"

Everything was going well, except that my shoulder was sore so I didn't go out much. I did not try to drive the car again, but on the 25th I took a long walk back to the Don River with Helen, the daughter of a family friend. I visited with many other friends as well, and church on Sunday provided another chance to see people. So my convalescence continued to be a pleasant one.

Thursday, September 30, I went to a show with my mother and later bought a bedroom suite at Eatons. Before the war my older brother was the only one of us earning money. As a result, he was the only one to have his own bedroom. I shared a room with my younger brothers. Now George was in Italy, and Douglas in the Navy, so I could fix up a room for my own. Mr. Smith, our next-door neighbour, was a carpenter, and he came over and built me some wall bookshelves. I painted the floor and the bookshelves myself, a slow job with one arm and shoulder immobilized. The bedroom suite arrived the next day, and my room was complete.

The days were slipping by quickly—only a few more days of leave. I checked in on Mr. Gill at Eatons and found work progressing on his installation of the rebuilt three-speed gears onto my new bicycle. This bicycle, which I considered so "modern" when it was bought, would of course be regarded as an admirable antique in the eighties—the age of the ten-speed.

On Wednesday, October 6, Graig skipped school to drive me down to Union Station to check my luggage through to New Brunswick. I was off that same night. Arriving in Montreal the next morning, I bought a pair of moccasins for Mother and sent them back with books for Graig. Then it was off on the 1515 train to Saint John and Pennfield Ridge. Back at the station, Dr. Christie examined my shoulder, ordered another week with the splint, and said that he was arranging for me to lecture in the Synthetic Trainer Building on Airmanship until my shoulder was better. There was to be no flying for a while!

I started my new job in the Airmanship Section on Tuesday the 12th under Pilot Officer Odlum. With my arm in a sling and flying forbidden,

I expected the days to go rather slowly, but I hadn't bargained for the effects of the weather. Whenever the station had inclement weather, rather than have the aircrew trainees sit around in the flight rooms, they were passed on to the Synthetic Trainer Building. Continual rain for the rest of the week kept me on the move as I organized films, lectures, and demonstrations for the aircrews. I was therefore quite pleased on Monday the 18th when the Doctor exchanged my splint for a sling and I was given a 48-hour pass. I spent my brief leave at Digby, Nova Scotia, with my brother Douglas, and on my return to Pennfield Ridge saw a film, *Phantom of the Opera.*

When I went back to Airmanship Section the next day, I found that I was now in charge. It kept me well occupied, lecturing, scheduling and marking exams, and preparing for "wet weather" programmes. I had submitted a plan to the Chief Flying and Chief Ground Instructors for a wet dinghy drill. I wanted to take the crews into the Saint John YMCA. The only cost, other than transportation for the afternoon's fifty-mile trip to Saint John, would be a five-cent charge to rent a towel for each aircrew member participating. The suggestion was welcomed and I received a personal note from the Wing Commander to congratulate me on my initiative. The letter also mentioned that I was occupying a Flight Lieutenant's position, and that the rank would eventually be confirmed.

Leading Stoker Douglas and his brother, Flying Officer Donald Fraser, at H.M.C.S. *Cornwallis*, Nova Scotia, 1943.

For the next week I continued with my Airmanship duties, including the arrangement of the dinghy drill at the YMCA, and spent my evening hours constructing a "Skyhook" mechanism for collecting airborne micro-organisms. I was still taking German lessons from Jack Rush, and in what spare time remained there were always letters to write. At last, on October 30, the doctor finally took my sling off and told me I could fly again.

A couple of days later I was heading for my evening German class when a trainee came running up to me saying that the flying instructor had not authorized the night's flying programme. When I went over to the Flight Office I found the flying crews milling around. More than a little peeved at the missing instructor, I took charge and saw that the crews were briefed on the weather and their cross-country routes. Having gotten the aircraft off the ground, I had to stay in the Flight Office and Control Tower until they returned safely after midnight.

For the first time in many weeks, I went flying on November 2. I took up an *Anson* in the morning and a *Bolingbroke* in the afternoon. These were lighter aircraft than the *Ventura,* and did not need as much physical strength to fly.

I finally completed the construction of my Skyhook tube, and the younger of the two nurses who had taken care of me while I was in the hospital, MacCallum by name, offered to sterilize the glass tube in the hospital sterilizer. Unfortunately, she cracked it in the process. Oh well, back to the drawing board! I decided to try using Pyrex tubing for my next attempt.

I was given a 48-hour pass on Sunday, November 7, and I used the first several hours of it luxuriously sleeping in. Then I cycled to Black's Harbour, the centre of the east coast sardine industry. One of the Australian pilot trainees at Pennfield had opened his food parcel from home one day to find, among other things, a tin of Connors Brothers' sardines. The can of Canadian sardines had been shipped all the way to Australia, only to return as a "special treat" to a point a few miles from its origin. We all had a good laugh over that one.

I was somewhat shocked to discover that no official notice was taken of Armistice Day, November 11, to commemorate the end of the First World War. The only thing out of the ordinary that day was that I had Course 19 off to Saint John for their dinghy drill at the YMCA. The crews seemed to enjoy it, especially as I didn't schedule the return of the bus to Pennfield until later that evening so we could spend the rest of the afternoon in Saint John.

The next few weeks held little excitement. I was kept tolerably busy at flights as duty instructor sending up student crews. An occasional trip into Saint John for a wet dinghy drill at the YMCA and a few rare hours of flying on air tests were almost my only other duties. Poor weather prevented much excitement or variation in activity. We had our first snowfall on November 16, causing two flights to divert to Moncton, one aircraft to circle base for four hours, and me to head to Saint John for a rug and a pair of galoshes. Rain and snow, with snow gradually becoming the more frequent, dominated the weather from then on. Chess, ping pong, a movie or two, letters received and sent, and the never-ending German studies filled the long evenings.

On 17 November a notice was posted concerning an RAF Advanced Armament Course. The qualifications included experience in operational flying, a university degree, and experience instructing on bombers. Successful applicants would be sent back to university for six months, and finally for another six months to an operational group. I felt that I was especially qualified for a position in that field, so I chased around the Orderly Room for the necessary forms and discussed the application with the Chief Ground Instructor. I was later called in to see the Chief Flying Instructor, who just wanted to let me know that he considered my application for the course very well-documented, and that he had given it his unrestricted recommendation.

I was feeling very pleased with this new turn of events until a few days afterward, when a signal from RAF Headquarters in Halifax indicated that my application had been turned down. The reason seemed to me to be very unfair: "Fraser's application for Advanced Armament Course not accepted because he is in the RCAF, not the RAF." I was disappointed of course, but after a few years in the Air Force one learned to take events with a "win some, lose some" attitude. I nevertheless made the somewhat futile gesture of applying for a similar course with the RCAF, although I didn't even know if they had such a program or not. At least RCAF Headquarters in Ottawa would know that I existed, and that RCAF aircrew with the RAF don't get all the RAF advantages. I was later informed that my application had been received and duly pigeonholed "for future reference".

On 5 December I was appointed the gruesome task of chairman of the Adjustment Committee. This position included the identification and correct disposal of the personal belongings of crashed aircrew. My first assignment involved the belongings of four airmen whose bodies had just been found after their *Ventura* disappeared one year earlier. I was more than happy to return to the "dull" task of writing out Christmas cards and answering letters from home later that day.

My responsibilities continued with the less morbid duties of an instructor and flight officer throughout December. My leisure-time round of German, chess, ping pong, and movies was brightened with the opening of a station hockey rink on the 13th. It was wonderful to be skimming over the ice again with skates and stick, something I hadn't been able to do for a few years. I also tested my skis, which were to give me hours of pleasure that winter.

With the frequent snowfalls, more and more students on cross-country flights were diverted to alternate bases. For a while we had a series of "forced landings" by our trainees at the USAAF base in Bangor, Maine. The students would stay there overnight, meanwhile stocking up on the very reasonably priced boxes of chocolates, silk and nylon stockings, and other items which were prohibitively expensive in Canada. Unfortunately, they would often have trouble starting their aircraft the next morning, after the sub-zero temperatures of the night.

On one such occasion our Flight Commander, Squadron Leader Ken Forsythe, decided that he should fly down with several mechanics in a *Bolingbroke* and get the trainee's planes back into the air and home to Pennfield. He was warmly welcomed by the American colonel, and while they talked shop, the mechanics quickly got all the *Venturas* on their way back to Pennfield. But when Ken tried to start up his aircraft, the cold engines refused to turn over. The recalcitrant machine was pushed into a comparatively warm hangar, and Forsythe spent the night at the base. He was up early the next morning to fly back, when, looking out over the tarmac, he saw three more *Venturas,* ostensibly force-landed by students on cross-country flights! After that episode Forsythe re-routed the flights either out over the sea or over the woods of northern New Brunswick. There were no more "engine problems" with the student planes.

On Thursday, December 23, I caught the evening train for Toronto, where I arrived at 2030 hours on Christmas Eve. I had been given a two-week Christmas leave, and I felt truly fortunate that I was one of the few lucky men in the services who could spend Christmas with his family. The holiday passed all too quickly. Thoughtful gifts, an over-abundance of delicious food, and the traditional, moving church services of the season marked my first days home. The rest of my first week's leave was filled with shopping, visits with friends, and a Cairngorm Scots Hogmanay dance. My mother's brother, Uncle Leslie, was visiting Toronto for Christmas. A bachelor banker from Vermont, Uncle Leslie often used to drive to Toronto in the prewar days in his red Oldsmobile convertible. The car was one of the great joys of his life, until on one of his return trips through New York he was rammed head-on by another car whose driver had fallen asleep. Uncle Leslie was thown from the car—he survived, but only after months in the hospital with multiple injuries. He was always edgy about driving after that. On his current trip he offered to give us his small 1937 V-8 Ford sedan, however an inquiry at Canadian Customs changed any such plans. Apparently the duty would have been about $300—almost the value of the car. So Uncle Leslie decided to take it back to the States after all, and I was delighted to accompany him for the trip.

We left early on the morning of Tuesday, January 4, arriving in the late afternoon at Utica, New York, where we spent the night. There was a potato growers' convention at our hotel, and bags of potatoes were everywhere. We escaped the earthy atmosphere that evening by going to a show. We reached my uncle's home in Rutland, Vermont the following afternoon with no mishaps, despite the wintry roads. He showed me around the town and introduced me to friends at the Masonic Lodge, then accompanied me on an overnight train to Montreal. After breakfast and another show we parted, Leslie returning to Vermont, and I to Pennfield Ridge. My leave was over.

Life at the station continued much as it had before I left, with frequent poor weather preventing anything over a minimal work load. I was still on the Adjustment Committee, and on January 12, 1944 the Medical Officer sent over a bag of belongings to be sorted and identified. I bent to my morbid task reluctantly. Inside the bag were the remnants of several purses and billfolds. When I pried the sticky mass apart, I discovered a number of small, white grubs crawling about. Nauseated, I dissected out the soggy dollar bills, identification papers, pictures of girlfriends, and scraps of paper. I needed a magnifying glass to get the required serial numbers of the dollar bills and record them. The bank would reimburse their value to the survivor's estates. My job didn't end with the identification process. Each member of the four-man crew had a different country of origin. One was a Canadian, one came from the United Kingdom, one from Australia, and one was a New Zealander. Each country had a different regulation for the disposal of personal effects. There was no problem with the Canadian's belongings—they were all to be shipped off to the surviving relatives in Canada. The United Kingdom ruling was that personal belongings, such as watches and rings, were to be shipped to relatives *via* the RAF in London, while clothes left behind in the locker were to be auctioned and the money thus obtained was to be added to the jewelry and included in the shipment. The same procedure was to be followed with War Bonds, British savings certificates that were bought for fifteen shillings in 1942 and would be worth twenty shillings seven years later. As for the Australian and New Zealander, additional correspondence was required before their estates were settled.

I posted the required notices for the auction of belongings and found that nobody would take on the job of auctioneer. I was thus unanimously "elected". A group of about twenty aircrew gathered for the auction and I explained the situation, as if everybody didn't know anyway, then started off the bidding. The uniform was first on the block, and it went quickly, as did the overcoat and then the other personal belongings. At last I came to the savings certificate. No bidding. After several attempts had failed to raise any interest in the certificate,

I gave up. Whether it was legal or not, I wanted to clear up the estate, so I finally bid the actual value of the savings certificate myself and entered it accordingly in the books. Seven years later, when I went to cash it in at a Toronto bank, I found that the pound had devalued considerably. After seven years of interest I received less for the certificate than I had originally paid for it.

I received a letter from Mother on January 13th, and learned that Graig, who had turned eighteen on January 5, had received a draft notice. Mother would soon have all four of her sons away in the war.

On the 17th I was called in to see the Canadian liaison officer, Group Captain McPherson. He asked for my personal history, how I liked being attached to the RAF, and what my future plans were. It seemed that something was brewing, although nothing immediate came as a result of the conversation. I concluded that it was just a regular check on the well-being of an RCAF man in the RAF, perhaps occasioned by the fact that my 26th birthday was coming up on January 23. On that date I learned that the Allies had landed at Anzio north of the Gustav line in Italy, Berlin had been raided again by the RAF, and the Russians were advancing. But the most exciting thing in our corner of the war was that I led a low-level group in formation flyings. My birthday went singularly unnoticed.

On January 25 the Wing Commander informed me that I was permanently posted as Officer in Charge of the instructional fuselage training. I was also given the task of investigating an accident—a tractor had run into a plane. Much of the day was spent interviewing witnesses.

The next week turned out to be a busy one. We had lectures as usual, and with Warrant Officer Charlie Painter on leave I was left shorthanded, although I managed to get away one evening for a "C" Flight party. The next morning I asked for a programme room to be set aside for emergency equipment demonstrations, and found myself presented with an old carpentry storage area. The place turned out to be in an awful mess, and I was at a dead end. How was I to get it remodelled with such a limited number of personnel? Suddenly I had an idea. The Station Guard House, where airmen convicted of minor offences were incarcerated for up to a week, offered a sensible solution, and I approached the Security Officer. Would he consider "lending" me inmates during the evenings so that they could be put to work cleaning my proposed demonstration room? He thought it a good idea, and so began a month-long effort. The walls and floors were scraped, varnished, painted, and waxed, and the room gradually began to take on a new appearance. I set up a survival tent on the floor, and placed various essential items in front of it: a compass, a small stove, a survival rifle, digging tools, and an axe. To the other side lay the sea survival equipment: a dinghy with a sail, water retainers, a Mae West, and some fishing line. I covered the walls with large photographs of actual rescue operations to aid me in my lectures.

The following two weeks held less excitement. The weather was snowy and cold, and flights were cancelled for a good part of the time. I spent my days lecturing and making illustrations for the demonstration room. I was joined, temporarily, by Pilot Officer Todd and Flying Officer Morish, who were awaiting their new postings, and I managed to arrange a bit of flying for them near the end of the week. On the 15th I had a conference with the Chief Ground and Chief Flying Instructors, who had expressed their satisfaction with my achievements, and I organized a wet dinghy drill for the next day. A letter from George informed me of his promotion to Captain.

On February 27, Mordie, White, Dixon, and myself were ordered to report to Trans Canada Airlines in Moncton the following day. We were given no clue what was wanted of us, but thought it must be important, for we were given a *Hudson* to fly down in despite the poor weather— lots of cloud and freezing rain. Our interview the following morning with the Vice-President of TCA was somewhat disappointing; we didn't feel that it justified the dangerous trip down. Apparently their outfit was short of pilots as their needs were going to encompass trans-Atlantic flights and they were doing some fishing in the Air Force. Before even asking me my plans, they looked over my credentials: a university degree, many hours of flying, and operational flying and instructing on twin-engine bombers, which were similar to their Lockheed *Lodestars.* With apparent approval of me, they finally asked about my plans for the future. I told them I enjoyed flying tremendously, but did not intend to make a career in it. I wanted to return to my graduate work at the university as soon as the war was over. Perhaps a bit disgruntled, they thanked me for coming down and asked if I would send in the next man. The interview was over.

In 1976 I was at a science conference in Winnipeg and stopped by for a medical check with Dr. Mathewson, who is conducting a long-term heart study on 3700 pilots. He mentioned that an old Flight Commander of mine from Pennfield Ridge, Squadron Leader Ken Forsythe, was now top dog with Air Canada. Before leaving the city I contacted Ken through the airline office, and was immediately greeted with a friendly, "Are you still catching bugs, Don?"

As soon as my interview was over I caught the train for Toronto, for I had been given a week's leave. By evening I was in a theatre with my mother, watching *Yeoman of the Guard.*

As usual, I spent my leave at home making rounds of visits. I saw an old friend of mine, Jimmy Hall, and his wife, Jeannie, at the University.

He and I had graduated together, but he had gone on to the University of Western Ontario for his Master's and was now studying in the Department of Zoology at the U of T. At the Eglinton Hunt Club RCAF medical research centre, I was given some special flying goggles and an oxygen mask by my friend Flight Lieutenant Jocelyn Rogers. When I dropped in at my old high school later that week, I was asked to give a lecture on aircraft recognition for my old Latin teacher, Bud Page. I must have impressed someone, for I was invited to return that Friday evening for an "at home" dance, at which my date and I had a great time.

By Tuesday, March 7, I was back on the job, but apparently my time there was growing short. The Saint John newspapers had already announced the station's demise: "Pennfield Ridge RAF Station closes soon", and although this was a bit of a surprise, it was not entirely unexpected. C.D. Howe had met with the RAF liaison officers some time earlier to phase out RAF stations in Canada, and Course 31 was the last to go. The Canadians with the RAF were to be posted to RCAF stations, and Joe Coles and Mordie went to become pilots for TCA.

While I was on leave, there had been a horrible flying accident in which an entire student crew was killed on a low-level cross-country formation flight. An instructor was flying the leading machine with two student crews in *Venturas* on each wing, when all of a sudden the student on the left clipped a water tower aerial and crashed. The rest of the flight returned to Pennfield. It was assumed that the student had disobeyed orders by flying under the minimum height of 250 feet. Photographs had been taken by the rear-mounted automatic camera in the instructor's machine, and when developed, these showed the student plane flying at a higher altitude than the instructor, meaning that the latter had been flying at less than 80 feet—grounds for a courtmartial. The court found him guilty of negligence, but the president of the court believed him to be generally a good pilot, so he gave him a suspended sentence and posted him directly overseas.

Sunday and Monday turned out to be rather drab, and aside from a church parade most of my time was spent indoors making spore tubes and labelling diagrams for the dinghy room. I also found Course 30 and 31 unloaded on me for the wet weather programme, as continual rain had put an end to all scheduled flights. On Tuesday I was interviewed, as were all other Canadians, for future posting. At my suggestion that I go back on ops in *Mosquitoes,* I was given a scrutinizing glance and brief reply: "No, too old."

"Ye gods," I thought, "too old at 27!" Squadron Leader Ball-Scilly then mentioned that I might be posted to Transport Command on *Dakotas* at Comox, British Columbia, and then sent on to India—a less than favourable prospect to my eyes. I did not want to be marooned in India with the war apparently coming to an end. Taking the bull by the horns, I said what I really wanted was a Flying Instructors Course at RCAF Station Trenton, Ontario. As was usual in the Air Force, he merely said he would look into it, and dismissed me.

The church stalwarts at RAF Station, Pennfield Ridge, N.B. S/L Guiness is in the centre, front row, the author on the far left.

Our *esprit de corps* quickly diminished with the station's announcement that it would close on May 18th. The RAF types could hardly wait to be sent back to England, and joked about a ship coming into Black's Harbour to pick them up.

The vernal equinox was that Tuesday, that is to say, the period of daylight was equal to that of darkness. Our basketball and boxing teams had been invited to compete against the United States Navy Seabees at Eastport, Maine, so we were off that evening by bus. There were only seven of us on the basketball team, all Canadians, but the boxing team consisted of RAF types from the phys-ed section of the station. All were experienced fighters, some with the cauliflower ears and bent noses so characteristic of their kind.

It wasn't long before we arrived at the USN Base in Eastport, and after a welcome in the mess, were ready for the games. Rumour had it that the Seabees had been flying in seven-foot players from as far away as Chicago and New York. We shrugged off this disarming bit of news until we were face to chest with our opponents. They were giants, all twenty-five of them. The five playing members lined up and went at the game as if it were the World Championship. After five minutes, when the score was about 10:2 in their favour, the Seabees called time and put in an entirely new team. We only had two spares, and changed team members accordingly. At half time we were completely fagged out, and the score was Seabees 35, RAF 6. Despite all our valiant efforts, the game ended with a final score of 72 to 11.

Then came the boxing matches. Everyone was crowded around the ring anxiously awaiting the boxers' entrance. Finally they came in, and the crowd roared. The first Pennfield representative was a bull-doggish, squat individual with a flattened nose and cauliflower ear. He measured his opponent as he moved slowly toward him. Suddenly, the RAF man let go with a sharp upper-cut, and the Seabee hit the floor. Struggling to get back on his feet, he staggered upright on the count of six. Another swing and down he went for the full count in the first round. Round 2 was much the same, save for a bloody nose the Seabee had acquired in the first few seconds of the round. Then something happened that I had read about but never seen, before or since. The American coach threw a white towel into the ring, and the fight was stopped. It was as much of a fiasco for the Americans as the basketball game had been for us. In the rest of the boxing matches only one Seabee seemed to have a chance, and he acquitted his team with a tie bout.

The competitions over, we all walked or crawled back to the recreation hall for some refreshments. Before leaving we loaded up with chocolates and nylon stockings, scarce and expensive items in Canada. Then it was back on the bus and homeward bound. The trip back seemed slow, and many of us dozed off in our seats. At the border the

Customs officer stepped in and shouted down the darkened corridor, "Did you win?" We sleepily grunted some sort of affirmative noise, and he said, "Then pass, friends." It was 0400 before we were back at base.

We had lovely weather on Saturday, accentuated by our narrow basketball victory over the Army at Camp Utopia later on that afternoon. Despite the weather I caught a head cold, and suffered miserably, remaining in bed all the next day.

On the 26th I went to church and took up the collection despite my badly infected throat. I later found out that Flying Officer Dixon and I were to report to Moncton for an RCAF transport squadron interview. Mordie and Bocking accompanied us when we took off the next morning. Squadron Leader Hoyt of the transport squadron offered Dixon a course with 164 Squadron pending a possible transfer to Trans Canada Airlines. When my turn came the Wing Commander looked at my records and noted that I had had an ear operation earlier in my career. I explained that I would rather take an Instructor's Course at Trenton than be posted to Transport Command, regardless of any potential employment with TCA. Again I was given no definite answer, and we flew back to base later that same day.

By this time half the students had left the base, so work was slowing down. I spent considerable time reviewing airmanship exams and course work with the remaining trainees.

On Monday, April 3rd, I went over to my office and started to close down the dinghy section, as we were to have our last wet drill that Wednesday. I came down heavily on several trainees who were late for the bus—the morale of the station personnel was obviously slipping.

Two days later I was invited to be head usher that day at Warrant Officer Paynter's wedding in nearby Black's Harbour. Paynter was a good friend and an industrious worker in my airmanship section. It was rather late notice, but nonetheless I made it to the local church early to see that all was in order for the ceremony. When I arrived I was greeted by the minister, groom, and best man. As soon as we had gone over the procedures, the other usher and I prepared to receive the guests. Most of them were from the bride's side, as she was a local girl with many friends and relatives.

Finally all the guests had arrived and been seated. Right on schedule, the minister took his place at the front of the church, the groom and best man followed, and the organ began to play softly. I was at the entrance of the church with the bride's mother, who was to be the last person up the aisle before the bridal procession. But an unexpected complication had arisen—the bride had not yet appeared. I rushed out to look down the road, but there was no sign of the bride's car. When I returned to the church the bride's mother was beginning to look more than a little anxious. The minister glanced toward us curiously, and though Paynter and his best man kept their eyes carefully forward, I could tell that they, too, were growing concerned. The organ played sedately on, and the congregation waited expectantly, with many a turned head.

To escape the strained atmosphere I went back outside, and after several long minutes saw a car in the distance, approaching rapidly on the dusty road. Was it the bride's car? The seconds ticked by. At last I saw the car slow to pull into the church driveway. Heaving a sigh of relief I ran over to meet them. As we walked hastily back to the church, they explained that a freight train had blocked their way, delaying them for over five minutes. But all was at last well, and a moment later the bride was gliding up the aisle on the arm of her father to the tune of the Wedding March.

After the excitement and joy of the wedding day, my responsibilities back at the base were mundane. After a few days of lectures and drills I went with the basketball team to RCAF Station Greenwood across the Bay of Fundy. We lost again, 44:30, but enjoyed ourselves all the same. The RCAF Touring Show was at Greenwood, so we stayed on for the night to watch it.

Courses at Pennfield wound to a close during the next few weeks. Rumour had it that the station was to become the home of an RCAF transport squadron after we left. My assessments of the students didn't take up too much of my time, so I spent several hours selling War Bonds. We played two more basketball games, one against some visiting Seabees from the US Navy base at Eastport and the other against an Army team from Camp Utopia. As usual, we lost both games, 60:33 and 50:29 respectively. One day I bicycled to Pocologan to fish, but had no luck whatsoever, succeeding only in losing my "Dart O' Reno", a treasured lure that my father had used.

On April 19 a cross-country *Ventura* from Course 31 ran into a power line stretched across the Saint John River. The entire city of Fredericton was blacked out. A rather shamefaced pilot returned safely a few hours later.

I learned on May 2 that I was to be posted to No. 9 Service Flying Training School, Centralia, Ontario, near London. In mid-June I would go on to an Instructor's Course at Trenton. By this time there was no more flying at the station. The *Venturas* were put in storage as students and instructors were posted out. On Friday, May 5, I was given all my back pay, and Saturday night I left for Toronto, where I was to spend a few days at home before going on to my new posting.

Chapter Twelve
More Instructing in Canada

NO. 9 SERVICE FLYING TRAINING SCHOOL at Centralia used twin-engine *Ansons* with *Jacobs* engines. Although I was officially assigned to the Navigation Flight, I did get in some flying as a pilot during my brief posting there. Apart from my lectures, I also worked part time in the Intelligence Library, and brought the war situation in Europe up to date on the wall maps. Flight Lieutenant Ivor Beckwith was helping me. We were slated to go on the Trenton Flying Instructor's Course together.

On June 5 I once again injured myself in a ball game. I was running for third, when my ankle twisted, and I ended up in the hospital with a sprain. I was awakened very early the next morning by shouts outside my window. The invasion of Europe had begun at 0630 that morning, and excitement on the station was high.

The remainder of my stay at Centralia was uneventful. Although I was released from the hospital the day after I went in, I had to use a cane for a couple of weeks, preventing much activity. The day before I left for London, Ontario, there was a CO's parade with both a pipe and a brass band, with the pipe band wearing the RCAF tartan kilt. (The Group Captain at Centralia had had the tartan specially designed, and it had been adopted by the whole Air Force.) On Saturday, June 17, I left for Toronto, and two days later Ivor Beckwith and I together caught the train to Trenton Air Station.

Our Flying Instructor's Course began on the morning of June 29th; I was to fly Cessna *Cranes* in C Flight. The day after I arrived, we had another CO's parade, and tested our planes later in the afternoon. The course was interesting, and I managed to keep quite busy most of the time, with ground school in the mornings, and flights later in the day. The meals at Trenton were the best we had seen on a station in some time. Our exercise programme was much improved with the addition of swimming.

I flew six hours on Saturday, July 1. My instruction patter was coming along well, but with the weather up and down as it was, the many flight cancellations forced my retreat to the Link trainer. We were given special lectures one afternoon by a Bell Telephone Communications Officer who, through the use of recorded patter and phased-in *Harvard* engine sounds, was able to advise us on an audible octave level to use when communicating during flights.

On the 15th I headed to Muskoka on an overcrowded train to meet my mother and Graig, who had driven over from Sparrow Lake to see me. My attempts to catch a fish that weekend were again in vain, and I returned to Trenton the next night.

From the 18th to the end of the month, my time was spent flying and practising for the approaching low-level bombing tests. I was grounded for a while with an eye infection, but managed to get along by periodically bathing it in a zinc sulphide solution. News of Hitler's attempted assassination provided us with new hope that it would all end soon. Flight Lieutenants Bull and MacWilliams were killed when their *Crane* crashed and was immediately engulfed in flames. The former had signed my log book only a week previously. As both air instructors and friends, their loss would be felt by all.

I managed to pass my low-level bombing test on *Harvards* and *Cranes* on August 4 with relative ease. After the tests I decided to do some instrument flying, and took up an airman with me to act as lookout. As I approached the runway to land, I gradually dropped into the circuit and throttled back to bring the undercarriage down. As I cut back the engine, the warning horn suddenly began screeching, and a red light on the instrument panel indicated that the undercarriage was not lowering. I climbed back up to 5,000 feet and dived steeply, hoping the wheels would lock into place. No dice. As I didn't have a radio in the plane, I dived low over the control tower several times to illustrate my predicament, waggling my wings as I approached. If the situation hadn't been so dangerous, it would have been quite exhilarating to sweep down on the tower. Finally a commotion on the ground below indicated that they saw me. A fire truck and ambulance waited expectantly for me to make my move. Quite a few airmen came rushing out as well, and watched me with ghoulish interest. I dropped into the circuit and approached for a landing. The red light was still on, meaning that the wheels were either still up, or in an unlocked position. I lowered full flap and my passenger and I checked our safety harnesses, preparing for the worst. Slowly, gently, I touched down, waiting for a screaming belly landing, or for the wheels to collapse, but we glided smoothly along the surface. I dared not apply the brakes too suddenly, but nothing happened, and I eventually came to a safe stop just to the side of the main runway. The Winco, glaring, pulled alongside in a jeep, and I could see he was ready to give me a blast. But when he climbed up beside me and heard the blaring horn, he merely said he'd have the chief engineer check it over. He even gave us a ride back to Flights in his car. I had survived another close call.

On August 9 I learned of my scheduled posting as a Flying Instructor on *Ansons* to No. 5 Service Flying Training School at Brantford, Ontario. The next day I cleared from the station and left for Toronto at 1515 hours.

By August I was at my new posting in Brantford. The first problem at hand was my lack of experience on *Ansons*. I had been trained on *Tiger Moths, Yales,* and *Harvards,* with less than ten minutes accrued on the *Anson,* and that was back at Cumberland in 1943. I realized that I needed to learn them inside and out to keep ahead of my students, but, as most flights were cancelled the first week because of rain, my chances to familiarize myself with the *Anson* were greatly reduced.

By the 23rd the weather had cleared, and I was able to get in a fair amount of practice, both night and day. I was finally getting used to the old *Annie.* Besides instructing, flying, and doing some duty pilot work, I was also being given administrative duties, and was in charge of a barracks block.

Even during short leaves I was able to make it to Toronto, and in mid-September I had two whole weeks to spend at home. On my first Saturday home I took my current girlfriend to a wedding and dance. Just a couple of days later I was downtown with another young woman. But I was not the Casanova that this makes me sound. On my way down Yonge Street I heard someone shouting my name at the corner of Bloor. It was Rosamond, a friend from university whom I had taken to a class dance in 1941 just before I left for overseas. She was as delightful as ever, but could not talk long as her office mates were throwing a going-away party for her in a nearby restaurant. Having been with Bell Canada since graduation, she was leaving to attend the Ontario College of Education to become a high school teacher.

Later that week I visited several other friends, and spoke at the morning convocation at NTCI. One evening I stopped in to see the Roseblade family, to tell them how their son Norman and I had flown together at Wick, and later at Limavady. My leave ended all too soon, and I caught the train back to Brantford on the 25th.

In early October I was transferred to the Armament Training Section, where I was to organize and instruct bombing exercises. On the 10th I had a harrowing experience, when I took one of my students up on a low-level flying exercise. The *Anson* was loaded with practice smoke bombs. Approaching the bombing range at 1000 feet, we began a dive toward the target. When he realized that we would overshoot, the student began pushing the control column forward in an attempt to correct his misjudgment. In his enthusiasm he was overcorrecting, and our dive was growing dangerously steep. Saying, "I have control," I began to slowly pull up to prevent a crash. Well, I almost had kittens.

The whole column came away in my hands, the wing nuts had not been fastened properly. Grabbing the student's controls I brought the plane back to a safe height at the last moment. Despite the student's shaking hands, we tried the dive again, this time with success.

One afternoon I led a nine-plane formation through somewhat dull skies. The independence I had learned on ops in Bomber and Coastal Command was a hindrance to this sort of flying, as I was unaccustomed to operating as part of a unit. In Coastal Command it was rare to see so much as one other plane when we went off on night sorties.

I was assigned to low-level bombing exercises during the week of October 14 to 20, and on one occasion flew to Niagara Falls with several of my students. We circled lazily above the awesome spectacle, taking in the exceptional view from our plane.

On October 22nd we experienced a change in weather, from the cool crispness that had become so characteristic of late to an almost hazy warmth. With Indian summer upon us, Dick Knight and I decided to take advantage of it and pooled our instrument flying time to take out an *Anson* for a six-hour flight. We went north over his home, then swung east to cross the Severn River and Sparrow Lake, where I took some aerial photographs of my "summer home". The sky was clear as we turned our *Annie* south toward Lake Simcoe, where fires burning in the peat bogs of the Holland marsh sent smoke swirling lazily into the warm air. Finally our adventure ended, and we reluctantly landed at Brantford in late afternoon.

On Monday we hastened to finish off our courses. The station would be closing next month, and the impending threat of being grounded, with no students to teach, hung over our heads. In the early evening we had a sports competition in which I played mixed doubles badminton with an athletic and comely member of the Women's Division of the RCAF. Between my partner's expertise and a bit of luck, we somehow managed to win first prize—a bottle of Scotch.

On the last day of October 1944 the Wing Commander announced that there was a surplus of pilots in Canada. Those pilots or other aircrew who had already been on operations in Europe and had guaranteed civilian jobs or wished to further their education could put in their resignations, which would in all likelihood be accepted. I considered the Winco's suggestion carefully, thinking of my future. Later that day I visited the Administration Officer to discuss my decision to return to graduate work. This officer was most helpful. He agreed with me, and pointed out that I had been recommended since 1943 for a promotion to Flight Lieutenant. He also noted that, with my pre-war COTC service, I was qualified for a Canadian Efficiency Decoration. Finally, he said that I should perhaps consider an RCAF Personnel Course, and he noted all three recommendations on my file before I left.

The last course at Brantford had their Wings Parade on November 2. There was quite a party afterward, for we all knew that the die was cast concerning the future of surplus aircrew now that there were no more students to teach. I wasted no time, and two days later I took advantage of a 48-hour pass to have an interview with the Dean of the Ontario College of Education in Toronto. I had always planned to be a teacher, and I was hoping the Dean could help me find the best avenue to that goal. Unfortunately, the College's courses for 1944/45 were already well under way, and I would not be able to gain admission until the following September, even if I were released from the RCAF right away. After this depressing conversation I headed for the University of Toronto to see the Registrar and Dr. Sifton about graduate work. I was welcomed with open arms. Registration would be no problem. I could start classes and research as soon as I obtained leave from the Air Force.

Back at Brantford on the 6th we learned that the station would officially close on the 19th, but that we would receive living allowances after the closing. I managed to salvage a number of navigation maps for future personal use before they were burned in the general clearing out. On Saturday the 11th the Commanding Officer announced that all aircrew would report Monday to Trenton for reposting. I was cleared out that afternoon. Some things happen fast.

Epilogue
The War is Over

MY STAY AT TRENTON WAS EXTREMELY BRIEF. The station did not really know what to do with the growing pool of redundant aircrew, and so sent almost everyone on extended leave until further notice. I went straight to Toronto to begin my graduate work at the University.

It took me a couple of weeks to decide which direction my research studies should take. After visiting a Director of the Ontario Department of Lands and Forests about an ecology or reforestation problem, and vainly attempting to contact the University pathology professor, I finally settled with the Geography Department on Agricultural Geography and Soils and with the Botany Department on Forest Ecology for my PhD research.

I would not be released from the RCAF until 20 March 1945. Until then, all pilots were still to be available on instant recall, should they be needed in Europe or the Pacific. In fact, when the *Luftwaffe* made its sudden and devastating raid on many continental Allied airfields on January 1, 1945, there was a flap in both London and Ottawa. Some of the pilots on final leave received telegrams ordering them to report to the RAF Transport Group at Dorval in Montreal, and they were on their way to England within a few hours. It was later found that their services were not required.

A few days after I started my graduate work I was asked to help demonstrate in a first-year Botany class twice a week. They were extremely short of help since there were very few graduate students available. I agreed, and an hour or so later was asked for similar assistance by a different professor. Altogether it involved class teaching for nine hours a week, at least six hours to set up labs, and another six hours or so to mark laboratory exercises. It did not leave much time for my research, but I struggled on. A few months passed and I spoke to the Chairman of the Department. Was there no remuneration for demonstrating? I knew there was, but didn't say so. He replied that he had thought I was getting enough final leave pay from the RCAF, and didn't need any more money. When I said that leave pay would soon stop and I would like to be considered on a par with the other demonstrators, he finally let the cat out of the bag. He'd been sending my demonstration fee to the graduate student who had handled the job before me until being drafted into the army, because, "poor fellow, he needed it more". So that was what they thought of returning veterans! I let him know my feelings on the matter—I was there to complete my studies and was demonstrating only to provide assistance to the professors. My research could only be prolonged by this, thus bringing me further expenses. The Chairman saw my point, and a cheque was soon in the mail.

U-249 with five officers and forty-seven ratings surrended to Commander H.J. Weir R.N., 10 May, 1945. The U-boat Captain is wearing a white cap.

(Imperial War Museum)

On May 8, 1945, I was sitting in the office of Reg Johnson, Chief, Research Division, Ontario Department of Lands and Forests, in the East Block of the Parliament Buildings, Toronto. We were discussing my proposed work with his division as Chief Soils Surveyor for the land use studies in an area south of James Bay. Suddenly we heard shouting, shrill whistles, and cheers outside his window. His phone began to ring. After a brief conversation he hung up the receiver. The war in Europe is over," he said. We sat quietly for a moment or two. "Aren't you going out to celebrate?" he asked.

"No," I replied. I had already lost five years of my life—I had no time for celebrations.

In mid-August 1945 I was steering a twenty-foot freighter canoe up the Abitibi River east of Cochrane, Ontario, with my survey party of summer students. We had been away from civilization for about ten days. I guided the canoe into a landing on the bank of the river and my student helpers hauled it out of the water. The Lands and Forests truck that was to be left at this point with the ignition keys under the mat, was, of course, not there. So I began to walk down the dirt road, hoping to find a house and telephone. A forest worker's pick-up truck approached, and I waved it down. When he heard that I'd been on the river for ten days, he said, "Then you haven't heard yet. They've dropped an atomic bomb on Japan."

I was shocked. Several seconds passed before I managed to reply that the war would soon be over.

"It ended yesterday," he said.

It was at last all over.

Selected Bibliography

Air Ministry. 1963. Operational Research in the RAF. Butter and Tanner Ltd., London.
— 1963. The Origins and Development of Operational Research in the Royal Air Force. Air Publication 3368. H.M. Stationery Office, London.
Anon. 1963. United States Submarine Losses, World War II. Office of the Chief of Naval Operations, Washington, D.C.
Anon. 1972 and 1976. La Marina Italianna. Nella Seconda Guerra Mondiale I Sommergibili Negli Oceani. Vol. XII and Vol. XIII. Ufficio Storico Marina Militare: Rome.
Andrews, C.F. 1969. Vickers Aircraft Since 1908. Putnam, London.
Barker, Ralph 1955. Down in the Drink. Great Pan, London.
Beesly, Patrick 1977. Very special Intellifence, Hamish Hamilton Ltd., London.
Bishop, Edward. 1971 Mosquito: Wooden Wonder, Ballantine Books, New York.
— 1974. Wellington Bomber, Ballantine, New York.
Botting, Douglas. 1980. The Giant Airships, Silver Burdett Co., Morristown, New Jersey.
Bowyer, Chaz. 1979. Coastal Command at War. Ian Allan Ltd., London.
Bryant, Ben. 1960. Submarine Commander, Ballantine Books, New York.
Buchheim, Lothar-Günther 1978. U-Boat War. Alfred A. Knopf Inc. New York.
Busch, Harald, 1955. U-Boats at War. Ballantine Books, New York.
Coombs, L.F.E. 1984. Cockpits of the RAF; Vickers Wellington In Aeroplane 12 (1) 54-58.
Deighton, Len. 1970. Bomber. Pan Books. London.
Doenitz, Karl, 1959. Memoirs: Ten Years and Twenty Days, Leisure Books, New York.
— 1964. Zehn Jahre and Zwanzig Tage. Athenaum Verlag, Frankfurt am Main, Bonn.
— 1980. 40 Fragen an Karl Dönitz. Bernard and Graete Verlag. München.
Eisenhower, Dwight D. 1948. Crusade in Europe. Doubleday and Company, Garden City, New York.
Frankland, Noble, 1970. Bomber Offensive: The Devastation of Europe. Ballantine, New York.
Frank, Wolfgang: 1955. The Sea Wolves. Ballantine Books, New York.

Fraser, D.A. 1974. Conquer the Darkness. Sentinel 4-6, Ottawa.

— 1980. Present at the Creation: Recollections of the very first Anti-submarine operations using the Leigh Light. Canadian Defence Quarterly Vol. 9 (4) 1-4, Toronto.

— and Gaertner, E.E. 1974. Atlantic Light Patrol. Cdn. Assoc. Geographers Ann. Meeting 74-75.

Galloway, Strome. 1981. The General who never was. Mika Publishing Co., Belleville, Ontario.

Gateway, John. 1975. Vickers Wellington: The Immortal Wimpey. In Weapons and Warfare, No. 4; 29-36.

Goodspeed, D.J. 1967. The Armed Forces of Canada: 1867-1967. Directorate of History, Can. Forces H.Q. Ottawa.

Green, William, 1967. Famous Bombers of the Second World War. Macdonald and Co., London.

Hastings, Max. 1979. Bomber Command, The Dial Press, New York.

Harris, Arthur 1947. Bomber Offensive, Collins, London.

Hezlet, Arthur. 1970. Aircraft and Seapower. Cox and Wyman Ltd., London.

Holliday, Joe. 1970. Mosquito. Doubleday, Canada, Toronto.

Johnson, Brian, 1978. The Secret War. BBC Corp. London.

Jones, R.V. 1978. Most Secret War. The Trinity Press, London.

Joubert, Philip. 1955. The Third Service, Jarrold and Sons, London.

— 1964. Fun and Games. Hutchison and Co., London.

Julian Marcel. 1967. The Battle of Britain. Fawcett Publ. Greenwich, Conn.

Lenton, H.T. 1972. British Submarines. Macdonald, London.

— 1965. German Submarines, 1. Macdonald, London.

   1965. German Submarines 2. Macdonald, London.

Lumsden, Alec. 1974. Wellington Special, Ian Allan, London.

Lund, Paul and Harry Ludlam. 1974. Night of the U-Boats, New English Library Ltd., London.

Lyall, Gavin (ed.) 1968. Freedom's Battle. Vol. 2. The War in the Air. 1939-45. Hutchison and Co. Publishers London.

Macintyre, Donald. 1956. U-Boat Killer. Corgi Books, Ealing, London.

Mars, Alastair. 1974. Submarines at War., Corgi Books, London.

Mason, David, 1968. U-Boat: The Secret Menace. Ballantine Books Inc., New York.

Morpurgo, J.E. 1972. Barnes Wallis. Longman Group, London.

Morse, Philip M., and George E. Kimball. 1970. Methods of Operations Research. The M.I.T. Press., Cambridge, Mass.

Moyes, Philip, J.R. 1964. Bomber Squadrons of the RAF and their aircraft. Macdonald: London.

Noli. Jean, 1974. The Admiral's Wolf Pack, Doubleday and Co., New York.

O'Neil-Dunne, Patrick. 1976. Sally: A Diary of a WAAF Backman and Turner, London.

Peillard, Leance. 1983. The Laconia Affair, Bantam Books, New York.

Preston, Antony, 1978. U-Boats. Bison Books, London.

Price, Alfred. 1967. Instruments of Darkness, William Kimber and Co. London.

— 1973. Aircraft *versus* Submarines. William Kimber and Co. London.

Richards, Denis, 1953. Royal Air Force, 1939-45, Vol I, H.M. S.O. London.

— and Saunders, Hilary St. George. The Royal Air Force Vol. II. The Fight Avails H.M.S.O. London.

Saunders, Hilary St. George. 1954. Royal Air Force: The Fight is Won. Vol. III. H.M.S.O., London.

Rhoer van der, Edward. 1978. Deadly Magic. Charles Scribners' Sons. New York.

Roscoe, Theodore, 1958. Pig Boats. Bantam Books, Montreal.

Robertson, Terence, 1957. The Golden Horseshoe, Pan Books, London.

Roskill, Stephen W. c. 1950. The War at Sea. Vols. I, II and III. H.M.S.O., London.

Rumpf, Hans. 1961. The Bombing of Germany, Frederick Muller, London.

Schaeffer, Heinz. 1957. U-Boat 977. Ballantine Books, New York.

Speer, Albert. 1971. Inside the Third Reich. Avon Books, New York.

Stacey, C.P. 1970. Arms, Men and Governments. Ottawa. The Queen's Printer for Canada, Ottawa.

Stevenson, William. 1976. A Man Called Intrepid. Harcourt Brance, New York.

Swettenham, J. 1979. Canada's Atlantic War., Samuel-Stevens, Publ. Toronto.

Terrell, Edward. 1958 Admiralty Brief, George Harrap, London.

Waddington, C.H. 1973. Operational Research Against the U-Boat. Elek Science, London.

Watson-Watt, Robert. 1959. The Pulse of Radar. The Dial Press, New York.

Watts, Anthony. 1976. The U-Boat Hunters. Redwood Burn, London.

— 1977. Axis Submarines. Arco Publ. New York.

Webster, Charles and Frankland Noble. 1961. The strategic offensive against Germany, Vols. 1, 2, 3, 4, H.M.S.O., London.

Werner, Herbert. A. 1972. Iron Coffins. Holt Rinehart and Winston, New York.

Winton, John. 1976. Air Bomber Power at Sea. Whitefriars, Press, London.

Young, Desmond, 1950. Rommel, Collins, London.

Index